Daily

Reading
Comprehension

GRADE 4

The following illustrations were created by the artists listed (provided through Shutterstock.com) and are protected by copyright: Bipsun (page 9); Denis Cristo (pages 9, 10); Norwayblue (page 10)

Writing: Lisa Klobuchar
Camille Liscinsky
James Spears
Editorial Development: Debra Housel
Leslie Sorg
James Spears
Copy Editing: Carrie Gwynne
Laurie Westrich
Art Direction: Cheryl Puckett
Cover Design: Cheryl Puckett
Design/Production: Carolina Caird
Yuki Meyer
John D. Williams

EMC 3614

Evan-Moor®

Visit
teaching-standards.com
to view a correlation
of this book.
This is a free service.

**Correlated to
Current Standards**

Congratulations on your purchase of some of the finest teaching materials in the world.

Photocopying the pages in this book is permitted for <u>single-classroom use only</u>. Making photocopies for additional classes or schools is prohibited.

For information about other Evan-Moor products, call 1-800-777-4362, fax 1-800-777-4332, or visit our website, www.evan-moor.com.
Entire contents © 2018 Evan-Moor Corporation
18 Lower Ragsdale Drive, Monterey, CA 93940-5746. Printed in USA.

CPSIA: McNaughton & Gunn, Saline, MI USA [1/2022]

Contents

How to Use *Daily Reading Comprehension*

Daily Reading Comprehension provides a unique integration of instruction and practice in both comprehension strategies and comprehension skills.

Strategies—such as visualizing or asking questions—are general, meta-cognitive techniques that a reader uses to better understand and engage with the text. **Skills**—such as finding a main idea or identifying a sequence of events—focus on particular text elements that aid comprehension. See page 6 for a complete list of strategies and skills covered in *Daily Reading Comprehension.*

The first six weeks of *Daily Reading Comprehension* introduce students to comprehension strategies they will apply throughout the year. Weeks 7–30 focus on specific skill instruction and practice. All 30 weeks follow the same five-day format, making the teaching and learning process simpler. Follow these steps to conduct the weekly lessons and activities:

STEP 1 The weekly teacher page lists the strategy or skills that students will focus on during that week and provides a brief definition of the strategy or the skills. Read the definition(s) aloud to students each day before they complete the activities, or prompt students to define the skills themselves. You may also wish to reproduce the comprehension skill definitions on page 8 as a poster for your classroom. Then reproduce the strategy visual aids on pages 9–14 and distribute them to students.

STEP 2 The teacher page provides an instructional path for conducting each day's lesson and activities. Use the tips and suggestions in each day's lesson to present the skills and introduce the passage.

STEP 3 Each student page begins with directions for reading the passage. These directions also serve as a way to establish a purpose for reading. Help students see the connection between setting a purpose for reading and improving comprehension.

STEP 4 Because much of reading comprehension stems from a reader's background knowledge about a subject, take a moment to discuss the topic with students before they read a passage. Introduce unfamiliar phrases or concepts, and encourage students to ask questions about the topic.

STEP 5 After students have read a passage, two comprehension activities give students an opportunity to practice the strategies and skills. In weeks 1–6, the first activity is an open-ended writing or partner activity that encourages students to reflect on the reading process, applying the weekly strategy. The second activity provides three constructed response items that practice the week's skills in a test-taking format.

In weeks 7–30, students complete the constructed response activity before practicing the strategy activity. The teacher page for these weeks offers suggestions for teaching the skills and gives tips for reminding students of the strategy(ies). Throughout the week, encourage students to refer to the strategy visual aids. Use the Student Record Sheet on page 15 to track student progress and to note which skills or strategies a student may need additional practice with.

Weekly Teacher Page

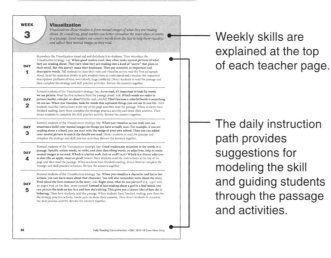

Weekly skills are explained at the top of each teacher page.

The daily instruction path provides suggestions for modeling the skill and guiding students through the passage and activities.

Strategy Visual Aid

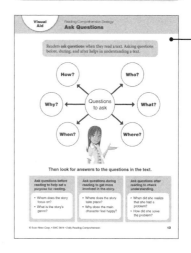

A definition and graphic image for each strategy help students to understand the concept and provide a reference as they complete the activities.

Daily Student Pages

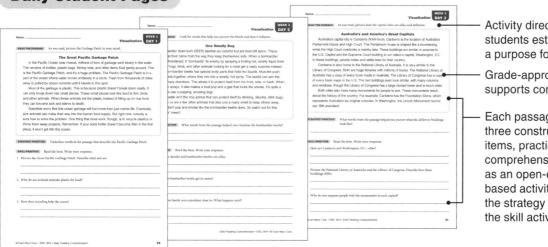

Activity directions help students establish a purpose for reading.

Grade-appropriate text supports comprehension.

Each passage is followed by three constructed response items, practicing specific comprehension skills, as well as an open-ended strategy-based activity. In weeks 1–6, the strategy activity precedes the skill activity.

Student Record Sheet

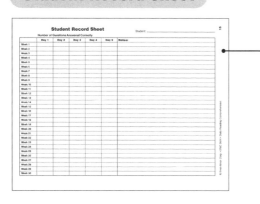

The record sheet allows you to record students' progress and identify areas in which individuals need improvement.

Comprehension Strategies and Skills

In *Daily Reading Comprehension*, students learn and practice the following commonly tested comprehension strategies and skills, all proven to increase students' abilities to read and understand a wide range of text types. Reproduce and post the strategy visual aids on pages 9–14. You may also wish to post or distribute copies of page 8, which provides a student-friendly list of skills and helpful questions that students can ask themselves as they read.

Strategies

Make Connections
Students make connections to the text to aid their comprehension. Connections can be made to personal experiences or to things the students have seen or read.

Visualization
Students make mental images of what they are reading. They learn to look for vivid language, including concrete nouns, active verbs, and strong adjectives.

Organization
Students learn to find the organizational pattern of a text. This allows them to anticipate what they are reading and helps them focus on the author's central message or important ideas.

Determine Important Information
Students learn to categorize information based on whether or not it supports an author's central message or is important for a specific purpose.

Ask Questions
Students learn to ask questions before reading to set a purpose for reading, during reading to identify when their comprehension breaks down, or after reading as a way to check their understanding of a passage.

Monitor Comprehension
Students learn to pay attention to their own reading process and notice when they are losing focus or when comprehension is breaking down. They then can employ another strategy to help them overcome their difficulty.

Skills

Main Idea and Details
Students identify what a passage is mostly about and find important details that support the main idea.

Sequence
Students look for the order in which things happen or identify the steps in a process.

Cause and Effect
Students identify what happens (effect) and why it happens (cause).

Fact and Opinion
Students determine which statements can be proved true (fact) and which statements tell what someone thinks or believes (opinion).

Compare and Contrast
Students note how two or more people or things are alike and different.

Make Inferences
Students use their background knowledge and clues from the text to infer information.

Prediction
Students use their background knowledge and clues from the text to figure out what will happen next.

Character and Setting
Students identify who or what a story is about and where and when the story takes place.

Fantasy vs. Reality
Students determine whether something in a story could or could not happen in real life.

Author's Purpose
Students determine why an author wrote a passage and whether the purpose is: to entertain, to inform, to persuade, or to teach.

Nonfiction Text Features
Students study features that are not part of the main body of text, including subheadings, captions, entry words, and titles.

Visual Information
Students study pictures, charts, graphs, and other forms of visual information.

Scope and Sequence

Comprehension Strategies

Skill	W1	W2	W3	W4	W5	W6	W7	W8	W9	W10	W11	W12	W13	W14	W15	W16	W17	W18	W19	W20	W21	W22	W23	W24	W25	W26	W27	W28	W29	W30
Monitor Comprehension	•						•		•				•		•				•			•			•		•	•		
Make Connections		•							•	•	•				•	•	•				•	•		•			•		•	
Visualization			•				•			•			•			•				•			•		•			•		
Organization					•					•		•				•			•				•	•						•
Determine Important Information						•		•				•		•					•		•			•		•				•
Ask Questions								•	•		•				•			•			•		•			•			•	

Comprehension Skills

Skill	W1	W2	W3	W4	W5	W6	W7	W8	W9	W10	W11	W12	W13	W14	W15	W16	W17	W18	W19	W20	W21	W22	W23	W24	W25	W26	W27	W28	W29	W30
Main Idea and Details	•			•				•					•						•						•					
Sequence					•	•		•					•						•						•					
Cause and Effect				•	•			•							•						•					•				
Fact and Opinion					•			•							•						•					•				
Compare and Contrast				•			•			•						•					•						•			
Make Inferences		•								•						•					•						•			
Prediction	•										•						•						•						•	
Theme	•						•				•					•							•					•		
Character and Setting	•									•						•							•					•		
Author's Purpose							•				•						•						•						•	
Nonfiction Text Features	•					•							•					•							•					•
Visual Information					•								•					•						•						•

How to Be a Good Reader

Ask yourself these questions to help you understand what you read:

Main Idea and Details	What is the story mostly about? What tells me more about the main idea?
Sequence	What happens first, next, and last? What are the steps to do something?
Cause and Effect	What happens? (the effect) Why did it happen? (the cause)
Fact and Opinion	Can this be proved true? Is it what someone thinks or believes?
Compare and Contrast	How are these people or things the same? How are these people or things different?
Make Inferences	What clues does the story give? What do I know already that will help?
Prediction	What clues does the story give? What do I know already that will help? What will happen next?
Character and Setting	Who or what is the story about? Where and when does the story take place?
Fantasy vs. Reality	Is it make-believe? Could it happen in real life?
Author's Purpose	Does the story entertain, inform, try to persuade me, or teach me how to do something?
Nonfiction Text Features	What kind of text am I reading? What does it tell me?
Visual Information	Is there a picture, chart, or graph? What does it tell me?

Readers **make connections** between the text and themselves, the world around them, or other things they have read and seen.

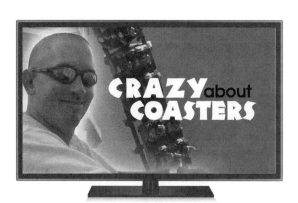

I read something about a wakeboarding contest in Santa Cruz, CA.

The Best Vacations TV show advertised an amusement park with six roller coasters.

I bet wakeboarding is kind of like snowboarding…

This guy reminds me of my uncle, who loves to ride roller coasters.

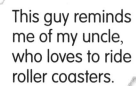

Readers use **visualization** to understand a text. Visualization is using details to create pictures in the mind and imagine what is happening in the text.

To use visualization, look for words that **describe**, such as adjectives, action verbs, adverbs, and concrete nouns.

When you read...

Mr. Flannery opened the box and said, "They have big heads and round bodies. And they sure do squeal like pigs."

Mr. Morehouse could not believe his ears. "But they are not pigs!" he insisted.

You may picture...

Readers use the **organization** of a text to understand what the text is about. Organization is the way an author chooses to share information.

To know a text's **organization**, pay attention to the words the author uses.

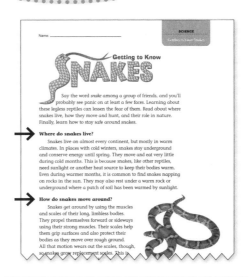

This text has a question-and-answer organization.

Organization of Text	Key Words and Phrases to Look for
Cause and Effect	leads to, result, cause, effect, impact, outcome
Sequence	first, second, third, fourth, etc…, next, then, after, before, last, finally
Compare and Contrast	like, alike, in contrast, similarly, different, unlike, on the other hand
Main Idea and Details	for example, also, one reason is, for instance, specifically
Question and Answer	who, what, where, when, why, how

Readers **determine important information** in a text. Determining important information is figuring out the main topic and staying focused on details related to that topic.

To **determine important information**, have a purpose for reading and look for information related to that purpose.

Identify a purpose for reading.

Do you have an activity to complete that is related to the text? Or do you need to get information from the text for any specific reason?

Begin by scanning a text for words or features that stand out.

What stands out when you look at the page? Are any words or phrases repeated? Are there any bold words or headings? These are clues that point to important ideas in the text.

Look for information related to your purpose for reading.

Find information that is related to the text that will help you complete the activity or help you get the information you need.

Identify the main topic of the text.

Look at headings, topic sentences, captions, and bold text.

Find details that relate to the main topic.

Look for key words that relate to the main topic.

Identify details that are not as important for understanding the main topic.

Avoid being distracted by unimportant details in the text.

Readers **ask questions** when they read a text. Asking questions before, during, and after helps in understanding a text.

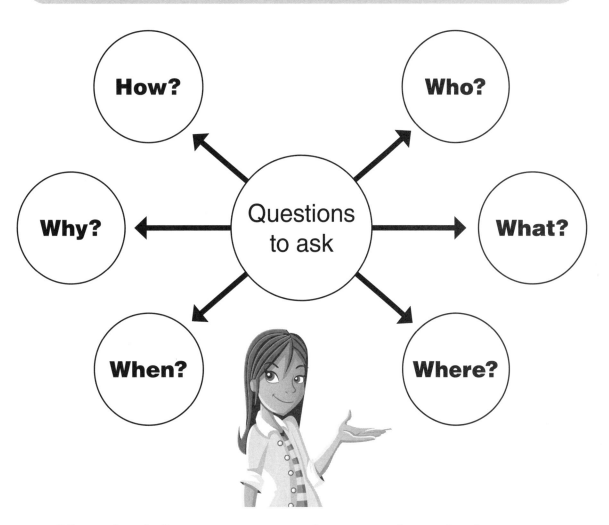

Then look for answers to the questions in the text.

Ask questions before reading to help set a purpose for reading.	Ask questions during reading to get more involved in the story.	Ask questions after reading to check understanding.
• Whom does the story focus on? • What is the story's genre?	• Where does the story take place? • Why does the main character feel happy?	• When did she realize that she had a problem? • How did she solve the problem?

Readers **monitor comprehension** when they read a text. Readers who monitor comprehension keep track of how well they understand the text.

To **monitor comprehension**, think about the text while reading it.

As Dad parked the car, I noticed people holding signs and shouting in the grocery store parking lot. It was a protest, and one of the signs had the words: "Unfair Pay, Unfair Treatment of Farm Workers" written on it. Another sign read, "Boycott California Grapes in 1966."

Use visualization. Create mental pictures and imagine what is happening in the text.

"The fields have no protection from the sun, so the farm workers get very hot while working," Dad said. "They're also expected to work long hours with no break. Usually, there's no bathroom facility. And it's exhausting, back-breaking work."

· long hours, no break
· no bathrooms

Make notes about the text. Use the margin of the text, a sheet of paper, or a device to write details that you think are important.

Break the text into chunks. Pause after every paragraph and think about what the paragraph is saying.

TIP: Compare reading a text to eating an apple. We don't eat a whole apple at once. We take one bite at a time and chew it before taking another bite. Monitoring comprehension is like taking one bite at a time.

Student Record Sheet

Student: _____

Number of Questions Answered Correctly

	Day 1	Day 2	Day 3	Day 4	Day 5	Notes:
Week 1						
Week 2						
Week 3						
Week 4						
Week 5						
Week 6						
Week 7						
Week 8						
Week 9						
Week 10						
Week 11						
Week 12						
Week 13						
Week 14						
Week 15						
Week 16						
Week 17						
Week 18						
Week 19						
Week 20						
Week 21						
Week 22						
Week 23						
Week 24						
Week 25						
Week 26						
Week 27						
Week 28						
Week 29						
Week 30						

Monitor Comprehension

When students monitor their comprehension, they keep track of how well they understand the material and identify when their understanding breaks down. Related activities include rereading, asking questions, taking notes, and paraphrasing what has been read.

DAY 1

Reproduce the *Monitor Comprehension* visual aid and distribute it to students. Then build background by showing students the location of the Arctic Ocean on a map or globe. Have students read the passage independently, and then introduce the *Monitor Comprehension* strategy. Explain: **Good readers monitor their comprehension by thinking about what they are reading.** Model the strategy: **I know that this is a nonfiction text that is telling me facts. It is important that I understand those facts. As I was reading, I realized I didn't understand how cold the Arctic Ocean is. So I reread the section titled "Size and Temperature." I figured out that the temperature must be almost as cold as ice because there is so much ice in the Arctic Ocean.** Have students complete the strategy practice activity and share their responses. Then have them complete the skill practice activity. Review the answers together.

DAY 2

Remind students of the *Monitor Comprehension* strategy and point out the instructions at the top of the page. Ask: **How would pausing and asking myself if I understand help me monitor my comprehension?** (It gives you a chance to think about what you read to make sure you understand it. It tells you if you need to read it again.) After students finish reading the passage, model the strategy: **I didn't understand why Dr. Fowler wanted to save so many different kinds of seeds. I reread the second paragraph and figured out that he wanted to save a variety of seeds to protect the crops that grow in different countries.** After students complete the strategy practice activity, have them share their responses. Then have them complete the skill practice activity. Review the answers together.

DAY 3

Remind students of the *Monitor Comprehension* strategy. Then say: **We are going to read about a Japanese holiday called Children's Day.** Build background by pointing out Japan on a map and asking volunteers to share what they know about Japanese culture. Then call students' attention to the instructions at the top of the page. Say: **One good way to monitor our comprehension is to recall the main idea of each paragraph.** After students finish reading, have them complete the strategy and skill practice activities. Review the answers together.

DAY 4

Remind students of the *Monitor Comprehension* strategy. Then read the title of the passage aloud. Say: **Sometimes, titles give us good clues as to what a passage is about. Thinking about the title as you read can help you understand the passage.** After students finish reading, have them complete the strategy and skill practice activities. Review the answers together.

DAY 5

Before students read the passage, build background by pointing out Mexico and Spain on a map. Explain that before Mexico was its own country, it was part of Spain. Then have students read the passage. Explain: **Sometimes it can be difficult to concentrate while reading. However, if you monitor your comprehension while reading, you can keep yourself on track.** Have students turn to a partner to complete the strategy practice activity by naming a specific action he or she could take to monitor comprehension. Ask volunteers to share their responses and discuss how those actions helped them stay focused while reading. For the skill practice activity, have students answer the items independently and then review the answers as a group.

READ THE PASSAGE   As you read, pause after each section to think about whether you understood the information.

I. Introduction

The Arctic Ocean is the smallest and coldest ocean in the world. It stretches from the North Pole to Asia, Europe, and North America. The Arctic Ocean is mostly covered in sea ice all year. It is home to walruses, polar bears, and whales. Because the ocean is so cold, few plants and animals can live there.

II. Size and Temperature

The Arctic Ocean covers 5.4 million square miles (14 million square km). It is smaller than all other oceans. It is also the shallowest ocean. The temperature of the Arctic Ocean stays around 32 degrees Fahrenheit (0 degrees Celsius). The large amount of sea ice in the ocean stops its temperature from changing too much. However, much of the ice in the Arctic Ocean is melting because of global warming.

STRATEGY PRACTICE   Was there any part of the passage that you did not understand right away? How did you figure it out?

_____

_____

SKILL PRACTICE   Read the item. Write your response.

1. What is the article mostly about?

_____

_____

2. What is the purpose of the side headings?

_____

_____

3. Name two continents that the Arctic Ocean does not touch.

_____

_____

READ THE PASSAGE   As you read, ask yourself, "Do I understand what I am reading?"

The Doomsday Vault

If you wanted to save one thing for the future, what would you pick? For Dr. Cary Fowler, it's an easy choice. He would save seeds. Dr. Fowler is the scientist who helped create the Svalbard Global Seed Vault in Norway, near the Arctic. Dr. Fowler is trying to collect and save seeds from every food crop in the world.

Why would anyone save seeds? Well, Dr. Fowler believes the world must be prepared in case something terrible happens. Some disasters, whether they are natural or caused by people, could destroy crops around the world. People wouldn't have food, and they might not be able to grow it. Dr. Fowler believes we must protect seeds today so we can grow crops in the future.

Today the seed vault has over 400,000 different types of seeds. Dr. Fowler hopes to one day have over 1 million types of seeds. He is asking countries around the world to deposit seeds into the vault so that the seeds can be withdrawn when we need them.

STRATEGY PRACTICE   Was there anything you read about the seed vault or Dr. Fowler that you did not understand? Write a question you had while you were reading.

_____

SKILL PRACTICE   Read the item. Write your response.

1. Why is the Svalbard Global Seed Vault important?

_____

_____

_____

2. Draw two conclusions about Fowler based on information from the text.

_____

_____

3. What does the word *deposit* mean? How can you tell?

_____

_____

READ THE PASSAGE   As you finish each paragraph, recall the main idea.

Children's Day in Japan

Every year on May 5, people in Japan celebrate a festival known as Children's Day. This festival celebrates the happiness of children and mothers across the country. It is a national holiday for everyone in Japan.

Children's Day probably began as a festival for boys around AD 600. People flew flags shaped like a fish called a *carp.* The carp is a symbol of strength and health. Each boy had his own flag, and the oldest boy in a family had the biggest flag. People still fly carp flags today. But in 1948, the Japanese government changed the festival so that it celebrated both boys and girls.

People in Japan do many things on Children's Day. They eat special treats, such as rice cakes wrapped in oak leaves. They also take hot baths in water that has the leaves of iris plants in it. These leaves are said to be good for a person's health. But the children in Tokyo, the capital of Japan, get something extra special. They compete in the Kids' Olympics on Children's Day. There is a torch relay and races for kids and their parents. So before you're too old, plan a trip to Japan to celebrate Children's Day, and have fun being a kid!

STRATEGY PRACTICE   How did thinking about the main idea of each paragraph help you better understand the passage?

_____

_____

SKILL PRACTICE   Read the item. Write your response.

1. What do the Japanese think of carp?

_____

_____

2. What happened to the Children's Day festival in 1948?

_____

_____

3. In which activity would you most like to participate on Children's Day? Why?

_____

READ THE PASSAGE   As you read, think about the title of the passage and how it helps explain what you are reading.

Real-Life Dragons

Stories about dragons that breathe fire and fly through the air are just make-believe. But some islands in the Indian Ocean are home to a very real reptile called the Komodo dragon. This giant lizard can grow to be 10 feet (3 m) long and weigh up to 150 pounds (68 kg). Komodo dragons don't have wings, or smoke coming out of their nostrils, but they have strong tails and a very nasty bite. A Komodo dragon has a powerful venom and knife-like teeth. When a Komodo dragon bites an animal, the animal usually goes into shock and dies quickly.

Although they can be dangerous, Komodo dragons usually don't attack people. In fact, in the past 35 years, Komodo dragons have attacked only five people. The Indonesian people who inhabit the same islands as the dragons believe that the lizards are special and should be treated with respect.

STRATEGY PRACTICE   Explain how the title helped you understand the passage.

_____

_____

SKILL PRACTICE   Read the item. Write your response.

1. How does the first sentence prepare the reader to understand the text?

_____

_____

2. Use quotation marks to cite the sentence in the text that tells how Komodo dragons differ from the dragons in fairy tales.

_____

_____

3. What is the main idea of the last paragraph?

_____

_____

READ THE PASSAGE   As you read, keep your attention focused on the facts about Santa Anna's life.

The Story of Santa Anna

Early Life

Santa Anna was born in Mexico in 1794, when Mexico was still owned by Spain. He began his career in the Spanish army when he was only 16. Santa Anna first fought against Native Americans in Mexico. Brave and smart, Santa Anna quickly became popular with the other soldiers. He was given many honors. When Santa Anna turned 22, he was made a captain in the army.

Politics

After Mexico declared itself independent of Spain, Santa Anna became a politician. He served as the president of Mexico many times. None of his terms were very long, and he was not a good president. Sometimes, he showed little interest in running a country. Other times, he was a dictator who favored the rich. He made many bad decisions that made the country poorer. However, Santa Anna claimed that he wanted to help Mexico. So every time Mexico was in trouble, he offered his "aid."

STRATEGY PRACTICE   What advice would you give someone who could not concentrate while reading the passage? Tell a partner.

SKILL PRACTICE   Read the item. Write your response.

1. Why does the first section have the side heading "Early Life"?

_____

_____

2. Was Santa Anna a good president? Support your response with two facts.

_____

_____

3. Summarize the text in two sentences.

_____

_____

Make Connections

This strategy helps students put what they are reading into context by helping them see the connections between the text and themselves, the world around them, and other things they have read or seen.

DAY 1

Reproduce the *Make Connections* visual aid and distribute it to students. Then introduce the strategy by explaining: **When good readers read, they will often be reminded of something they have seen, done, or read before. This helps them better understand the situation, the details, or the feelings involved in what they are reading. But it is important to stay focused on the text and not be distracted by the connections you make.** Next, have students read the instructions at the top of the passage and then read the passage. When students have finished reading, model a connection you made with the text (e.g., When I was in fourth grade, I could not take part in the science fair because I had the chickenpox.). Direct students to complete the strategy and skill practice activities. Review the answers together.

DAY 2

Remind students of the *Make Connections* strategy and ask them if they have ever been told they were wrong about something when they knew they were right (e.g., someone said you did something you didn't do). Say: **You can use that experience to make a connection with this passage.** Direct students to read the passage. After students have finished, instruct them to complete the strategy practice activity. Ask volunteers to share their responses. Have students discuss how they answered the question based on their own experiences. Then direct students to complete the skill practice activity. Review the answers together.

DAY 3

Point out to students that when they read about a place, they can make connections to what they are reading by thinking about similar places they know of. Have students read the directions at the top of the page. Ask: **Have you ever been to a community garden? What about a community center or local park? Think about those places as you read.** Direct students to read the passage and complete the strategy practice activity. Invite volunteers to share their responses. Then have students complete the skill practice activity. Review the answers together.

DAY 4

Remind students of the *Make Connections* strategy. Have students read the directions at the top of the page. Then say: **Good readers can connect what happens in a story to their own lives. As you read, think about what you would do if you were in a similar situation. How would you behave? What would you say?** Direct students to read the passage and complete the strategy practice activity. Invite volunteers to share their responses. Then have students complete the skill practice activity. Review the answers together.

DAY 5

Remind students of the *Make Connections* strategy. Tell students they are going to read about a new way that scientists study hurricanes. Have students share what they know about hurricanes. Then direct students to read the passage. After they finish reading, have students complete the strategy practice activity. Ask students how making a connection to something they would like to study could help them better understand the passage (e.g., think about how to study something, new ideas for studying something). Then have students complete the skill practice activity. Review the answers together.

Think about the way Henry and Lauren behave and what it reminds you of.

Game Day

The rain continued to pour throughout the gloomy Saturday afternoon. Lauren and Henry were dressed in their dark blue uniforms. Lauren's uniform had more dirt stains than Henry's did because she loved stealing bases and sliding into home. She was the best base stealer on the team.

Lauren pounded her fist into her glove as she watched the rain fall in steady sheets. Every couple of minutes, she would sigh loudly, which caused the window to fog up. Henry was reading a comic book and eating an apple and some crackers. He kicked off his shoes and grabbed a pillow from the couch.

"Aren't you worried?" Lauren asked him. "What if it doesn't stop raining?"

"I hope it rains all day," Henry said. "I'm having a great time, and besides, we can play next week. This is the final issue of *Captain Smoke*."

The telephone rang. Henry and Lauren nervously looked at each other. Their mother answered it. "Hello, Coach Donna," she said. After a short pause, she said, "Okay, I'll let them know. We'll see you next week."

STRATEGY PRACTICE   Describe a time when you could not do something you wanted to do because of the weather.

_____

_____

SKILL PRACTICE   Read the item. Write your response.

1. Describe the setting of this story.

_____

_____

2. Why does Lauren pound her fist into her glove?

_____

3. Which sibling enjoys baseball less? How do you know?

_____

_____

READ THE PASSAGE   As you read, think about how Galileo acted differently from other people.

Galileo's Wild Idea

When Galileo (GAL-ih-LAY-oh) was a boy in Italy in 1574, he studied science. As he grew older, Galileo became interested in studying the stars. At that time, most people believed the sun moved around Earth. Galileo wanted to prove that Earth moved around the sun.

Galileo got his idea after he read a book and learned more about stars. Galileo studied Jupiter with a telescope. The telescope helped Galileo find some of Jupiter's many moons. He saw that the moons moved around Jupiter. Now he knew that some things in the solar system did *not* move around Earth!

Galileo wanted to tell everyone about his idea, but he had a problem. Some of Italy's rulers did not like the idea that Earth was not the center of the universe. They called Galileo a troublemaker and threatened to kill him if he did not say that his ideas were wrong. Galileo agreed, and instead of being killed, he spent the rest of his life in prison. However, Galileo was right! Today we know that the planets move around the sun.

STRATEGY PRACTICE   How do you think Galileo felt when he was forced to say that his ideas were wrong?

_____

_____

SKILL PRACTICE   Read the item. Write your response.

1. What is the theme of the text?

_____

_____

2. What was the stance of Italy's leaders?

_____

_____

3. Draw a conclusion about the text. Include a quote from the text to support your conclusion.

_____

_____

READ THE PASSAGE   As you read, think about the things that people do at a community garden.

Growing a Community

Every Saturday morning, people come to work in the community garden. Some people grow their own vegetables. Other people grow flowers. One person even made a goldfish pond! The garden is a busy place, especially on sunny days.

A few years ago, the garden didn't exist. There was just a run-down parking lot in the spot. Most people said it was only good for growing weeds and collecting trash. But the people in the community saw that the space could be used to make a garden.

Now the community garden has 50 plots. Each plot is used by a different person or family. Even some of the local stores have a plot. They grow produce that they sell to people in the community. The fruits and vegetables are fresh, tasty, and healthful.

Sometimes, special events take place in the garden, such as music concerts or gardening classes. Other times, schools bring students to the garden to learn about plants and insects. The garden offers much more to the community than just a place to dig in the dirt.

STRATEGY PRACTICE   Describe a public place where you enjoy spending time.

_____

_____

SKILL PRACTICE   Read the item. Write your response.

1. What would be a good location for a community garden?

_____

_____

2. What do you think people meant when they said the old lot was "only good for growing weeds and collecting trash"?

_____

_____

3. What is the theme of this text?

_____

_____

READ THE PASSAGE As you read, think about how Kate behaves and whether you know anyone like her.

Kate's Vacation

When Kate came back to school after the winter holiday, she told everyone in her class about the snowman she had built. "It was 15 feet tall. It was so huge that I needed a ladder to put the hat on top of its head," Kate said.

During lunch, Kate told everyone what a great snowboarder she was. "I was going faster than anyone else on the hill," Kate said. "I think I set a world record."

During recess, Kate explained to everyone how she had built an igloo from the snow. "It had five rooms," Kate said. "We almost moved into the igloo because it was twice as big as our house."

Just then, it began to snow. All the kids cheered as big white flakes drifted down from the sky. Sarah, who had listened to Kate's stories all day, smiled. She said to Kate, "Now you can make us a giant snowman and an igloo! And we can watch you set a new record on your snowboard!"

Kate's face turned bright red. She quietly went back inside and didn't say anything else about her winter vacation.

STRATEGY PRACTICE What would you have said to Kate to help her change her behavior?

_____

_____

SKILL PRACTICE Read the item. Write your response.

1. Use three adjectives to describe Kate. Explain your choices.

_____

_____

2. Why did Kate's face turn bright red?

_____

_____

3. What did Kate learn from this experience?

_____

_____

READ THE PASSAGE   Think about what it might be like to be a scientist who studies hurricanes.

Hurricane Plane

You might know that wind vanes tell you which way the wind is blowing and that thermometers tell you how hot or cold it is outside. But did you know that airplanes can be used to study hurricanes?

On November 1, 2007, an aircraft flew through a dangerous hurricane. People on the ground controlled the plane, so nobody was inside it. However, it was full of equipment used to take pictures and record data as the plane passed through the storm.

While large planes can safely fly over a hurricane, looking at a hurricane from above doesn't tell scientists everything they want to know. This is because most hurricanes get their energy from warm water in the ocean. Scientists wanted to learn more about what happens where that warm ocean water meets the air in a hurricane. So, they sent in the small remote-controlled plane. The plane studied how clouds form and measured the temperature of the air and water. It also recorded many images of the storm.

Scientists are still studying the information they collected using the plane. Many hope it will help them better understand how hurricanes form and move so that people can be better prepared when a hurricane comes.

STRATEGY PRACTICE   Describe a type of weather you would like to study.

_____

_____

SKILL PRACTICE   Read the item. Write your response.

1. What is the purpose of the hurricane plane?

_____

_____

2. Where do hurricanes form?

_____

_____

3. What is the importance of studying hurricanes?

_____

_____

Visualization

Visualization allows readers to form mental images of what they are reading about. By visualizing, good readers can better remember the main ideas or events in a passage. Good readers use sensory words from the text to help them visualize and adjust their mental images as they read.

DAY 1

Reproduce the *Visualization* visual aid and distribute it to students. Then introduce the strategy to students. Say: **When good readers read, they often make mental pictures of what they are reading about. They turn what they are reading into a kind of "movie" that plays in their mind. But this doesn't mean they daydream. They pay attention to important and descriptive words.** Next, tell students to close their eyes and visualize as you read the first paragraph of the passage aloud. Read the sentences slowly to give students time to understand and visualize the important descriptions (millions of tons, swirl slowly, huge problem). Direct students to read the passage and then complete the strategy and skill practice activities. Review the answers together.

DAY 2

Remind students of the *Visualization* strategy. Say: **As we read, it's important to look for words we can picture.** Read the first sentence from the passage aloud. Ask: **Which words are easier to picture: *beetles*, *colorful*, or *alone*?** (*beetles* and *colorful*) **That's because a colorful beetle is something we can see. When you visualize, look for words that represent things you can see in real life.** Have students read the instructions at the top of the page and then read the passage. When students have finished reading, have them complete the strategy practice activity and share their answers. Then direct students to complete the skill practice activity. Review the answers together.

DAY 3

Remind students of the *Visualization* strategy. Say: **When you visualize as you read, you can sometimes build your mental images on things you have actually seen. For example, if you are reading about a school, you can start with the image of your own school. Then you can adjust your mental picture to match the details you read.** Direct students to read the passage and complete the strategy and skill practice activities. Review the answers together.

DAY 4

Remind students of the *Visualization* strategy. Say: **Good readers pay attention to the words in a passage. Specific action words, or verbs, and clear describing words, or adjectives, help us make mental images as we read. Which is a better verb, *look* or *seek*?** (seek) **Which is a clearer adjective to describe an apple, *sweet* or *good*?** (sweet) Have students read the instructions at the top of the page and then read the passage. When students have finished reading, direct them to complete the strategy and skill practice activities. Review the answers together.

DAY 5

Remind students of the *Visualization* strategy. Say: **When you visualize a character and his or her actions, you can learn more about that character. You will also remember more about the story. Read aloud the first sentence in the story.** Ask: **Right away, what do you picture?** (e.g., a girl with an angry look on her face, arms crossed) **Instead of just reading about a girl in a foul mood, you can picture the look on her face and how she's sitting. This gives you a clearer idea of how she is behaving.** Then have students read the passage. When students have finished reading, pair them for the strategy practice activity. Invite pairs to share their answers. Then direct students to complete the skill practice activity. Review the answers together.

As you read, picture the Garbage Patch in your mind.

The Great Pacific Garbage Patch

In the Pacific Ocean near Hawaii, millions of tons of garbage swirl slowly in the water. The remains of bottles, plastic bags, fishing nets, and other items float gently around. This is the Pacific Garbage Patch, and it's a huge problem. The Pacific Garbage Patch is in a part of the ocean where water moves endlessly in a circle. Trash from thousands of miles away is pulled by ocean currents until it travels to this spot.

Most of the garbage is plastic. This is because plastic doesn't break down easily. It can only break down into small pieces. These small pieces look like food to fish, birds, and other animals. When these animals eat the plastic instead of filling up on real food, they can become sick and starve to death.

Scientists worry that this ocean garbage will hurt more than just marine life. Eventually, sick animals can make their way into the human food supply. But right now, nobody is sure how to solve the problem. One thing that does work, though, is to recycle plastics or throw them away properly. Remember, if your soda bottle doesn't become litter in the first place, it won't get into the ocean.

STRATEGY PRACTICE   Underline words in the passage that describe the Pacific Garbage Patch.

SKILL PRACTICE   Read the item. Write your response.

1. Picture the Great Pacific Garbage Patch. Describe what you see.

_____

_____

2. Why do sea animals mistake plastic for food?

_____

_____

3. How does recycling help the ocean?

_____

_____

READ THE PASSAGE   Look for words that help you picture the beetle and how it behaves.

One Smelly Bug

Bombardier (bom-buhr-DEER) beetles are colorful but are best left alone. These beetles get their name from the way they keep themselves safe. When a bombardier beetle is threatened, it "bombards" its enemy by spraying a boiling hot, smelly liquid from its body. Frogs, birds, and other animals looking for a meal get a nasty surprise instead.

The bombardier beetle has special body parts that hold two liquids. Muscles push these liquids together, where they mix into a smelly, hot spray. The beetle can aim the liquid in many directions. This allows it to protect itself from the front, side, or back. When the beetle sprays, it also makes a loud pop and a gas that looks like smoke. It's quite a surprise to see a popping, smoking bug!

The beetle isn't the only animal that can protect itself by stinking. Skunks, stink bugs, and musk ox are a few other animals that also use a nasty smell to keep others away. But they don't pop and smoke like the bombardier beetle does. So watch out for this "explosive" insect!

STRATEGY PRACTICE   What words from the passage helped you visualize the bombardier beetle?

_____

_____

SKILL PRACTICE   Read the item. Write your response.

1. Explain how skunks and bombardier beetles are alike.

_____

_____

2. How did the bombardier beetle get its name?

_____

_____

3. A bombardier beetle sees a predator close by. What happens next?

_____

_____

_____

READ THE PASSAGE   As you read, picture how the capital cities are alike and different.

Australia's and America's Great Capitals

Australia's capital city is Canberra (KAN-bruh). Canberra is the location of Australia's Parliament House and High Court. The Parliament House is shaped like a boomerang, while the High Court overlooks a nearby lake. These buildings are similar in purpose to the U.S. Capitol and the Supreme Court building in our nation's capital, Washington, D.C. In these buildings, people make and settle laws for their country.

Canberra is also home to the National Library of Australia. It is very similar to the Library of Congress. Both are huge libraries with millions of books. The National Library of Australia has a copy of every book made in Australia. The Library of Congress has a copy of every book made in the U.S. The two buildings even look similar, with many columns and windows, though the Library of Congress has a large domed tower and is much older.

Both cities also have many monuments for people to see. These monuments teach about the history of the country. For example, Canberra has the Foundation Stone, which represents Australia's six original colonies. In Washington, the Lincoln Monument honors our 16th president.

STRATEGY PRACTICE   What words from the passage helped you picture what the different buildings look like?

_____

_____

SKILL PRACTICE   Read the item. Write your response.

1. How are Canberra and Washington, D.C., alike?

_____

_____

2. Picture the National Library of Australia and the Library of Congress. Describe how these buildings differ.

_____

_____

3. Why do you suppose people visit the monuments in each capital?

_____

_____

READ THE PASSAGE   As you read, try to visualize the ancient Copper Scroll.

The Oldest Treasure Map

You've probably read stories or seen movies about treasure maps. Maybe a pirate was looking for buried treasure. Maybe an explorer was seeking a lost fortune. Most treasure maps are made up by storytellers, but one treasure map is very real and very old.

The Copper Scroll is a treasure map like no other. Instead of being written on paper or animal skin, this map is written on copper. The map is from the Middle East and is over 2,000 years old. Because it is made from copper, the map didn't hold up very well over time. Researchers had to cut the map into strips and then carefully put them back together.

The map's writing is difficult to read, so people aren't sure what it says. Most think the map lists the places where silver and gold were buried. But so far, none of the treasure listed on the map has been found. However, the map is still important. It has helped researchers learn more about how people spoke and wrote thousands of years ago.

STRATEGY PRACTICE   Underline words from the passage that give you a mental picture of the Copper Scroll.

SKILL PRACTICE   Read the item. Write your response.

1. Picture researchers putting the map back together. Describe the setting.

_____

_____

_____

2. Why are people unsure what the Copper Scroll says?

_____

_____

3. How is this treasure map different from other treasure maps?

_____

_____

_____

READ THE PASSAGE   As you read, picture how Tammy behaves.

Tammy's Troubles

Tammy was in a foul mood. Her parents had insisted that she was too young for a cell phone, no matter how much she begged. "But Sun and Alicia have cell phones!" Tammy cried. "If I don't get one, I won't be popular."

"Having a cell phone doesn't make you popular," Tammy's dad said. He was always saying stuff like that, as if he knew what it was like to be in fourth grade. "Besides," Dad said, "your school doesn't allow cell phones, and you can call your friends from the house as soon as you finish your homework."

"But I can't send them text messages," Tammy replied.

"You can use e-mail," Mom said. "Cell phones are expensive. We want you to wait until you can pay for part of the cost before you get one."

"By that time I won't need one," Tammy said. "Nobody will know who I am. I might as well move to a deserted island."

"In that case, I'll get you some empty bottles and some paper," Dad said. "Bottle messages are way cooler than text messages."

"Ugh," sighed Tammy.

STRATEGY PRACTICE   Describe how you picture Tammy.

_____

_____

SKILL PRACTICE   Read the item. Write your response.

1. Name three reasons why Tammy's parents are against her getting a cell phone.

_____

_____

2. Compare an e-mail to a text message.

_____

_____

3. Describe Tammy's facial expression at the end of the story.

_____

_____

Organization

By looking at how a passage or selection is organized, students can better understand the author's intent, as well as predict what information is likely to appear later in the text. Texts are often organized sequentially, around main ideas and details, according to causes and effects, or by comparison and contrast.

DAY 1

Reproduce the *Organization* visual aid and distribute it to students. Then introduce the *Organization* strategy. Say: **By looking at the organization of a passage, we can get a better idea of what the author is trying to tell us. Sometimes the author will use certain words to signal how the information is organized.** Tell students they are going to read a passage that gives information about how to organize a neighborhood party. Say: **Look for words such as *first, next, during,* and *after* to help you understand the order of events that the author describes.** Then have students read the passage. When students have finished, have them complete the strategy practice activity. Ask volunteers to share their responses. Then direct students to complete the skill practice activity. Review the answers together.

DAY 2

Point out to students that by knowing the organization of a passage, good readers can pay more attention to important details and work less hard to understand what the passage is about. Then say: **We are going to read a passage about eating healthful snacks. The author of this passage included both facts and opinions about healthful snacks. As you read, think about how the facts and opinions are organized.** Have students read the instructions at the top of the page and then read the passage. When students have finished reading, direct them to complete the strategy and skill practice activities. Review the answers together.

DAY 3

Remind students of the *Organization* strategy and point out the instructions at the top of the page. Say: **Another way that a passage may be organized is by cause and effect.** (If necessary, review the terms *cause* and *effect.*) **When we read these types of passages, we are looking for what happens and why it happens.** Tell students they are going to read about storm water—the water that runs down sidewalks and streets during a storm. Explain that students can look for cause-and-effect signal words (*because, as a result, therefore,* etc.) as they read to help them understand this kind of text. When students have finished reading, direct them to complete the strategy and skill practice activities. Review the answers together.

DAY 4

Remind students of the *Organization* strategy. Explain to students that the passage they are about to read is a biography. Ask: **What do we usually find in biographies?** (dates, names, important events in a person's life, etc.) Then say: **I expect to see this passage organized around important dates in the life of this person in the order that they happened.** Have students read the passage. When students have finished reading, direct them to complete the strategy practice activity and share their responses. Then direct students to complete the skill practice activity. Review the answers together.

DAY 5

Remind students of the *Organization* strategy and say: **Persuasive writing usually begins with a clear statement of what the author believes. The author then gives facts supporting that opinion and includes a possible objection, or reason you might disagree with him or her. When you read persuasive writing, pay attention to how it is organized. This will help you decide if you agree with the author or not.** Have students read the passage and complete the strategy practice activity. Discuss students' answers. Then have them complete the skill practice activity. Review the answers together.

As you read, notice how the tips for giving a neighborhood party are organized.

A Neighborhood Party

A neighborhood party is a great way to raise money for a charity, to celebrate a holiday, or to get to know the people in your neighborhood. There's no better way to bring the community together than to throw a party!

Before you begin, you first need to figure out where to have the party. Churches or community centers are often available for neighborhood events. If the weather is nice, many people prefer to have the party outside. It could be at a park or on a street that has been blocked off for you ahead of time.

Next, ask your friends and neighbors to help. Volunteers are important for making sure the party runs smoothly. Get plenty of people to help tell others about the party, set up the party, and clean up after the party. A volunteer can post fliers or pass out cards to people in the neighborhood.

During the party, be sure to have lots of things to do. Many parties feature activities for kids, such as relay races or face painting. At most parties, food and drinks are served. The best parties are when everyone brings something to share. After all, that's what being part of a neighborhood is about!

Underline the words in the passage that helped you understand the order of events.

Read the item. Write your response.

1. What is the first step in planning a neighborhood party?

_____

_____

2. What else has to happen before the start of the party?

_____

_____

3. Picture your neighborhood having a party. Describe three activities you would enjoy doing.

_____

_____

READ THE PASSAGE   As you read, look for facts and opinions about healthful snacks.

Smart Snacks

It's not hard to see why cheeseburgers, fries, pizza, and ice cream are popular. They're delicious! But not everything that tastes good is good for you. The next time you need to feed, consider smart snacks.

Nearly everyone loves french fries made from potatoes. Did you know that other root vegetables taste great, too? Root vegetables include beets, carrots, and sweet potatoes. They contain important vitamins and minerals, and they can all do the jobs a potato can do. Raw carrots are crunchy and satisfying. Cooked beets and sweet potatoes are full of flavor. Peel them and cut them into strips, just like fries. Give them a try! You'll forget all about french fries.

Discovering new foods can be fun. Plus, if you eat healthful foods, you'll be less likely to get sick. You'll also have more energy to run and play. And you will be able to think more clearly and for longer periods of time. So start snacking smartly!

STRATEGY PRACTICE   Underline two facts in the passage and draw a box around two opinions.

SKILL PRACTICE   Read the item. Write your response.

1. What is the author's opinion of root vegetables? How do you know?

_____

_____

_____

2. What are three benefits of healthy eating?

_____

_____

3. Does the author make a good case for healthy eating? Explain.

_____

_____

_____

READ THE PASSAGE   As you read, look for reasons why storm water is harmful.

When It Rains, It Pollutes

Have you ever noticed small "rivers" of water running down the sides of streets after a heavy rain? That's storm water, and it is a big source of water pollution.

In cities, the roads and sidewalks cover much of the ground. Therefore, they block the ground from soaking up water. As a result, storm water collects on the pavement or flows through gutters. Most cities have storm drains that channel the storm water out of the city. This keeps cities from flooding, but it has an unwanted effect. It dumps a lot of dirty water into lakes, rivers, and the ocean.

So how does storm water pollute? Well, if you have ever walked down the sidewalk, you have probably noticed trash in the street. Storm water carries this trash with it as it flows. As a result, bags, cans, and bottles end up in lakes and rivers. So do oil and gasoline left behind by cars. This is because when rain hits the streets, it picks up trash and waste from cars and washes it into the storm water.

Scientists and people who plan how cities are designed want to find a way to stop storm water from being such a hazard. They think planning better, having trees and grassy areas, and teaching people not to litter will help.

STRATEGY PRACTICE   What words from the passage helped you understand that the author was showing a cause-and-effect relationship?

_____

SKILL PRACTICE   Read the item. Write your response.

1. Why is storm water a problem?

_____

_____

2. Why does storm water build up in cities?

_____

_____

3. If no one littered, would that affect the storm water problem? Explain.

_____

_____

READ THE BIOGRAPHY   Think about how the author organized the information in the passage.

Dinosaur Discoverer

Roy Chapman Andrews was an American explorer born in 1884. He liked traveling to different places and studying animals. Andrews wanted to find fossils that would tell him more about early humans. Instead, he found something that changed what everyone thought about dinosaurs.

Andrews and his team made many trips to Asia during the 1920s. There, they found dinosaur fossils, as well as fossils from different mammals, including a type of early rhinoceros. Andrews sent his discoveries to the American Museum of Natural History in New York. They liked what he found and encouraged him to keep searching.

Andrews' most interesting discovery was made in 1923 in the Gobi Desert of Mongolia. He and his team became the first people to find dinosaur eggs. Until this discovery, scientists weren't sure whether dinosaurs laid eggs or gave birth to live babies.

In 1927, the Boy Scouts of America made Andrews an honorary Scout. He was the first person to receive this award. Today, Andrews is regarded as a model explorer and adventurer.

STRATEGY PRACTICE   List three important dates in Andrews' life in the order given in the passage. Tell what happened on those dates.

_____

_____

_____

SKILL PRACTICE   Read the item. Write your response.

1. What was the purpose of Andrews' trips to Asia in the 1920s?

_____

2. What important discovery did Andrews make that changed our knowledge of dinosaurs?

_____

_____

3. How did the American Museum of Natural History benefit from Andrews' exploration?

_____

_____

READ THE LETTER   As you read, think about how Troy organized the main points of his letter.

Dear Editor,

I believe I have an idea that will solve the town's money problems. We need $50,000 for the new library. Every year, more than 10,000 people visit during the Pecan Festival. So this year, we should turn the Pecan Festival into a fundraiser for the library!

In the past, admission to the festival has been free. But if we charge five dollars per person this year, we should be able to raise the money we need.

Also, we should sell our famous pecan sticky buns at the festival. We can even set up a kitchen in the middle of the festival and show people how to make them. If some of the bakeries and restaurants from town donate ingredients or lend us bowls, ovens, and mixers, it will help us raise money for the library.

Some will say that people won't come to the Pecan Festival if we charge a fee. This is silly. While $50,000 is a lot of money for our town, five dollars for each visitor is almost nothing. People will gladly donate. This is the only way to raise money for our new library.

Sincerely,

Troy Henson

STRATEGY PRACTICE   How did the organization of the letter help you understand the author's view? Were you convinced? Why or why not?

_____

_____

SKILL PRACTICE   Read the item. Write your response.

1. Write the two facts that Troy establishes in his first paragraph.

_____

_____

2. Quote one of the author's opinion statements from paragraph 4.

_____

3. Why does Troy think that some people will be against his idea?

_____

Determine Important Information

When readers determine important information, they identify the type of text they are reading and then concentrate on finding the essential ideas, events, or details in that text. For nonfiction, determining the important information often means finding the main idea. For fiction, it means understanding essential plot points, themes, or character actions.

DAY 1

Reproduce the *Determine Important Information* visual aid and distribute it to students. Then introduce the *Determine Important Information* strategy to students. Explain: **Good readers look for information that helps them understand what they are reading or answers a question they have.** Point out the ad on the student page and ask: **What are we looking at?** (an ad for a kind of racer) **What information do we usually find in ads?** (the name of the thing being sold, how much it costs, etc.) **Would this ad be better or worse if the picture of the Fast Flyer was not here? Why?** (It would be worse because you couldn't see what the racer looked like.) **So, the picture of the Fast Flyer is important information if you want to know what it looks like.** Direct students to read the instructions at the top of the page, study the ad, and complete the strategy and skill practice activities. Review the answers together.

DAY 2

Remind students of the *Determine Important Information* strategy. Point out the charts on the page. Say: **When you see two things together, such as these charts, it's helpful to study the relationship between them. First look for the information they have in common. Then you can look for the information one chart tells you that the other chart does not.** Have students read the directions at the top of the page. Then have students study the charts. When students have finished, direct them to complete the strategy and skill practice activities. Review the answers together.

DAY 3

Point out the table of contents on the page and ask: **Why do books have a table of contents?** (to tell us what information is in a book and to help us understand how it is organized) **When we read different kinds of text, the information that is important is often different. Would you expect to find a main idea statement or a character's description in a table of contents?** (no) Point out the bold text to the left of each lesson title. Say: **This book is divided into lessons. What type of book has lessons?** (instruction books, textbooks, etc.) Then point out the numbers to the right of the lesson titles. Ask: **What do these numbers tell us?** (what page each lesson begins on) Have students read the instructions at the top of the page. Then direct students to study the table of contents and read the text. When students have finished, direct them to complete the strategy and skill practice activities. Review the answers together.

DAY 4

Remind students of the *Determine Important Information* strategy. Have students look at the Web page briefly, and then ask: **What did you notice first?** Allow volunteers to share their answers, and then say: **I noticed the title of the Web page first. This is important information that tells me what I am reading about. When I look at this Web page, the title, picture, and timeline tell me different kinds of information.** Have students read the directions at the top of the page and the Web page. When students have finished, direct them to complete the strategy and skill practice activities. Review the answers together.

DAY 5

Remind students of the strategy. Then ask them what they see at the top of the page. (a recipe) Say: **A recipe tells what is in a dish and how to prepare it. It tells you important information that you may not know without reading the recipe.** Allow volunteers to share their experiences of cooking with a recipe. Have students read the instructions at the top of the page and study the recipe. Then direct students to complete the strategy and skill practice activities. Review the answers together.

READ THE ADVERTISEMENT   Study the ad and think about the information it tells you.

The *Fast Flyer* is the NUMBER 1 racing machine!
The *Fast Flyer* outraces <u>all other racers</u>!

The *Fast Flyer* is the first choice for people who are serious about racing!

Add the paddle attachments to make the *Fast Flyer* the first-ever water racer!
Only $199!

Rocket pack coming soon!

The *Fast Flyer* is a bargain at **$799**, but for a limited time, you can buy your very own *Fast Flyer* for just **$499**.

STRATEGY PRACTICE   What are two important things to know about the Fast Flyer? Explain why they are important to know.

_____

_____

SKILL PRACTICE   Read the item. Write your response.

1. What is the purpose of this ad?

_____

2. What does the information inside the starbursts tell the reader?

_____

_____

3. How much money can a person save by buying the Fast Flyer on sale? Explain.

_____

_____

READ THE CHARTS   Study the information in each chart and think about how they work together.

Raise Money for Scouts and Earn Prizes!

IF YOU SELL...	YOU CAN EARN...
10 candles OR **10** boxes of cookies	1 prize from **Column A**
20 candles OR **15** boxes of cookies	1 prize from **Column A** AND 1 prize from **Column B**
25 candles OR **20** boxes of cookies	2 prizes from **Column A** AND 1 prize from **Column B**

PRIZES

COLUMN A	COLUMN B
• model rocket	• sticker book
• jigsaw puzzle	• baseball
• paint set	• harmonica
• earbuds	• checkers set

STRATEGY PRACTICE   If you wanted to earn a prize for a friend, how would you use the information?

_____

_____

SKILL PRACTICE   Read the item. Write your response.

1. What items are the Scouts selling? How do you know?

_____

_____

2. How does the chart on the left relate to the chart on the right?

_____

_____

_____

3. What is the fewest number of candles a Scout must sell to earn a prize in Column B?

_____

READ THE INFORMATION Think about what the lesson titles tell you about the book.

CONTENTS

Coming Up with a Story

Even though comic books contain mostly pictures, they still tell a story. And just like stories told with only words, the stories in comic books must be planned and worked on.

Many of the stories you read in comic books are first written as **scripts**. The writer includes many details to help the artist visualize the story before he or she makes the first sketches for the book.

STRATEGY PRACTICE In what kind of class might you use this book? Explain.

_____

_____

SKILL PRACTICE Read the item. Write your response.

1. Based on this table of contents, what would be a good title for this book? Explain.

_____

_____

2. In which lesson would the text that's to the right of the table of contents appear? How do you know?

_____

_____

3. You want to draw an elephant. What page would you turn to and why?

_____

READ THE WEB PAGE Think about how the information is arranged.

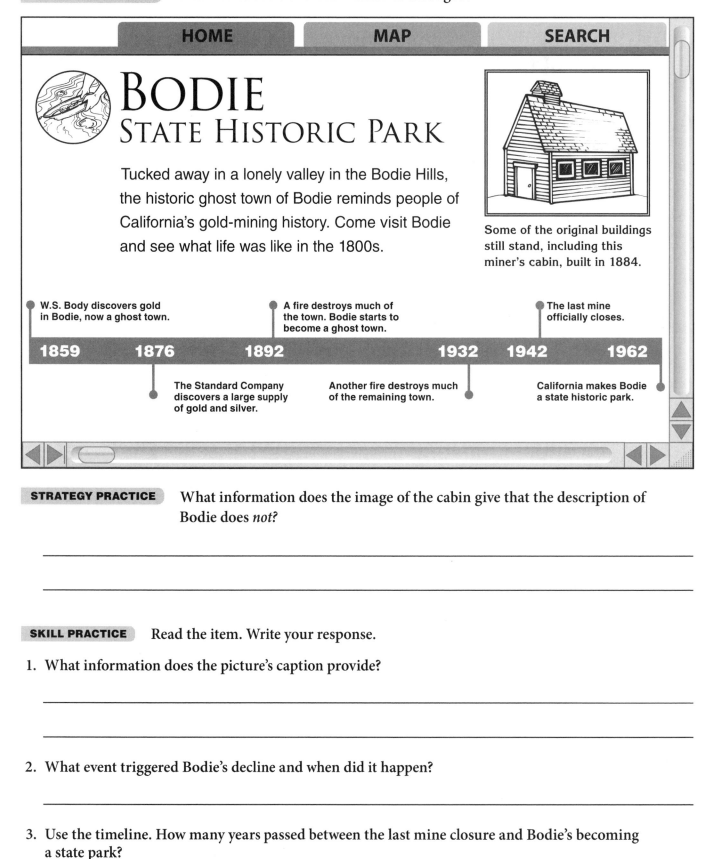

HOME   MAP   SEARCH

BODIE
STATE HISTORIC PARK

Tucked away in a lonely valley in the Bodie Hills, the historic ghost town of Bodie reminds people of California's gold-mining history. Come visit Bodie and see what life was like in the 1800s.

Some of the original buildings still stand, including this miner's cabin, built in 1884.

W.S. Body discovers gold in Bodie, now a ghost town.

A fire destroys much of the town. Bodie starts to become a ghost town.

The last mine officially closes.

1859   **1876**   **1892**   **1932**   **1942**   **1962**

The Standard Company discovers a large supply of gold and silver.

Another fire destroys much of the remaining town.

California makes Bodie a state historic park.

STRATEGY PRACTICE What information does the image of the cabin give that the description of Bodie does *not*?

_____

_____

SKILL PRACTICE Read the item. Write your response.

1. What information does the picture's caption provide?

_____

_____

2. What event triggered Bodie's decline and when did it happen?

_____

3. Use the timeline. How many years passed between the last mine closure and Bodie's becoming a state park?

_____

Name: _____

READ THE RECIPE   Think about the information you would need to know to follow this recipe.

MYrecipes.com

Sweet Party Mix

Rating: ★★★★ (85 users)
Submitted by: Taylor Klark   **Prep Time:** 15 minutes
Cooking Time: 1 hour   **Servings:** 24

Ingredients

- 1 box crispy cereal
- 6 ounces toasted pecans
- ½ cup molasses

- 5 ounces slivered almonds
- ¾ cup butter
- 1½ cups brown sugar

Directions

1. Preheat the oven to 220 degrees. Lightly grease a large baking pan.

2. In a large bowl, mix the cereal, pecans, and almonds.

3. Melt the butter in a saucepan over low heat. Add the molasses and sugar, and mix until you have a syrupy paste.

4. Add the paste to the bowl of cereal and nuts. Stir well.

5. Pour the nut and cereal mixture into the pan. Cook for 1 hour.

STRATEGY PRACTICE   Why do you think a rating is included for this recipe? Why is it important?

_____

_____

SKILL PRACTICE   Read the item. Write your response.

1. Why are there three main parts of this text? What does each part tell you?

_____

_____

_____

2. What is the purpose of the ingredients list?

_____

3. You have 45 minutes before you leave for the party. Can you make this recipe? How do you know?

_____

_____

Ask Questions

By asking questions, readers can set a purpose for reading or make sure they understood what they have read. Good readers ask questions to involve themselves with the text and often ask questions before, during, and after reading.

DAY 1

Reproduce the *Ask Questions* visual aid and distribute it to students. Then introduce the strategy to students. Explain: **One way good readers stay focused and check their understanding is to ask questions. You can ask questions before, during, and after reading. When we ask questions before we read, we set a purpose for reading. The questions we ask can guide our reading.** Tell students they will read about a place that helps children with special needs. Then read the title of the passage aloud. Prompt students to think of questions about what they might read. Model by asking: **Where can you swim with dolphins?** Have students write their own questions in the space provided for the strategy practice activity. Tell students they will look for these answers as they read. Then direct students to read the passage and complete the skill practice activity. Invite students to share whether their initial questions were answered.

DAY 2

Review the *Ask Questions* strategy. Say: **When we ask questions during reading, we are monitoring our comprehension and focus. Asking a question while reading helps us pay attention to what we are reading and sometimes alerts us to information that we don't understand.** Have students read the instructions at the top of the page. Then tell students to think of a question about solar power as they read the first paragraph. Direct students to write that question in the space provided for the strategy practice activity. Have students read the rest of the passage and invite volunteers to share whether or not their questions were answered. Then direct students to complete the skill practice activity. Review the answers together.

DAY 3

Remind students of the *Ask Questions* strategy. Tell students that asking a question after they read is a good way to check that they understood what they have read. Say: **When we ask questions after we read, we are reviewing what we have read to make sure we understood it. We ask ourselves the types of questions that we find on tests or in our textbooks.** Have students read the instructions at the top of the page and the passage. Then direct students to complete the strategy practice activity and ask each other their questions. Discuss as a class how asking and answering those questions helped confirm their understanding of the passage. Finally, direct students to complete the skill practice activity. Review the answers together.

DAY 4

Review the *Ask Questions* strategy by asking: **When you read, when should you ask questions?** (before, during, and after reading) Tell students they are going to read a passage about a sport called rugby. Ask: **What questions do you have about rugby before you read?** (e.g., How is rugby played? What equipment do you need?) Invite volunteers to share their questions. Then remind students to ask themselves questions as they read. Have students read the instructions at the top of the page and the passage. When students have finished, have them share the questions they asked themselves as they read, as well as any remaining questions they have. Discuss the questions and answers as a class. Then direct students to complete the strategy and skill practice activities.

DAY 5

Remind students of the *Ask Questions* strategy. Tell students they are going to read about a dog named Bo who is a husky. Explain that huskies were bred to live in cold climates and to pull sleds. Then have students read the instructions at the top of the page and the passage. When students have finished, pair them or complete the strategy practice activity as a group. Discuss the questions and their answers as a class. Then direct students to complete the skill practice activity independently. Review the answers together.

Daily Reading Comprehension • EMC 3614 • © Evan-Moor Corp.

READ THE PASSAGE   As you read, think about how the author feels about the trip.

Swimming with Dolphins

When my sister Gina was born, she had a problem with her heart. She had five operations before she was three years old. She had trouble walking, playing with other children, and going to school.

Our parents wanted to take Gina to a special place in Florida where she could swim with dolphins. Gina was scared because she had never been around dolphins before. We had also never traveled that far as a family.

When we got to Florida, we saw where the dolphins lived. It was a place where kids with special needs like Gina could come and spend time. I thought it was going to be a vacation, but it wasn't. Gina had to work hard every day for a week.

The trip was amazing. Gina laughed and clapped when she saw the dolphin, and the dolphin squeaked and splashed when it saw Gina. They swam together all day. Gina was able to move her body more than she normally did at home. Mom and Dad were proud of Gina. I was, too.

STRATEGY PRACTICE   Write two questions you had about the passage before you read it.

_____

_____

SKILL PRACTICE   Read the item. Write your response.

1. Why did the author write this text?

_____

_____

2. Use text evidence to explain why Gina has special needs.

_____

_____

3. Did Gina enjoy the trip? What makes you think so?

_____

_____

_____

READ THE PASSAGE Ask yourself questions as you read to help you stay focused on what the author is saying.

Using the Sun at Night

My house gets energy from the sun. That kind of energy is called "solar power." We use it to power the lights, the television, and the computer. It also powers the stove and toaster. It even runs the heater in the winter and the air conditioner in the summer.

We collect the sun's energy with large solar panels on our roof. These panels turn the sun's energy into electricity. Some of the electricity gets used right away, and some of it is stored so we can use it at night.

In the winter, getting enough sunlight can be hard. So sometimes we have to use electricity from the power company. But we need less of this electricity than we would without our solar panels.

The sun is a good source of energy because it will never run out. It is also cleaner than some other kinds of energy and is becoming less expensive, too. In the future, more people will have panels like ours on their roofs.

STRATEGY PRACTICE What is the most important question you would ask the writer about solar power?

_____

_____

SKILL PRACTICE Read the item. Write your response.

1. Why did the author write this text?

_____

_____

2. Which season is the best for making solar energy and why?

_____

_____

3. How is using solar panels similar to getting electricity from the power company?

_____

_____

READ THE PASSAGE   As you read, ask yourself what Mr. Kim wants and what lesson he learns.

Noisy Neighbors

Mr. Kim couldn't take it anymore. He needed peace and quiet. But his two neighbors, Ms. Abrams and Mr. Green, were the noisiest people he had ever known!

In the house on the left, Ms. Abrams gave tuba lessons. In the house on the right, Mr. Green worked on cuckoo clocks. And in the middle was Mr. Kim—sad, tired, and crabby. Then he had an idea. He would pay his neighbors to move!

"Oh boy!" Ms. Abrams said when Mr. Kim offered her $200 to move away.

"Hot dog!" said Mr. Green when Mr. Kim offered him the same deal.

The next day, he saw Mr. Green carrying his clocks to Ms. Abrams' house and Ms. Abrams carrying her tuba to Mr. Green's house.

"I thought you were both moving," Mr. Kim said.

"We are," Mr. Green said. "Ms. Abrams is moving into my old place, and I'm moving into hers." Mr. Kim nearly fainted. What would he do?

The next day, Mr. Green and Ms. Abrams visited Mr. Kim. "We know why you asked us to move," Mr. Green said. "So we got you this." And they gave Mr. Kim a very fancy set of earmuffs. Finally, peace and quiet!

STRATEGY PRACTICE   What questions do you still have about the passage?

_____

_____

SKILL PRACTICE   Read the item. Write your response.

1. Did this really happen? Explain your opinion.

_____

_____

2. What was the author's purpose for writing this story?

_____

_____

3. Describe a lesson that Mr. Kim learned.

_____

_____

Name: _____

READ THE PASSAGE   As you read, ask yourself questions to help you think about the similarities and differences between rugby, football, and soccer.

The Rugged Sport of Rugby

My cousin Chris plays rugby. He says it's similar to football and soccer, but some things are different.

A rugby field is called a "pitch." However, Chris's rugby team plays on the soccer field since it's the same size as a pitch.

To score points, players kick, carry, or throw the ball down the pitch. A rugby "goal" is like a football touchdown, and it is worth five points. A rugby "drop goal" is like a football field goal. For both drop goals and field goals, you kick the ball between two posts to score three points.

The pitch is crowded during a rugby game. That's because each team has 15 players on the field at once. That is more players than in football and soccer, both of which have 11 players.

The ball that players use in rugby is similar to a football. It is made from leather and is shaped like an oval. But it doesn't have laces, and the ends are less pointed than a football's ends.

Chris enjoys playing rugby and hopes to join a league soon. I might join, too.

STRATEGY PRACTICE   Do you think rugby is more like football or soccer? Why?

_____

_____

SKILL PRACTICE   Read the item. Write your response.

1. Why did the author write this text?

_____

2. How is rugby like soccer?

_____

_____

3. How is rugby like football?

_____

_____

_____

READ THE PASSAGE   As you read, think about how the narrator feels about Bo.

Slow Down, Bo!

Bo is a husky that was born in Alaska, but he lives with us in Minnesota now. I walk Bo in the morning and afternoon. During every walk, I usually end up shouting, "Slow down, Bo!"

When Bo was in Alaska, he liked to pull sleds and run fast. He worked with a team of other dogs to pull a sled over snow and ice. Bo was very fast and strong, and his team won several dog-sled races. Many people enjoyed rooting for Bo to run.

Whenever we go on walks, Bo starts out running. He jerks me down the sidewalk and pulls me around the park. I have to dig my heels into the ground and pull Bo back with a sharp tug. This is the only way Bo will stop. I have to wait for him to calm down before we start walking again.

Some people think it is funny when they see Bo trying to race instead of walk with me. "Go, Bo! Go!" they shout and laugh.

"No, Bo! Oh please, no!" I yell. I don't think it is very funny because it feels like Bo is likely to pull my arms off. Mom says Bo will eventually learn how to walk slowly and not try to run everywhere. I hope he's a fast learner.

READ THE PASSAGE   What is one question you have about Bo, huskies, or the author?

_____

_____

SKILL PRACTICE   Read the item. Write your response.

1. Why do you think this family adopted Bo?

_____

2. Does Bo frustrate the writer? Explain.

_____

_____

_____

3. Will things be different for the writer in another month? Tell why or why not.

_____

_____

Main Idea and Details
Students look for the central idea or message of a passage or story. They also find details that best support the main idea.

Sequence
Students look for the order of events or steps in a process.

DAY 1

Point out to students that reading comprehension almost always involves looking for the main idea and details. Explain: **Each passage has a main idea, and each paragraph in the passage has its own main idea. Also, within each paragraph, there are important details that support the main idea of the passage or paragraph. The title can give us a good idea of what the paragraphs in a passage will mostly be about. According to the title, what do you think this passage will be about?** (one of Jupiter's moons) **As you read each paragraph, look for sentences that tell you about this moon.** Have students read the instructions at the top of the page. Then remind them of the *Monitor Comprehension* strategy (Week 1). Tell students to stop after each paragraph and determine that paragraph's main idea. Then direct students to read the passage and complete the skill and strategy practice activities. Review the answers together.

DAY 2

Ask students to recall what a main idea is and what details are. (The main idea tells what something is mostly about, and details are important information that support the main idea.) Then remind students of the *Visualization* strategy (Week 3). Say: **As you read, make a mental image of what is being described. This will help you recall the important details more easily.** Then have students read the passage. When students have finished, direct them to complete the skill and strategy practice activities. Review the answers together. Invite volunteers to share their drawings and explain which words from the passage helped them decide what to draw.

DAY 3

Introduce the *Sequence* skill to students. Say: **Sequence can refer to the order of things in a series, the order of things based on when they happen, or the order of steps or instructions that need to be followed.** Tell students they will read about how emperor penguins care for their eggs. Say: **As you read, underline words in the passage that tell you what happens first, second, and so on. Underlining is a good way to help you monitor how well you understand the sequence of events.** Have students read the passage. When students have finished, direct them to complete the skill and strategy practice activities. Review the answers and the words that students underlined in the passage.

DAY 4

Remind students of the *Sequence* skill. Then say: **You are going to read a passage about how hurricanes form. The formation of a hurricane involves several steps. As you read, number each step.** Model by reading the first sentence of the second paragraph and saying: **The first thing that happens is that the ocean waters begin to warm up. I'll write the number *1* next to this sentence. This will help you understand the sequence.** Then remind students of the *Visualization* strategy. Say: **You can also make a mental picture of each step. This will help you remember the process better.** Then have students read the passage. Direct students to complete the skill and strategy practice activities. Review the answers together and have students share how they numbered the sentences in the passage.

DAY 5

Tell students they will practice both the *Main Idea and Details* and *Sequence* skills as they read a passage about a mixed-up aunt. Review the *Monitor Comprehension* strategy. Then say: **Before you read the passage, read each item in the skill practice activity. Then, as you read the passage, you can look for the information that you need to respond to the items.** Have students read the passage and complete the skill and strategy practice activities. Review the answers together.

READ THE PASSAGE   Stop after each paragraph and tell yourself what it is mostly about.

Life on Jupiter's Icy Moon

Jupiter is the largest planet in our solar system and is made up of many different kinds of gases. It is so big that 1,300 Earths could fit *inside* Jupiter! And it has 63 moons. Some of its moons are like small planets, and others are pieces of frozen rock and ice. Studying Jupiter's moons has helped scientists learn more about the solar system. But the moon that scientists are most interested in is Europa (yur-OH-pa).

The conditions on Europa make it the most likely place other than Earth to have life in our solar system. It is covered in a layer of ice, and some scientists believe a liquid ocean lies beneath the icy surface. If this is true, Europa may have simple forms of life in these oceans. The creatures on Europa would probably be too small to see without a microscope. But the idea of anything at all living on Europa is very exciting.

Right now, we cannot explore Europa because it is too cold and too far away to send people there. The spacecrafts and robots we have are not sturdy enough to land on the surface. But scientists have big plans. In the future, they hope to send one robot to melt some of the ice on Europa's surface, and another robot to swim through its oceans. The information that these robots gather could change what we think about life beyond Earth.

SKILL PRACTICE   Read the item. Write your response.

1. Why are scientists so interested in Europa?

_____

_____

2. What detail from the text helps you to imagine the size of Jupiter?

_____

_____

3. What is the last paragraph's main idea?

_____

_____

STRATEGY PRACTICE   As you were reading, which paragraph was easiest to understand? Why?

_____

_____

Think about the main idea of the passage. Picture the important details in your mind.

A Frog with . . . Claws?

Animals have many ways of defending themselves. Some use poison or bad smells. Others hide or use camouflage to keep from being seen. But one animal with a really weird defense is the hairy frog. This tiny frog lives in Central Africa and has hair-like strands on the lower part of its body. But the strangest part about this frog is its claws!

When the hairy frog is threatened, it will break the biggest of the three toe bones in each of its feet. The broken bone then juts out of the skin as a type of "claw." It looks like a small thorn on the bottom of the frog's foot. But this claw isn't the same as the claw on a cat or dog. It is made of bone instead of keratin (KARE-uh-tin), the material that animal claws and your fingernails are made of. Also, the hairy frog can't pull its claws back into the skin like most animals can. Instead, the skin and bone slowly heal.

The hairy frog isn't the only amphibian to use its bones as a weapon. The ribbed newt can cause its sharp ribs to poke out through its skin. To make things worse, the ribs are covered in poison! So, hungry fish or birds looking for a quick snack get a painful poke in the mouth instead. Who knew such tiny creatures could be so dangerous?

SKILL PRACTICE Read the item. Write your response.

1. How does the hairy frog's claws differ from a dog's claws?

   _____

   _____

   _____

2. Describe how the ribbed newt defends itself.

   _____

   _____

3. Write the main idea of the last paragraph in your own words.

   _____

   _____

STRATEGY PRACTICE On a separate piece of paper, sketch the foot of a hairy frog as you visualized it from the passage.

READ THE PASSAGE   Underline words that help you understand what happens and when it happens.

A Patient Parent

Adults may tell you that it's tough being a parent. Just tell them that they have it easy compared to the emperor penguin. This parent has one of the toughest jobs in the world.

Emperor penguins mate in Antarctica in March or April. The female lays an egg in May or June. Then the mother penguin carefully passes the egg to the father, who balances it on top of his feet. The penguins must be very careful not to drop the egg, as it can crack or freeze if it touches the ground.

The mother leaves to find food, and the father waits patiently for the egg to hatch. This usually takes at least 60 days. During that time, the father doesn't eat, and he must stay very still so he doesn't hurt the egg.

By the time the chick hatches, the father is very weak. But he must feed the baby if the mother has not yet returned. He does this by making a special liquid in his throat. Luckily the mother penguin usually returns within a few days after the chick hatches. She feeds the chick and takes care of it so the father can go get food for himself. By this time, the male has gone 115 days without eating. Talk about a devoted dad!

SKILL PRACTICE   Read the item. Write your response.

1. Who keeps the egg warm for the first two months? Cite text evidence.

_____

_____

2. Why does the father penguin grow weak?

_____

3. What happens after the mother penguin returns?

_____

_____

STRATEGY PRACTICE   Look at the words you underlined as you were reading. Use them to write a summary of the sequence of events described in the passage.

_____

_____

_____

READ THE PASSAGE   Picture what happens during each stage of a hurricane.

A Storm Is Brewing

When people talk about the seasons, they usually mean winter, spring, summer, and fall. But did you know there is also a hurricane season? For people living in the United States, hurricane season starts in June and ends in late November. Although hurricanes and tropical storms can happen at other times, most storms form during the summer and fall months.

In early summer, warm temperatures cause the oceans to warm up, especially near the equator. As water from the ocean evaporates, it carries a lot of heat into the atmosphere. This usually creates a storm. Sometimes storms will blow away, but some storms start spinning. They spin faster and faster and become hurricanes.

The winds of a hurricane can grow to be as strong as 200 miles per hour (320 km per hour). And as the hurricane grows, it begins to travel north. The hurricane moves heat away from the warm part of the ocean in the south into parts of the ocean in the north. As the hurricane does this, it cools and becomes weaker. Eventually, it disappears.

By November, ocean and air temperatures are too cool for hurricanes to form. But by June, hurricane season is sure to start all over again.

SKILL PRACTICE   Read the item. Write your response.

1. Where does a hurricane form, and in what direction does it travel?

_____

_____

2. About how many months of the year are in the hurricane season? How do you know?

_____

_____

3. Think of pictures you have seen of an area affected by a hurricane. What does it look like?

_____

_____

STRATEGY PRACTICE   Which step in the way a hurricane forms was easiest to picture in your mind? Summarize it.

_____

_____

READ THE PASSAGE   Think about the main idea and the order of events in the story.

Mixed-Up Aunt Hilda

June and I were very excited because Mom's sister, Aunt Hilda, was coming to visit all the way from South Africa. Aunt Hilda studied zebras there, and she told many interesting stories. She was really funny, too, because she did everything backward.

"I wonder if we'll have breakfast for dinner," June said. "Or maybe Aunt Hilda will wash clothes in the dishwasher and dishes in the washing machine again."

"I sure hope not. Her visits are getting expensive," said Dad, who was looking out the window and waiting for Aunt Hilda's taxi to arrive. "Oh, here she is!"

Aunt Hilda came through the door. "Good morning!" she said, even though it was late in the afternoon. We laughed, which made Aunt Hilda blush. Aunt Hilda then passed out presents. She gave me a new doll and June a toy robot. She gave Mom a new tie and Dad some fancy perfume.

"I'm so hungry, I could eat a fly!" Aunt Hilda said.

"We're having chicken salad instead," Dad said. "Why don't you get ready for dinner, Hilda." Aunt Hilda walked into the bathroom, put on her pajamas, and walked past us to the guest bedroom. June and I started giggling.

"It must have been a very long flight," Mom said.

SKILL PRACTICE   Read the item. Write your response.

1. How does the author use dialogue to add details to the story?

_____

_____

2. How does Hilda prepare for dinner?

_____

_____

3. Write two details that support the idea that Hilda is odd.

_____

_____

STRATEGY PRACTICE   As you were reading, what did you think was the oddest thing that Aunt Hilda did?

_____

Cause and Effect

Students practice identifying cause-and-effect relationships by looking for what happens (the effect) and why it happens (the cause).

Fact and Opinion

Students determine whether details in a text can be proved (facts) or represent what someone thinks or feels (opinions).

DAY 1

Introduce the *Cause and Effect* skill to students. Say: **When something happens, it is the *effect*. The thing that makes it happen is the *cause*.** Model by walking to the light switch and turning off the lights. Ask: **What caused the lights to go out?** (flipping the switch) **What is the effect of flipping the switch?** (The lights went out.) Say: **Often a writer will use causes and effects to explain a problem and how to solve or prevent it. The passage you will read is about "brain freeze," or the headache people sometimes get from eating ice cream. As you read, look for the causes and effects of a brain freeze.** Then remind students of the *Determine Important Information* strategy (Week 5). Point out that identifying important information helps you find causes and effects. Direct students to read the passage and complete the skill and strategy practice activities. Review the answers together.

DAY 2

Review the *Cause and Effect* skill with students. Say: **Fiction writers often use cause-and-effect relationships to create a problem for the characters or to start a chain of events that move the plot forward. Understanding what happens and why it happens in a story is important.** Then remind students of the *Ask Questions* strategy (Week 6). Say: **As you read, think of questions you might ask the main character in order to better understand her thoughts and feelings.** Then direct students to read the passage before completing the skill and strategy practice activities. Review the answers together.

DAY 3

Introduce the *Fact and Opinion* skill to students. Say: **Remember that a fact is something that is true and can be proved. An opinion is a personal thought or viewpoint.** Write *Leaves make food for plants* and *Leaves are beautiful* on the board. Ask: **Which one is the fact?** (Leaves make food...) **We can look up this information about leaves. Can I prove that leaves are beautiful?** (no) **It is an opinion. Often, writers use both in the same piece of writing. It is up to you to figure out which details are facts and which are the author's opinions.** Tell students they will read about a popular tourist spot called Lake Tahoe. Point out its location on a map. Then remind students of the *Determine Important Information* strategy. Read the strategy practice activity instructions. Say: **As you read, think about which details are facts that could be found in a textbook.** Then direct students to read the passage before completing the skill and strategy practice activities.

DAY 4

Review the difference between fact and opinion with students. Then say: **You are going to read a review of a TV show. As you read, pay attention to whether the details are facts or opinions.** Then remind students of the *Ask Questions* strategy. Say: **Pause after each paragraph and ask yourself a question about that paragraph. This will help you think more about what you are reading.** Then direct students to read the passage and complete the skill and strategy practice activities. Review the answers together.

DAY 5

Tell students they will practice both the *Cause and Effect* and *Fact and Opinion* skills. Explain that they will read a passage about skunks. Say: **As you read, think about what skunks do and why they do those things. Also, look for the author's opinions about skunks and other creatures.** Then direct students to read the passage and complete the skill and strategy practice activities. Review the answers together.

READ THE PASSAGE   As you read, think about the causes and effects of a "brain freeze."

Brain Freeze

Have you ever eaten ice cream on a hot day and suddenly felt a sharp pain in your head? If so, you had a very common experience that some people call a "brain freeze."

Brain freezes are caused when cold food or drink touches the roof of your mouth. Nerves in your mouth send a signal to your brain. Your brain then turns the signal into a sharp pain. However, the pain does not go to your mouth where the cold is—it stays in your head.

Most brain freezes last for less than 30 seconds. But if you want to make it go away quicker, you can try a couple of tricks. When you start to get a brain freeze, push your tongue against the roof of your mouth. This sometimes warms up your mouth so that the nerves don't send the signal that causes a headache. You can also try preventing brain freeze from the start by eating and drinking more slowly. If you take smaller bites or sips and wait longer between them, your mouth won't get as cold. Of course, sometimes a cold drink or an ice-cream cone on a hot day is just too good to enjoy slowly!

SKILL PRACTICE   Read the item. Write your response.

1. What causes a brain freeze?

_____

_____

2. If you have a brain freeze, what can you do right away to try and stop it?

_____

_____

3. How does eating and drinking slowly help prevent brain freeze?

_____

_____

STRATEGY PRACTICE   What is the most important piece of information to remember from the passage if you do *not* want to get a brain freeze?

_____

_____

Think about what happens in the story and why it happens.

Coaster Kingdom

Megan could hardly stay in her seat as her dad pulled the car into the parking lot of Coaster Kingdom, the biggest roller coaster park in the state. Today was Megan's 11th birthday, and she was sure she was finally tall enough to ride the scariest coaster, the Dragon. The Dragon's tracks were made from wood, not metal. Megan knew that wooden tracks were slower than metal ones, but wooden tracks also swayed and creaked, especially on windy days like today.

Megan's father paid for their tickets, and she excitedly took his hand. She wanted to hurry to the coaster, but her dad was thirsty after the long car ride. They stopped at the food court and shared a frozen lemonade and a warm, sugary churro. After their snack, Megan led her dad to the entrance of the Dragon. A sign shaped like a friendly dragon stood in front of the gate. The dragon was holding one hand up, and the message read, "You must be at least this tall to ride this coaster." Megan beamed and ran up to the sign. She stood on the tips of her toes and thought tall thoughts. Her father, however, was not smiling.

"I'm sorry, honey," he said. "Let's go check out the other rides. There are still plenty of fun things we can do today."

SKILL PRACTICE   Read the item. Write your response.

1. What was Megan looking forward to at Coaster Kingdom? How do you know?

_____

_____

_____

2. Why did Megan and her dad stop at the food court?

_____

3. How did Megan react to the dragon sign? Explain why she reacted that way.

_____

_____

STRATEGY PRACTICE   Underline the information in the passage that helped you figure out why Megan's dad said he was sorry and suggested that they go on other rides.

READ THE PASSAGE   Think about which details are facts and which tell how someone thinks or feels.

The Lake on Top of a Mountain

Imagine a lake as blue as the summer sky, surrounded by thousands of pine trees and towering mountains. It sounds like something from a storybook, but Lake Tahoe is a real place in the Sierra Nevada mountains, along the border of California and Nevada.

Lake Tahoe is the best spot for camping, skiing, sailing, fishing, and hiking. In fact, people come during every season to enjoy the lake and mountains. However, Lake Tahoe is best known for its snow sports. Most of the small towns surrounding Lake Tahoe have lodges where families can go to ski or snowboard. These resorts are much more fun to stay at than the ones in other parts of the country.

Thousands of people visit Lake Tahoe each year, but the area was popular long before California and Nevada were even states. Native Americans from the Washoe (WASH-oh) tribe traveled through the mountains and spent their summers at Lake Tahoe. In fact, the name *Tahoe* comes from a Washoe word meaning "big water." The Washoe were expert hunters who used the land and water for their food supply. They even created many legends about the lake. The best one is about a giant bird-like monster that lived in the middle of the lake and ate people!

While people now use Lake Tahoe mostly for fun, it is still important to keep the water and land clean. California and Nevada work together to make sure these natural resources are used wisely. It would be terrible if the lake and mountains became too polluted for everyone to enjoy. There is no place as beautiful or fun for a vacation as Lake Tahoe.

SKILL PRACTICE   Read the item. Write your response.

1. What are two opinions stated in the second paragraph?

_____

_____

2. Write three facts about Lake Tahoe.

_____

3. What is the author's favorite Washoe legend? How do you know?

_____

_____

STRATEGY PRACTICE   Underline two sentences from the passage that you might find in a book about Lake Tahoe's history.

READ THE REVIEW   Pay attention to which statements are facts and which are opinions.

New Reality Show Is a Real "Dog"

As a dog lover who will watch anything about dogs, I had high hopes for *Dog Academy*. The reality TV show follows a group of badly behaved puppies that go to training school. The school is known for being tough on pets and even tougher on their owners. Unfortunately, the show is toughest on the people who watch it!

The best part of *Dog Academy* is a construction worker named Jim and his tiny poodle, Mitzi-Witzi. Jim is over 6 feet (1.8 m) tall, has a thick brown beard, and is bald. He squints and scowls and yells at everyone on the show, but as soon as he is with Mitzi-Witzi, he begins to coo and talk like a baby. Watching them play together is really funny. The show would be much better if it focused only on Jim.

The worst part of the show is Kalen, who is one of the dog trainers. Kalen is a horrible person. She is rude to people and says mean things to them about their pets. When Honkers, a brown pug, chewed up one of Kalen's sneakers, Kalen told Honkers' owner that she had never met such a dumb, smelly dog. There is no reason to act that way. It's just cruel!

The show itself is very boring. The puppies are cute, but no one besides Jim and Mitzi-Witzi has much personality. If you are looking for something to watch on Thursday nights, there are much better shows than *Dog Academy*.

SKILL PRACTICE   Read the item. Write your response.

1. When does this show air and who are its human stars?

_____

_____

2. Would you like to see an episode of *Dog Academy*? Explain.

_____

_____

3. What is the reviewer's opinion of *Dog Academy*? How do you know?

_____

STRATEGY PRACTICE   Write a question you thought of while reading the passage. If you found the answer, write it, too.

_____

_____

READ THE PASSAGE Think about what happens and why it happens. Look for statements that tell what the writer thinks or believes.

Save the Skunks!

When people think about the need to protect animals, how many think of skunks? People dislike skunks for several reasons. Skunks can get into garbage cans. They sometimes carry diseases. And worst of all, of course, they can spray people and pets with a disgusting smelling liquid. But skunks play an important role in their environment.

Skunks are great to have around because they eat other pests. For example, a skunk will eat dangerous scorpions and spiders. Having a skunk around is much better than being bothered by those creepy creatures. Another reason to protect skunks is that they eat animals that are already dead. This helps keep forests and neighborhoods clean.

It's also important to remember that skunks are in our neighborhoods because we have come into their habitats. It's unfair to want the skunks to leave when they were here first! So the next time you catch a whiff of skunk spray, smile and hold your nose. Think about the good work that this peaceful animal is doing to keep your neighborhood clean and safe.

SKILL PRACTICE Read the item. Write your response.

1. What are three reasons that people dislike skunks?

_____

_____

2. Explain why skunks are good for a neighborhood.

_____

_____

3. Does the author prefer spiders to skunks? How do you know?

_____

_____

STRATEGY PRACTICE What information from the passage is important to know if you want to convince people to protect skunks?

_____

Compare and Contrast

Students practice comparing and contrasting by looking at the similarities and differences between two or more people or things.

Make Inferences

Students practice making inferences by using clues in a passage to understand what is being implied or inferred.

DAY 1

Introduce the *Compare and Contrast* skill to students. Say: **When we look at the similarities and differences between two or more things, we are comparing and contrasting.** To reinforce the concept, you may want to draw a Venn diagram on the board and label the diagram *french fries* and *potato chips.* Invite volunteers to list the similarities and differences between the snack foods. Then tell students they are going to read about different kinds of puddings from around the world. Remind students of the *Make Connections* strategy (Week 2). Say: **As you read, think about whether you have eaten or would like to eat the kinds of pudding described.** Have students read the instructions at the top of the page and the passage. When students have finished reading, direct them to complete the skill practice activity. Review the answers together. Have students complete the strategy practice activity in pairs. Invite volunteers to share their responses.

DAY 2

Remind students of the *Compare and Contrast* skill. Then tell students they are going to read an essay that compares mice and rats. Remind students of the *Monitor Comprehension* strategy (Week 1). Say: **As you read, draw a plus sign (+) next to each detail that tells how the animals are alike. Draw a minus sign (–) next to each detail that tells how the animals are different.** Have students read the instructions at the top of the page and the passage. When students have finished reading, direct them to complete the skill practice activity. Review the answers together. Have partners complete the strategy practice activity and share their responses.

DAY 3

Introduce the *Make Inferences* skill to students. Say: **A writer doesn't tell us everything that happens, because doing so would make what we are reading boring, or because the extra information is not that important. Instead, the writer relies on us to make inferences as we read. When we infer, we use clues from the text and our prior knowledge to figure out the information that is not included.** Then tell students they are going to read a passage about a drawing that comes to life. Remind them of the *Make Connections* strategy. Say: **Whenever you make an inference, you have to make a connection with what you are reading. You can't make an inference without thinking about your prior experience.** Direct students to read the passage and complete the skill and strategy practice activities. Review the answers together.

DAY 4

Remind students of the *Make Inferences* skill. Say: **When we make inferences, we use our background knowledge and clues from the text to fill in information we haven't been told directly.** Then tell students they are going to read a passage about a boy who cooks for his tired father. Remind students of the *Monitor Comprehension* strategy. Say: **As you read, think about the clues in the passage that help you make inferences about the food the boy makes.** Then have students read the passage. When students have finished reading, direct them to complete the skill and strategy practice activities. Review the answers together.

DAY 5

Tell students they will practice comparing and contrasting and making inferences by reading about snow skiing and water-skiing. To build background, show pictures of the sports or invite students who have skied to describe the experience. Direct students to read the instructions at the top of the page and the passage. When students have finished reading, direct them to complete the skill and strategy practice activities. Review the answers together.

READ THE PASSAGE Think about the similarities and differences between kinds of puddings from around the world.

A Pudding by Any Other Name

When you think of pudding, do you picture a bowl of creamy chocolate or vanilla dessert? Most people in the United States probably think of pudding in the same way. But there are many kinds of puddings, and not all of them are sweet.

In England, *pudding* can refer to desserts or to side dishes that are eaten with breakfast, lunch, or dinner. These puddings are usually not sweet. They can include butter, flour, spices, and even meats, such as sausage. A blood pudding is a salty side dish made with sheep's or cow's blood that is cooked until it is thick. Yorkshire pudding is almost like a bread and is often served with roast beef. And Christmas pudding is a sweet bread pudding that is served during holidays. It is not creamy like the milk-based puddings most of us are used to, though.

Other countries have puddings, too. Rice pudding is a sweet dessert popular in India and some parts of the United States. It is made with milk, sugar, rice, and spices such as cinnamon. Noodle kugel (KOOH-gul) is a side dish that comes from Eastern Europe. It is a baked mixture of noodles, eggs, butter, and cottage cheese.

Whether you like a creamy, sweet pudding or a salty, starchy pudding, you can travel almost anywhere and find a pudding to suit your tastes.

SKILL PRACTICE Read the item. Write your response.

1. Which puddings are sweet?

_____

_____

2. Name three of the puddings that are served as side dishes.

_____

_____

3. Which pudding mentioned in the text would you not want to try and why?

_____

_____

STRATEGY PRACTICE Tell a partner what kind of pudding you like to eat. If you do not like pudding, tell your partner why.

READ THE ESSAY   Think about the similarities and differences between mice and rats.

Mice and Rats

People use the words *mouse* and *rat* when talking about small, furry animals with big ears, a pointy nose, and a long tail. However, there are many different kinds of rats and mice, such as the Norway rat, black rat, house mouse, and deer mouse. The most common rat that people usually see is the Norway rat, while the house mouse is the most common mouse that people find in their homes.

If the differences between a rat and mouse confuse you, you are not alone. Norway rats and house mice both come from the same relative, which lived millions of years ago. As a result, they have many traits in common. Both Norway rats and house mice have long tails, whiskers, and round ears. They can also be similar colors, including gray, brown, white, and black.

However, there are many differences between Norway rats and house mice. The Norway rat is much bigger than the house mouse. A Norway rat can weigh over ten times as much as a house mouse and is usually three times as large. Also, a Norway rat has big feet and small ears compared to the size of its body. But a house mouse has small feet and big ears compared to the size of its body. And its tail is longer than its body, while a Norway rat's tail is shorter.

Now the next time you see something scurrying around the corner, you can tell whether it's a rat or a mouse before you yelp and scare it away.

SKILL PRACTICE   Read the item. Write your response.

1. You catch a quick glimpse of a rodent. How can you tell if it's a mouse or a rat?

   _____

   _____

2. How are a Norway rat's ears and feet the opposite of a house mouse's ears and feet?

   _____

   _____

3. Why do the house mouse and Norway rat share so many traits?

   _____

   _____

STRATEGY PRACTICE   Tell a partner how writing plus and minus signs helped you stay focused.

Use clues from the passage to make inferences.

Carolina's Strange Trip

Marcia woke up early on Saturday. Her twin sister, Carolina, was still asleep in her bed. Marcia tiptoed into the kitchen. The sun was barely peeking over the hills as Marcia gazed out the window and ate her cereal.

After Marcia finished her breakfast, she found her crayons and paper. She drew a picture of Carolina sailing in a small wooden ship on a giant blue ocean. Just as Marcia finished coloring Carolina's red hair, Marcia heard her sister cry out in surprise. Marcia raced up the stairs and opened the bedroom door to see Carolina sitting in the middle of a tiny boat. The floor and the rest of the room had disappeared. In their place was a wide blue ocean, just like in the picture that Marcia drew.

"Get me out of here!" Carolina cried. "I'm getting seasick!" Marcia raced downstairs again and looked at her picture. The expression on Carolina's face in the picture had changed. She was no longer smiling, and her skin was a little green.

Marcia quickly drew a yellow helicopter above Carolina. Then she drew a friendly firefighter helping Carolina aboard the helicopter. She even drew a large mug of hot chocolate for Carolina to sip. As soon as she finished drawing, Marcia heard a loud whirring sound upstairs. Marcia smiled and raced to her bedroom once again.

SKILL PRACTICE   Read the item. Write your response.

1. What will Marcia see when she opens the bedroom door this time?

_____

_____

2. What can you infer about Marcia's relationship with Carolina from this story?

_____

_____

3. What might Marcia have found in her room if she'd drawn a picture of Carolina in a rodeo?

_____

STRATEGY PRACTICE   Describe how you would have felt if you were Marcia.

_____

_____

READ THE PASSAGE   Use clues from the passage and your own knowledge to make inferences.

Fernando Cooks

Fernando watched Dad walk slowly through the door and sink into his favorite chair. Dad had started a new job and worked from very early to very late. He rarely had time to make dinner or help Fernando with his homework before he needed to go to sleep.

Tonight, Fernando had decided that he would help out by making dinner. It was going to be a surprise.

"Wait right there, Dad," Fernando said. "You're not going to believe this!" Fernando pulled the appetizers from the oven. What were supposed to be mini corn dogs from the freezer now looked like lumps of charcoal. "A little ketchup will fix these guys," said Fernando. He smothered the burned corn dogs in ketchup and took them to Dad. Dad wrinkled his nose but tried to smile at Fernando.

"Thanks, son," he said. "These look...interesting."

Fernando's next course was salad. He pulled a few leaves from a head of lettuce and placed them in two small bowls. He didn't notice the dirt that stuck to the leaves. Fernando then poured half a bottle of ranch dressing over each salad.

Next, Fernando slid the chicken into the oven. The chicken was still frozen, so he turned the oven to its hottest setting. "This is going to be great!" Fernando said.

SKILL PRACTICE   Read the item. Write your response.

1. Why did Fernando's dad wrinkle his nose at the corn dogs?

_____

_____

2. Will the salad taste good? Explain.

_____

_____

3. What is going to happen to the chicken that's in the oven?

_____

_____

STRATEGY PRACTICE   Underline the clues from the passage that helped you make inferences so you could answer the items above.

READ THE PASSAGE   Think about how snow skiing and water-skiing are alike and different.
Use clues from the passage and your background knowledge to make inferences.

Skiing Year-round

Skiing on water and skiing on snow have been popular sports for many years. In both types of skiing, people use long, flat boards to glide across a surface. But the similarities end there.

Snow skiing has been around for at least 5,000 years. Scientists in Norway have found cave drawings that show people skiing. There are two types of snow skiing. Cross-country skiers pump their arms and legs to push themselves forward over snow. In downhill skiing, skiers rely on gravity to build up speed as they slide down a slope.

Water-skiing is a newer sport than snow skiing. It first began around 1920, though people disagree on exactly when. While snow skiers always use two skis, water-skiers stand on either one or two skis, and the skis are wider than snow skis. Also, water-skiers don't move themselves forward. Instead, they hold on to a rope as a boat pulls them.

Skiing is a good sport for people who like to be active all year long. Winter weather is perfect for snow skiing, while the warm days of summer make water-skiing a great way to cool off.

SKILL PRACTICE   Read the item. Write your response.

1. Describe two ways in which snow skiing and water-skiing are similar.

   _____

   _____

2. Describe two ways in which snow skiing and water-skiing are different.

   _____

   _____

3. Why is 1920 the earliest that the sport of water-skiing could have begun?

   _____

   _____

STRATEGY PRACTICE   Describe one more detail about water-skiing or snow skiing that you know.

_____

_____

Character and Setting

Students practice analyzing character and setting by looking at the traits and motivations of a character and where and when a passage's events take place.

Theme

Students practice identifying the theme by looking for the central message or lesson in a passage.

DAY 1

Introduce the *Character and Setting* skill to students. Say: **The characters are who or what a passage is mostly about. Good readers study a character's traits. This means they know what the character looks like or what the character says, does, and believes. The setting is where and when a passage takes place. Good readers think about how the setting affects the characters and the story.** Name the titles of common stories, such as "Little Red Riding Hood," and ask volunteers to name the characters and settings. Then tell students that they are going to read a biography about a famous chemist. Build background by explaining that a *chemist* is a type of scientist who studies the properties of chemicals. Say: **Studying the character and setting of a biography helps us better understand why the author thinks this person is important to write about.** Then remind students of the *Organization* strategy (Week 4). Say: **Biographies are often organized according to chronological order, or the order in which events happen. Pay attention to the order of events as you read.** Have students read the passage and complete the skill and strategy practice activities.

DAY 2

Review the definitions of *character* and *setting* with students. Then tell students they are going to read a passage about a girl on a long hike. Say: **Sometimes, characters change by the end of a story. They may learn or realize something new that causes them to act or think differently. Sometimes, the setting plays a role in this change.** Then remind students of the *Visualization* strategy (Week 3). Say: **As you read the passage, picture the setting. This will help you better understand how and why the character changes.** Have students read the passage and complete the skill and strategy practice activities. Review the answers together.

DAY 3

Introduce the *Theme* skill to students. Say: **A theme is a lesson or view about life that the author wants to share. Often, the theme is not clearly stated in a story. You must think about the events in the story to understand the theme.** Tell students they are going to read a passage about a puppy. Say: **As you read, think about the lesson the author is trying to teach by showing what happens to the puppy.** Then remind students of the *Organization* strategy. Say: **Think about why the author wrote the story in the order he or she did. How does that order affect the theme?** After students finish reading, direct them to complete the skill and strategy practice activities.

DAY 4

Tell students they are going to read a folk tale. Then review the definition of *theme*. Say: **A folk tale usually has a moral or lesson about life. This is the story's theme. For example, the theme of "The Tortoise and the Hare" is that taking your time and never stopping your work pays off.** Then remind students of the *Visualization* strategy. Say: **If you visualize what is happening in the story, you may find it easier to understand the theme.** Have students read the passage and complete the skill practice activity. Then pair students and have them complete the strategy practice activity. Have partners share their responses.

DAY 5

Tell students they will practice studying the characters, setting, and theme by reading a funny story about an unusual family. Encourage students to pay attention to who the main character is and what kind of lesson he learns. Then remind students of the *Organization* strategy. Say: **As you read, think about how the story is organized around what the characters say and how the order of the dialogue helps the story build.** Have students read the passage and complete the skill and strategy practice activities. Review the answers together.

READ THE BIOGRAPHY   Think about the important events in Percy Julian's life.

A Chemist with Solutions

The story of Dr. Percy Julian is an example of one person's hard work, determination, and courage. Percy Julian was born in 1899 in Alabama. Because he was African American, he was not allowed to go to the same schools as white children. The schools he attended did not teach science. And yet, he became fascinated with the science of chemistry. Chemistry is the study of what substances are and how they react with one another.

After college, Percy wanted to go to graduate school so he could become a chemist. But one school after another turned him down because of his skin color. Finally, Harvard University accepted him. He got his master's degree in 1923. Then he went to Europe. In 1931, Percy Julian became Dr. Percy Julian, doctor of chemistry.

For the rest of his life, Dr. Julian worked with chemicals found in plants. He knew that some plants had chemicals that could heal people. But it would take too many plants to have enough of the chemicals, so he created those same chemicals in a lab. That meant more people could get the medicines they needed. He developed chemicals that treated people with eye diseases. He created chemicals used to ease the pain that some people have in their bones. Dr. Julian also used chemicals to invent many new products. One of his products helped fight fires, and another kept food from spoiling.

After working at a company in Chicago for many years, Dr. Julian opened his own lab. Then he started a school that trained young people to be chemists. Dr. Percy Julian died in 1975. Today, his discoveries continue to help millions of people.

SKILL PRACTICE   Read the item. Write your response.

1. Name two difficulties that Dr. Julian had to overcome.

_____

_____

2. Write two conclusions you can draw about the main character. How do you know?

_____

_____

3. What is the setting in which Dr. Julian spent his time when working?

_____

STRATEGY PRACTICE   Discuss with a partner why it made sense for the passage to be organized in chronological order. How did it help you understand what you were reading?

Think about the characters and setting of the passage.

Wendy's Walk

Wendy was hot, tired, and bored. She trudged along behind her brother, Bill, as they hiked up the steep trail to the cabin at the fire lookout tower. Buzzards circled lazily in the sky above them, and Wendy wondered whether they would eat her bones if she died out here. The sun was too hot, the trees and bushes were ugly, and the hike was boring.

"Almost there!" Bill said cheerily. This was his first summer working as a fire spotter at the state park. He would be staying on top of a mountain all summer, watching for fires in the forest. He was excited and had not noticed how tired Wendy had become.

Finally, Wendy couldn't take another step unless she rested first. She sat in the shade of a tall pine tree and drank lemonade from her canteen. Bill continued on for a few more moments before realizing that Wendy was no longer behind him.

"Sorry," he said, returning and sitting beside his sister. "I forgot your legs are shorter than mine." Wendy stuck her tongue out at her brother but then quickly smiled when he handed her some dried strawberries and peanuts from his backpack. "If you chew them together, it's like making a peanut butter and jelly sandwich in your mouth," he said.

The strawberries and peanuts tasted delicious. Wendy closed her eyes, stretched her arms and legs, and wiggled her toes in her hiking boots. She heard a songbird twittering in a nearby bush and caught the smell of wildflowers. Suddenly the sun didn't seem so hot, and the trees weren't as ugly anymore.

SKILL PRACTICE   Read the item. Write your response.

1. When and where does this story take place?

_____

_____

2. Use text evidence to draw a conclusion about Bill.

_____

_____

3. How does Wendy's mood change from the start to the end of the story? Why?

_____

_____

STRATEGY PRACTICE   Underline the details in the passage that were easy for you to visualize.

READ THE PASSAGE   Think about the lesson that Cinder learns.

Curious Cinder

Cinder was a curious puppy. She liked to sniff flowers, bark at cats, and explore her neighborhood. One day, Cinder noticed a strange-looking animal searching for something to eat. It was snooping around the trash cans on the other side of the fence that enclosed Cinder's yard. The animal was furry and small like a cat, but it had black fur with white stripes and a large, bushy tail.

Cinder wanted to meet the animal, so she began looking for a way out of the yard. She whined and dug and hopped and barked. This got the attention of Rupert the cat, who had been napping in the sun. He stretched his legs and arched his back.

"I would leave that skunk alone if I were you," said Rupert, yawning. "You're just asking for trouble."

"What do you know?" Cinder replied. "You're just a silly cat. I'm a curious puppy, and I do what I want." Cinder finally found a hole in the fence that was big enough to squeeze through. Cinder trotted right up to the skunk and said hello.

"Yikes!" shouted the skunk, startled. He quickly raised his big, fluffy tail and sprayed Cinder with a foul-smelling oil.

"Ugh!" cried Cinder, who now smelled awful. "This stinks!"

SKILL PRACTICE   Read the item. Write your response.

1. How did the cat try to help the puppy?

_____

2. What did Cinder learn?

_____

_____

3. How would you describe Cinder before she meets the skunk?

_____

_____

STRATEGY PRACTICE   Underline the advice that Rupert gives Cinder in the story. Then explain why you think the author put it there instead of at the end of the story.

_____

_____

READ THE FOLK TALE   Think about the lesson that the story teaches.

The Boulder and the King

There was once a wise king who was ready to stop being the king. So he ordered some workers to roll a large boulder onto the road that led through town. Then the king hid nearby and watched to see if anyone would move the huge rock from its place in the road. This person would become king.

The first man to pass by was the city's wealthiest person. He bitterly complained that he was too rich to have a boulder in his way. As he walked around the boulder, he shouted, "I must let the king know how angry I am!"

Soon the town's smartest person came to the boulder in the road. She complained loudly that the king should do a better job of keeping the roads clear. Then she, too, walked around the boulder.

Finally, a farmer came along, carrying a load of vegetables. As soon as he arrived at the boulder, he set down his vegetables and tried to move the rock. "Other people might need to use this road," the farmer said to himself. "If I can move it, then I should do so."

After much hard work, the farmer finally succeeded in rolling the boulder off the road. He then noticed a hole where the boulder had been. Inside the hole was a box. The farmer opened the box to find the king's crown and a note. The note read: "For your hard work and for caring about others, you are now the king!"

SKILL PRACTICE   Read the item. Write your response.

1. What kind of text is this (tall tale, fable, realistic fiction, etc.)? How do you know?

_____

_____

2. What is the theme of this story?

_____

_____

3. What lesson did the king teach his subjects?

_____

_____

STRATEGY PRACTICE   Describe to a partner how you visualized the king watching the farmer move the boulder.

READ THE PASSAGE Think about the type of people the Rowlands are and the lesson that Greg learns.

The Amazing Rowlands

Greg Rowland sat in the living room, feeling miserable. His father was a famous magician. His mother was an expert archer and acrobat. And his older sisters were lion tamers. Everyone in Greg's family was amazing, except for Greg. The most exciting thing he could do was to make grilled cheese sandwiches.

"Why so glum?" his mother asked, walking into the living room on her hands.

"I feel very un-amazing," Greg said.

"That's silly," said Greg's father, who appeared in the room in a puff of purple smoke. "You're the most amazing Rowland of all!"

"That's impossible," Greg said. "I can't do magic, I roll sideways whenever I try a somersault, and I'm not brave enough to pet a kitten, much less a lion."

"Yes, but who helps me practice my new tricks?" Dad asked. "And who points out when I make a mistake or when people can see the rabbit wriggling under my hat?"

"And who makes sure my bow and arrows are all in good shape?" asked Mom.

"And who helps us clean out the lions' cages?" called Greg's sisters from the kitchen.

Greg's mother rolled into a sitting position on the floor beside him and ruffled his hair. "You don't have to be flashy to be amazing, son," she said.

SKILL PRACTICE Read the item. Write your response.

1. Why does Greg feel bad?

_____

_____

2. Where does the story take place?

_____

3. What does Greg's family want him to understand?

_____

_____

STRATEGY PRACTICE Why do you think the author chose Greg's mother to speak first and last in the story? How did the order of who spoke when help you follow the theme?

_____

_____

Author's Purpose
Students identify the author's reason for writing about a subject.

Prediction
Students practice using clues from a passage to predict what will happen next.

DAY 1

Introduce the *Author's Purpose* skill to students. Say: **Authors write for several reasons, including to entertain us with a story, to inform us about a topic, to teach us how to do something, and to persuade us to take action or think a certain way. By understanding the author's purpose, we can better understand the main ideas that the author is trying to tell us.** Tell students they are going to read instructions for making a soda bottle "rocket." Then remind them of the *Ask Questions* strategy (Week 6). Say: **These are instructions meant to be used with a product called the Acme Rocket Launcher. As you read, ask questions about the product and look for information that the author gives you.** Then have students read the passage and complete the skill and strategy practice activities.

DAY 2

Remind students of the *Author's Purpose* skill and review the common reasons authors write (to entertain, to inform, to teach, and to persuade). Tell students they are going to read an essay that gives an opinion about a school lunch menu. Then remind students of the *Make Connections* strategy (Week 2). Say: **As you read, think about what is offered for lunch at our school. This will help you better connect with the author and understand her point of view.** Have students read the passage and complete the skill and strategy practice activities. Review the answers together.

DAY 3

Introduce the *Prediction* skill to students. Say: **When we make a prediction, we use clues from the text and our background knowledge to predict what will likely happen next.** Model by telling students about a time when you were able to successfully predict what would happen. For example, say: **I saw a boy walking down the hall not looking where he was going. I predicted that he would bump into someone, and he did.** Explain the clues and the background knowledge used to make the prediction. Then remind students of the *Ask Questions* strategy. Say: **Asking questions about what you have read is a good way to check your predictions.** Have students read the passage. When students have finished, direct them to complete the skill practice activity. For the strategy practice activity, pair students and have them share their questions and answers with the group.

DAY 4

Review the *Prediction* skill with students. Then tell students they are going to read about African killer bees. Say: **As you read this nonfiction article, pay attention to the main ideas and details. They will help you make predictions about how these bees behave.** Then remind students how to use the *Make Connections* strategy. Say: **As you read, think about your own experience with bees or what you have heard or read about them.** Then have students read the passage and complete the skill and strategy practice activities. Review the answers together.

DAY 5

Tell students they will practice both the *Author's Purpose* and *Prediction* skills by reading a story about a turtle who decides to take a vacation. Then remind students of the *Ask Questions* strategy. Say: **Asking questions before you read is a good way to set a purpose for reading. It helps you know what to focus on as you read.** Model by pointing out the title of the story. Say: **This title makes me wonder how a turtle could go on vacation. Will this be a realistic story or fantasy?** Direct students to think of their own question and write it in the space provided for the strategy practice activity. Then have students read the passage and complete the skill practice activity. Invite volunteers to share what they wrote for the strategy practice activity.

READ THE INSTRUCTIONS   Think about why the author wrote the instructions.

Build Your Own Bottle Rocket!

Now that you have your very own **Acme Rocket Launcher**, you can create and launch rockets that show off *your* personality and creativity.

All you need is your **Acme Rocket Launcher** and a few simple household materials:

- a 20-ounce (.6 L) plastic soda bottle
- permanent marker
- scissors
- poster board
- colored markers or paints
- glue

What to do:

1. Clean the soda bottle completely and allow it to dry.

2. Use the permanent marker to draw three small triangles and one large triangle on the poster board. Cut out the triangles.

3. Roll the large triangle so that two of its sides touch and it forms a pointed cone. This is the rocket's nose cone. Glue the sides of the cone so that it hold its shape.

4. Glue the nose cone to the bottom of the bottle to make the top of the rocket.

5. Glue the smaller triangles to the other end of the soda bottle, around its opening. This is the bottom of the rocket. The triangles will be the tail fins.

6. Follow the launching instructions included with your **Acme Rocket Launcher** and have a <u>blast</u>!

SKILL PRACTICE   Read the item. Write your response.

1. What was the author's purpose in writing this text?

_____

_____

2. Why did the author include the numbered list?

_____

_____

3. Where would the reader find these instructions?

_____

_____

STRATEGY PRACTICE   Write a question you thought of while you were reading. If you found the answer, write it, too.

_____

READ THE ESSAY   Think about why the author wrote the essay.

Taco Tuesdays

Every Monday, fourth-grade students at Jackson Elementary have art class. Every Tuesday, we have music class, and Wednesday is computer class. Each week, the class schedule is the same. However, the cafeteria menu is *not.* The menu changes from week to week, and the weekly menu that we are given is often wrong. The cafeteria should have a menu that is the same each week and that offers delicious foods.

By having a menu that stays the same each week, students, teachers, and parents would know what food to expect every day. This would help us know whether to bring a lunch from home if we don't like what is being served. Also, we wouldn't need a new menu printed out each week. This would save time and paper.

People might think that fourth-graders would get tired of eating the same thing every week. But if the meals are fun and delicious, we won't mind. Most of us would rather eat our favorite foods again and again than have many kinds of foods that taste bad. For example, everyone likes tacos. If every Tuesday was taco day, then we would enjoy coming to school on Tuesdays more!

It's not fun to go to lunch expecting hamburgers, only to be served creamed corn. And it's just as bad to bring a lunch from home because the menu said we'd be eating boiled fish sticks when the cafeteria is really serving pizza. So let's make the food better and the menu predictable.

SKILL PRACTICE   Read the item. Write your response.

1. Who wrote this text and why? How do you know?

_____

_____

2. Write three reasons that support the author's stance.

_____

_____

3. What is the author's main point in the third paragraph?

_____

STRATEGY PRACTICE   Do you agree with the author? Why or why not?

_____

READ THE PASSAGE   Use clues from the story and your experiences to predict what Jason will do next.

Jason and His Guitar

Jason admired the new guitar he had received for his birthday. It was shiny and black, with red flames decorating the body. "This guitar is awesome!" Jason said. "I'm going to practice every day until I know at least three songs!"

The next day, Jason spent the afternoon looking through his microscope at rainwater he had collected from the backyard. His guitar sat in the corner of his room.

Two days after his birthday, Jason spent the afternoon trying to wrap Biscuit, the family cat, in aluminum foil. Jason was trying to make her the first astronaut kitty. Biscuit was yowling sadly. Jason's microscope sat in the corner of his room, next to his guitar.

Day after day, Jason found something new to do that he had not done the day before. The pile of equipment and supplies in the corner of his room grew.

"How is the guitar practice coming along?" Mom asked. She was making sandwiches for lunch and watching Jason dig through the recycling bin for cans he could use to make a tin-can telephone.

"Huh?" Jason said, looking up. "Oh, yeah. I'll get around to it. I'm waiting until I feel the music."

"I wish you'd feel the need to clean your room," Mom said, handing Jason his lunch.

SKILL PRACTICE   Read the item. Write your response.

1. What is Jason likely to do after he eats lunch?

_____

_____

2. Use two adjectives to describe Jason. Support your answer with text evidence.

_____

_____

3. How will Biscuit behave the next time that she sees Jason? Why?

_____

_____

STRATEGY PRACTICE   Write a question that can be answered with information from the passage. Then have a partner answer your question.

READ THE PASSAGE   Use clues from the passage and your own knowledge of bees to make predictions about the African killer bee.

Flight of the Killer Bees

The African killer bee might sound like a terrifying insect, but its name isn't entirely accurate. Its real name, in fact, is the Africanized bee. And although it can be dangerous, it does not fly around killing people.

Africanized bees first came to North America from Brazil. Beekeepers in North America wanted a honeybee that could live in warm climates. The bees from Brazil were better suited for the warmer weather. However, some of the bees escaped into the wild. They formed groups called colonies. These colonies started moving north. They have now spread through the southern parts of Texas, New Mexico, Arizona, and California. However, the bees do not seem to be moving farther north. Some scientists believe this is because the bees only do well in warm climates.

Africanized bees do not try to find people to sting. However, these bees are easy to upset. For instance, they do not like the sound of motors. And they are more likely to attack than other bees are. African killer bees will also chase their victim, sometimes as far as a quarter of a mile. Therefore, if you see a swarm of bees flying toward you, move away quickly but calmly and try to go indoors. You never know what mood those bees could be in!

SKILL PRACTICE   Read the item. Write your response.

1. How would Africanized bees react to the sound of a lawn mower? How do you know?

_____

_____

2. What kind of weather would be bad for Africanized bees? Support your answer with text evidence.

_____

_____

3. What should you do if a swarm of bees comes after you?

_____

STRATEGY PRACTICE   Write two other facts you know about bees, or describe an experience you have had with bees.

_____

_____

READ THE PASSAGE Think about why the author wrote the story. Use clues from the passage and your own experiences to make predictions. Complete the strategy practice before you read.

Turtle Goes on Vacation

Turtle was wise and hardworking, and he had delivered the mail for many years. Turtle had worked for so long that no one, not even Turtle, could remember when he had last taken a day off. So Turtle's friends wanted him to have the best vacation ever.

"Go see the world," said Stork, who delivered babies to very surprised parents. Stork traveled great distances because she could fly. But Turtle could not fly and did not think one day off was long enough to see the world.

"Sleep in," said Bear, who was thinking of the warm cave where he had spent all winter. Turtle enjoyed sleeping in the mud during winter, but it was spring now.

"Find a new place to live," said Hermit Crab, who had recently traded his old shell for an empty tin can. "My new place smells like peaches!" But Turtle was not able to leave his shell the way that Hermit Crab could.

"You should go see a movie," said Owl, who worked at night. "I hear there is a new movie about owls that is supposed to be quite good."

Turtle smiled politely at Owl and nodded his head. He then called his cousin, Frog, and asked if she was free the next day. Turtle smiled broadly at Frog's reply.

SKILL PRACTICE Read the item. Write your response.

1. What is the author's purpose for writing this text?

_____

2. Why didn't Turtle like the other animals' suggestions?

_____

_____

3. What do you think Frog said to Turtle? What makes you think so?

_____

_____

STRATEGY PRACTICE Write a question you have about what might happen in the story. If you find the answer as you read, write it, too.

_____

Nonfiction Text Features

Students practice identifying and comprehending common features of nonfiction text.

Visual Information

Students examine and evaluate information that is depicted visually.

DAY 1

Introduce the *Nonfiction Text Features* skill by pointing out the title and headings in the chart on the student page. Say: **Nonfiction writing often includes features that are not part of the main body of text but contain important information about the topic. Good readers know how to use these features to help them understand what they read.** Tell students they are going to read information on a chart about the food groups. Then remind students of the *Determine Important Information* strategy (Week 5). Say: **In a chart, column headings give important information. Read them first to determine what the topic of each column will be.** Then have students read the chart and complete the skill and strategy practice activities. Review the answers together.

DAY 2

Remind students of the skill by pointing out the index on the student page and having students identify some of its features (headings, entry names, page numbers, references to other entry names, etc.). Ask: **What does an index tell us?** (the pages where we can find information about a certain topic) Tell students that the index they will read is from a nonfiction book about the environment. Then review the *Organization* strategy (Week 4). Ask: **How is an index organized?** (The main entries are listed in alphabetical order, and so are the subentries under each main entry.) Read the instructions for the strategy practice activity aloud. When students finish reading the index, direct them to complete the skill and strategy practice activities. Review the answers together.

DAY 3

Introduce the *Visual Information* skill to students. Say: **Not all information is delivered in the form of words. Pictures, graphs, and other visual features can also tell us information.** Point out the flowchart on the student page and say: **A flowchart gives us information based on choices we make. This flowchart helps us choose something to eat.** Model how to read the chart, starting in the upper-left corner. Then remind students of the *Determine Important Information* strategy. Say: **As you study the flowchart, pay attention to the questions and arrows linking the parts of the chart. This will help you better understand how the choices you make are important.** When students have finished studying the chart, direct them to complete the skill and strategy practice activities. Review the answers together.

DAY 4

Review the *Visual Information* skill with students. Say: **Information can be presented and understood with pictures, graphs, diagrams, maps, and other visual features. Knowing how to interpret and understand visual information is as important as being able to read words.** Tell students they are going to read a paragraph and study a map about climate zones in the United States. Then remind students of the *Organization* strategy. Say: **As you study the map, pay attention to how the labels and shading help organize the information visually**. When students have finished reading, direct them to complete the skill and strategy practice activities.

DAY 5

Tell students they will read a flier in order to practice both the *Nonfiction Text Features* and *Visual Information* skills. Remind students of the *Determine Important Information* strategy. Say: **Use the pictures and text features to help you determine what information is important to know if you want to hire this pet sitter.** When students have finished reading, direct them to complete the skill and strategy practice activities.

READ THE CHART   Use the column headings to help you understand the chart.

The Food Groups

GRAINS	VEGETABLES	FRUITS	DAIRY	MEAT AND BEANS
Eat 6 ounces daily	**Eat 2½ cups daily**	**Eat 2 cups daily**	**Eat 2 to 3 cups daily**	**Eat 5½ ounces daily**
• Eat whole-grain cereals, breads, crackers, rice, and pasta. • 1 ounce is about 1 slice of bread, 1 cup of cereal, or ½ cup of cooked rice or pasta.	• Eat a lot of green vegetables, such as broccoli and spinach. • Eat plenty of orange vegetables, such as carrots.	• Eat a variety of fruits, including berries, citrus fruits, and fruits with pits or cores. • Choose fresh, frozen, or dried fruits. • Limit fruit juices.	• Eat low-fat or fat-free milk, yogurt, and other dairy products. • If you can't have milk, choose foods and drinks that have calcium added to them.	• Choose low-fat or lean meats, poultry, and fish. • Bake or broil meat. • Eat other foods high in protein, such as beans, peas, nuts, and seeds.

SKILL PRACTICE   Read the item. Write your response.

1. Look at the "Meat and Beans" column. Why are beans included with meat? How do you know?

_____

_____

2. Which is better for you: an orange or orange juice? How do you know?

_____

_____

3. What does the chart advise for people who cannot eat dairy products?

_____

_____

STRATEGY PRACTICE   What information in the chart would be helpful to someone who is trying to figure out how much food from each group to buy? Explain your answer.

_____

_____

_____

READ THE INDEX   Read this index from a nonfiction book about the environment.

INDEX

A

Accidents, *see* **Disasters**

Acid rain, 44

Air pollution, 19, 40–45

Alaska, 79–85
  glaciers, 80
  map, 82
  special animals, 83

Alternative fuels, 199–206
  batteries, 200, 201
  natural gas, 201, 202
  solar energy, 201, 204–206

Arctic Ocean, 109–114
  climate change, 110–112
  map, 109

B

Bahamas, 59–61
  climate, 59
  environmental research, 61

Brazil
  natural resources, 92–94
  oil production, 94

C

Carbon dioxide, 162
  common sources, 162
  effects, *see* **Greenhouse gases**

Carbon monoxide, 165–170
  from cars, 166

Climate, 59, 80, 110–112, 166
  Bahamas, 59
  climate change, 80, 110–112, 166

SKILL PRACTICE   Read the item. Write your response.

1. Which two topics listed in the index have maps? How do you know?

   _____

   _____

2. What would you expect to read about on page 93?

   _____

   _____

3. What is the purpose of an index?

   _____

   _____

STRATEGY PRACTICE   How is the index organized? How is its organization different from a table of contents?

   _____

   _____

READ THE MENU   Think about how the design of the menu would help you choose a meal.

Andy's Diner Kids' Menu

Can't decide what to have for dinner? Let us help you choose! Read the question
in each box and follow the arrow that matches your answer.

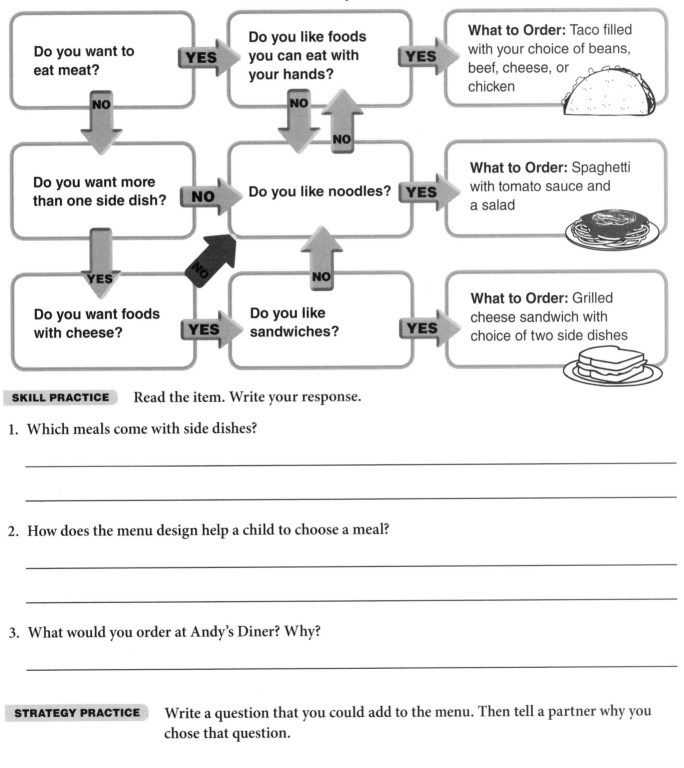

SKILL PRACTICE   Read the item. Write your response.

1. Which meals come with side dishes?

_____

_____

2. How does the menu design help a child to choose a meal?

_____

_____

3. What would you order at Andy's Diner? Why?

_____

STRATEGY PRACTICE   Write a question that you could add to the menu. Then tell a partner why you
chose that question.

_____

READ THE INFORMATION   Read the paragraph and study the map.

United States Climate Zones

According to the Department of Energy, there are four climate zones in the United States: *Cold, Temperate, Hot-Humid,* and *Hot-Arid.* Areas with cold climates have mild summers and cold winters. Areas with temperate climates have warm summers and cool winters. Hot-humid climate zones have mild winters, hot summers, and plenty of rain. Hot-arid climate zones have hot summers, mild winters, and little rainfall.

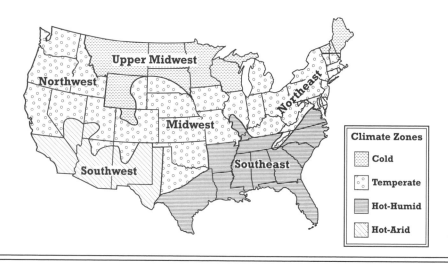

SKILL PRACTICE   Read the item. Write your response.

1. What is the name of the climate zone that has cool winters and warm summers? Name one region that is in this zone.

_____

_____

2. Is Texas in a single climate zone? How do you know?

_____

_____

3. Describe the climate zone of the Southeast.

_____

STRATEGY PRACTICE   Why is a different style of shading used for each climate zone on the map? How did this help you understand what you were looking at?

_____

_____

READ THE FLIER Think about the text features and visual information that the author uses.

Hire the Best-and Bravest-Pet Sitter in Town
If you have an unusual pet, call ME! (Duke K.)

I will watch any pet because
I am not afraid of anything!*
I like...

- bugs and slugs
- bats and rats
- frogs and dogs

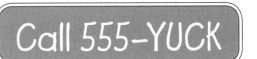
Call 555-YUCK

*Except for geese. They are mean.

I will keep your spider warm and safe, as long as I don't have to feed or touch it.

I will watch your snake (unless it is venomous).

Dad says I am not allowed to watch lions, tigers, or bears, unless they play football.

SKILL PRACTICE Read the item. Write your response.

1. Why did Duke create this flier?

_____

_____

2. How could you contact Duke?

_____

3. What kind of pets would Duke refuse to pet sit? How do you know?

_____

_____

STRATEGY PRACTICE Write two questions you would ask Duke if you wanted him to watch your pet.

_____

_____

Main Idea and Details

Students look for the central idea or message of a passage or story. They also find details that best support the main idea.

Sequence

Students look for the order of events or steps in a process.

DAY 1

Review the *Main Idea and Details* skill with students. Say: **Writers do not always clearly state the main idea of a passage or paragraph. Sometimes you have to figure out what the main idea is.** Model by reading the first paragraph aloud. Say: **This paragraph is introducing fungi.** *Fungi is the plural of fungus.* On the board, write: "Fungi are living things that do not make their own food." Then say: **I took the more important details from the sentences and formed a main idea statement. To help you monitor your comprehension and find the main idea, pause after you read each paragraph and ask yourself, "What is this paragraph mostly about?" Then check to see if your main idea matches the details in the paragraph.** Then remind students of the *Monitor Comprehension* strategy (Week 1). Read the instructions for the strategy practice activity aloud. Then say: **As you read details about fungi, write three facts you learn in the space provided for the strategy practice activity.** When students have finished reading, invite volunteers to share the facts they wrote. Then have students complete the skill practice activity.

DAY 2

Review the concept of *Main Idea and Details* with students by saying: **Good details tell us more about the main idea. They further explain what the author wants you to know about a topic.** Tell students they are going to read about a carousel designed by kids. Then remind students of the *Visualization* strategy (Week 3). Say: **As you look for details, notice which ones help you picture the carousel in your mind.** After students finish reading, have them complete the skill and strategy practice activities. For the strategy practice activity, invite students to draw on a separate piece of paper.

DAY 3

Remind students of the importance of paying attention to sequence as they read a passage. Say: **By understanding sequence, or order, we can understand nonfiction texts that tell about a process. As you read this passage about making a balloon for a parade, pay attention to the steps involved in making the balloon.** Then remind students of the *Monitor Comprehension* strategy. Read the instructions for the strategy practice activity aloud. Say: **Asking questions is a good way to monitor your comprehension.** Have students write questions in the space provided for the strategy practice activity as they read the passage. After students finish reading, have them complete the skill practice activity. Review the answers together and invite volunteers to share the questions they wrote.

DAY 4

Review with students the importance of the *Sequence* skill. Say: **Many actions are performed in a certain sequence. Understanding sequence will help you understand the order of those events.** Tell students they are going to read a story about the steps a girl follows when she bowls. Then remind students of the *Visualization* strategy. Say: **As you read, think about how the sequence described helps you picture what is happening.** When students have finished reading, have them complete the skill and strategy practice activities. Review the answers together.

DAY 5

Tell students they will practice both the *Main Idea and Details* and *Sequence* skills. Then remind students of the *Monitor Comprehension* strategy. Say: **Thinking about how you read different kinds of text is a good way to monitor your comprehension. As you read the paragraph, the supply list, and then the directions, think about what you do differently to read each of them.** When students have finished reading, direct them to complete the skill and strategy practice activities. Review the answers together.

READ THE PASSAGE   Make sure you understand the facts about fungi (FUN-geye or FUN-jeye).

Fascinating Fungi

Do you like pizza with fungus on it? You do if you eat mushrooms on your pizza. Mushrooms are a type of fungus, and so are molds. They are living things that grow best where conditions are damp and warm. Unlike plants, fungi do not make their own food. Fungi take what they need from whatever they are growing on.

Fungi are not particular about where they feed. A peach that's getting soft is a perfect place for mold to grow. Mold will settle on the peach and attach itself with fine threads. These spread rapidly and form black, white, pink, or green fuzz. A moist shower curtain may not sound as tasty as a peach, but to mold it's just as nutritious! And in the woods, fungi flourish. They are everywhere and help dead plants and animals break down and rot.

There is no one shape or color of fungi. Many fungi have names based on the types of mushrooms they produce. Small yellow buttons of fungi are called fairy cups. Shiny globs of slimy fungi are known as witches' butter. Red mushrooms trimmed with tiny fibers are called eyelashes. But no matter what they are called, all fungi are fascinating!

SKILL PRACTICE   Read the item. Write your response.

1. What is the main idea of this text?

_____

_____

2. How do fungi get nutrients? Cite text evidence.

_____

_____

3. Give two details that support this statement: Mushrooms come in different shapes and colors.

_____

_____

STRATEGY PRACTICE   In your own words, write three facts about fungi.

_____

_____

_____

READ THE PASSAGE   Stop often to make sure you understand the main idea and important details.

Red Cow and Purple Whale

Imagine a zebra with horizontal stripes and plaid legs. Picture a red cow with a large square body and bright green legs. Think about a giraffe that looks like a huge, fat, yellow pencil. These animals actually exist. They're just some of the figures on a fantastic carousel, or merry-go-round, in a park in Harlem, New York.

The ride is called Totally Kid Carousel because the animals were designed by kids. An artist named Milo Mottola was hired to make the merry-go-round. He invited children to the park. Dressed in armor made of foam rubber, he explained that carousels go back to the time of knights. He gave drawing lessons to the kids and told them to let their imaginations loose.

Milo had a tough time choosing the winning drawings. Once he did, he made the animal figures look exactly as they had been drawn. "I wanted the merry-go-round to be as magical as the children who ride it," said Mottola. Each original drawing hangs in a frame over its animal figure on the carousel, and the kids' signatures are carved into the wooden floor.

So if you visit the carousel, climb onto the bright orange swordfish, or tickle the giant purple whiskers of the pink cat. The Totally Kid Carousel is a totally fun ride.

SKILL PRACTICE   Read the item. Write your response.

1. Which animal described in the text would you like to ride on? Why?

   _____

   _____

2. Write the main idea of paragraph 2 in your own words.

   _____

   _____

3. How did Mottola give credit to the kids who drew the pictures for the carousel?

   _____

   _____

STRATEGY PRACTICE   Draw one of the animals that you visualized on the carousel.

Think about the steps in making the balloon.

Big Balloons

A 50-foot-tall (15-meter-tall) orange and black cat named Garfield drifts by with his thumb up. A 529-pound (240-kg) Mr. Potato Head passes high above you. The biggest stars in Macy's Thanksgiving Day Parade in New York City don't march. They float. They're giant balloon characters.

The enormous balloons take about one year to create. Each balloon first begins as a carefully drawn sketch. Experts make sure the balloon will float easily and safely. Once the sketch is approved, artists create a clay model. It is an exact replica of the balloon character, but much smaller in size. Next, workers make a painted model to test the details and colors that will be used for the finished balloon. The balloon is then ready to be made at its full size, in sections. Each section is formed of strong fabric. All the sections are then sealed together to create the character's shape.

A few weeks before the parade, each section of the balloon is checked for leaks. The balloon's final inflating takes place the night before the parade. The balloon is held down with nets, ropes, and sandbags. Trucks filled with helium gas stand nearby. Workers use long hoses to pump the helium into the balloon. About six hours later, the balloon finally has a shape and is ready to greet the world.

SKILL PRACTICE Read the item. Write your response.

1. What is the first step in creating a Macy's Thanksgiving Day Parade balloon?

_____

2. Describe what happens after the model is painted.

_____

_____

3. Why do workers inflate the balloon the night before the parade?

_____

_____

STRATEGY PRACTICE Write two questions you have about making huge, helium-filled balloons.

_____

_____

Visualize the steps in Carly's method of bowling.

Carly Likes Strikes

Carly loves the sound of bowling pins crashing against each other. She likes watching a bowling ball hurl down the lane. Carly bowls twice a week. She belongs to two leagues. She has her own bowling ball, too. It has orange and brown spirals that remind her of a giant marble. She also likes the way the pins rattle when she makes them fall.

Carly has a method for bowling that helps her focus. When it's Carly's turn to roll, she first wipes her hands. Next, she tugs on her bowling glove so that it fits her hand just right. Then, she walks over to the ball rack. After she twirls the ball twice, she slips her fingers into the holes. Carly then picks up the ball and faces the pins. She holds her bowling ball so that her thumb lines up with the first pin. Her wrist is steady and straight. She takes a deep breath and then goes into motion. Her steps are quick and sure. She reaches the line and rolls the ball with a smooth swing. Carly pumps a fist as if that final action will cause the pins to fall.

Read the item. Write your response.

1. What does Carly always do just before she lifts the bowling ball from the ball rack?

   _____

   _____

2. When does Carly take a deep breath?

   _____

   _____

3. Picture Carly just after she's thrown the bowling ball. What is she doing?

   _____

   _____

Look back at the passage. Underline two steps in Carly's process that were easy for you to picture in your mind.

READ THE INSTRUCTIONS   Think about how you read the different kinds of texts.

A Vegetable Bouquet

What can you do if you don't want to eat your vegetables? Turn them into art! You can use paints to transform vegetable slices into blooming "flowers."

You will need:

- white art paper
- watercolors
- tempera paints
- paintbrushes
- paper plates
- salt
- sliced vegetables such as cucumber, onion, and bell pepper

1. On the art paper, use watercolors to paint a vase sitting on a table. Let the paint dry.

2. Paint the background with watercolors. While the paint is wet, sprinkle some salt over it to add texture. When the paint is dry, shake off the excess salt.

3. Pour one color of tempera paint onto each plate.

4. Dip a vegetable slice into a paint color. Press the slice onto the paper to print a flower "blossom" above the vase.

5. Repeat, using the other vegetables to create different colors and shapes of blossoms.

6. Use green paint to add stems and leaves.

SKILL PRACTICE   Read the item. Write your response.

1. Could you use only one of the types of paint in the list? Explain.

_____

_____

2. Would it be better to use fresh or cooked vegetables? Why?

_____

_____

3. Describe what this craft project looks like when it is finished.

_____

_____

STRATEGY PRACTICE   Explain what you did differently to read the list of supplies as opposed to the numbered steps.

_____

_____

Cause and Effect

Students practice identifying cause-and-effect relationships by looking for what happens (the effect) and why it happens (the cause).

Fact and Opinion

Students determine whether details in a text can be proved (facts) or represent what someone thinks or feels (opinions).

DAY 1

Review the *Cause and Effect* skill with students. Say: **An effect is something that happens. The cause is why the effect happened.** Tell students they will read about a different kind of school that was created in Australia. Then remind students of the *Determine Important Information* strategy (Week 5). Say: **As you read, look for the important information that helps you understand why the school was created and what effect it could have on students.** When students have finished reading, have them complete the skill and strategy practice activities. Review the answers together.

DAY 2

Review the *Cause and Effect* skill with students. Tell them they are going to read about three places with unusual library systems—Kenya, northern Thailand, and Indonesia. Explain that in these places, transportation is challenging. Help students find the places on a world map. Say: **Pay attention to details about each place mentioned in the passage. These details will help you understand the causes and effects in the passage.** Then remind students of the *Ask Questions* strategy (Week 6). Say: **As you read, think about questions you may have about how people in these areas get books.** When students have finished reading, have them complete the skill and strategy practice activities. Review the answers together.

DAY 3

Review the *Fact and Opinion* skill with students. Say: **A fact can be proved. An opinion is what someone thinks or believes.** Tell students they will be reading a baseball fan's opinion of the Philadelphia Phillies' team mascot, the Phanatic. Point out that *phanatic* is a play on *fanatic*, which is where the word *fan* comes from. Ask students if they can guess why the Phillies' mascot spells its name with a *ph* instead of an *f* (to match the *ph* in *Philadelphia* and *Phillies*). Then remind students of the *Determine Important Information* strategy. Say: **As you read, look for information that provides support for each fact or opinion.** When students have finished reading, direct them to complete the skill and strategy practice activities.

DAY 4

Tell students they are going to read about the clothes worn by a cowboy. Then say: **Some writers include facts and opinions about a topic in the same paragraph. Pay attention to which details are facts and which are opinions.** Then review the *Ask Questions* strategy. Say: **By asking questions about a passage, we think about what else we need to know to fully understand it.** Tell students to read the passage and complete the skill and strategy practice activities. Review the answers together, and invite volunteers to share the questions they wrote.

DAY 5

Tell students they will practice both the *Cause and Effect* and *Fact and Opinion* skills as they read a passage about a strange animal called a hagfish. Say: **Hagfish live deep in the ocean and have some unique characteristics. As you read, look for causes and effects of the hagfish's unusual traits. Also, pay attention to the opinions the writer includes to describe his feelings about hagfish.** Then remind students of the *Determine Important Information* strategy. Say: **Look for information that you think is the most important for understanding the life of a hagfish.** After students finish reading, have them complete the skill and strategy practice activities. Review the answers together.

READ THE PASSAGE   Think about the causes and effects of attending a school through the Internet.

School Is a Click Away

The country of Australia has a vast area of land called "the outback," where few people live. If you live in the outback, chances are you're far from any town. And that means you're a long way from a school. So what do you do if you can't go to school? Well, school comes to you. Over 100 kids in the outback attend ASSOA—Alice Springs School of the Air. ASSOA students are connected by the Internet.

Some lessons happen in real time. When students log in, their teacher appears on their computer screens. She can talk to students, show an art project, or explain a science experiment. She can't see the students, but she can hear them. Students communicate with their teacher and with each other over the Internet, using their computers. But because students are in a "virtual" classroom and not at a physical school, they must still have a home tutor. The tutor can be a parent or a hired teacher. All tutors are trained to help students understand and complete their work.

ASSOA tries to create a school community. Every two weeks, students attend a virtual school assembly. Three times a year, all students travel to the town of Alice Springs. For an entire week, they leave the virtual classroom and enter a real one.

SKILL PRACTICE   Read the item. Write your response.

1. Why do students attend ASSOA?

_____

_____

2. What is the purpose of the virtual school assemblies?

_____

_____

3. Why do all ASSOA students have tutors?

_____

_____

STRATEGY PRACTICE   Look back at the passage. Underline the sentences that contain the most important information for someone who wants to know how attending an online school might affect a student.

READ THE PASSAGE   Think about why some places in the world have traveling libraries instead of buildings with books.

Libraries to Go

In the small villages of Kenya, Africa, most kids want to read books. But no roads lead to their homes, only miles and miles of sand. Cars and trucks are useless. So library books arrive on the backs of camels. Camels can handle the sand *and* the books. Two camels, a camel driver, and a librarian walk to the villages. One camel carries about 400 pounds (180 kg) of books, and the other carries a tent. At each village, the librarian sets up the tent and displays the books inside. Two weeks later, the camels return with new books.

Some people in the mountains and jungles of northern Thailand get books in a different way. Their "libraries" are carried by elephants. These massive mammals can handle the difficult journey. Because of their size, they can carry heavy loads of books in metal cases. The metal protects the books from the heavy rains that fall in the area.

Indonesia has its own challenges. This country is made up of over 17,000 islands. Therefore, most people travel by boat, and so do their library books. A wooden library boat holds about 500 books packed in boxes. Boxes of books are left in villages and are traded for new books a few weeks later.

For people who live in a remote area and can't get to a library, a library that comes to them brings more than books. It brings a whole world of information.

SKILL PRACTICE   Read the item. Write your response.

1. How do library books get delivered to jungle areas in Thailand?

_____

_____

2. Where and why do library books travel by boat?

_____

_____

3. Describe a temporary library in a small town in Kenya.

_____

_____

STRATEGY PRACTICE   Write a question you had as you read the passage.

_____

READ THE PASSAGE   Notice which details are facts and which are opinions.

One "Phantastic" Mascot

Baseball games are fun to watch, except when players can't hit the ball. So when I'm bored, I pay attention to the team mascot. I'm a fan of the Philadelphia Phillies. Our mascot is a huge creature covered in bright-green fur. He's the Phillie Phanatic. Although the Phanatic has a beak, it's not like any beak I've ever seen. His beak looks like a megaphone, and his tongue seems longer than a snake. The Phanatic will dance with the fans, steal their popcorn, and sit in their laps. Of course, he also gets them to cheer for the Phillies. The funniest thing he does is load up his hot dog launcher and shoot hot dogs into the crowd. The hot dogs are smeared with mustard and relish, and they are wrapped up and ready to eat.

I think the name "Phanatic" is perfect because it describes Phillie fans. We're fanatics! We get carried away when it comes to cheering for our team. Unlike the Phillies, a lot of teams have a mascot that goes with their team name. For example, the Orioles, Blue Jays, and Cardinals all have bird mascots that look like the real birds. I think that's kind of boring. I'll take our crazy-looking bird any day. No mascot is as "phun" as the Phanatic!

SKILL PRACTICE   Read the item. Write your response.

1. What is the author's opinion about the Philadelphia Phillies' mascot? Cite text evidence.

   _____

   _____

2. Write three things that the Phillie Phanatic may do during a game.

   _____

   _____

3. Identify the two facts given in the second paragraph.

   _____

   _____

   _____

STRATEGY PRACTICE   Underline the information in the passage that tells you what the Phanatic looks like.

READ THE PASSAGE   Notice which sentences are the writer's opinions and which are facts.

The Right Clothes for the Job

I think it would be great to have a job like my dad's. He's a cowboy who takes care of cattle on a big ranch. Most people think Dad's work is tough. He does his work on horseback much of the time. But Dad says his horse is a great partner. And the clothes he wears help him get the job done, too.

My dad has worn the same cowboy hat for a long time. The crease down its middle is permanently filled with dirt. The wide brim has kept the sun out of his eyes and the rain and snow off his face for years.

When Dad's work gets rough, he wears leather chaps over his jeans. They protect him from thorny cactuses and prickly bushes. And it's very dusty on the range during the hot, dry summer, so Dad ties a red bandana around his neck. When the dust blows, Dad pulls up the bandana to cover his nose and mouth.

To me, Dad's boots are the best! They're golden brown, just like honey, with stitching down the sides. I once wondered why cowboy boots have high heels. Dad says the heels prevent his feet from slipping through the stirrups.

I know that Dad is a good cowboy. But his clothes make him look good, too!

SKILL PRACTICE   Read the item. Write your response.

1. Are there any opinions in the second paragraph? How do you know?

_____

_____

2. "Dad's boots are the best!" Is this a fact or an opinion? Explain.

_____

_____

3. Why does Dad wear chaps?

_____

_____

STRATEGY PRACTICE   Write a question you have about cowboy clothing.

_____

_____

Name: _____

READ THE PASSAGE Notice how the author uses facts and opinions to describe hagfish. Pay attention to the causes and effects of a hagfish's physical traits.

Icky or Interesting?

I've talked to a lot of fishermen, and they all agree. They believe that the ugliest and strangest fish of all is the hagfish. Some call the slimy hagfish a true monster of the deep. I think hagfish are gross but in an interesting way.

For one thing, a hagfish has an unusual body. It is long and slippery like an eel, but it is not an eel at all. A hagfish has four hearts and two brains. Its eyes are covered with skin, so it is nearly blind. But it has four thick, whisker-like organs called *barbels* that wiggle like fingers out of its snout. These barbels and the hagfish's single nostril help the fish find food.

The hagfish's way of defending itself has resulted in its nickname, "slime eel." Large glands run along the sides of the hagfish's body. When danger is near, the glands secrete slime. And this is no ordinary goo. A hagfish's slime has fibers that make it very sticky. The fish can ooze a bucketful of slime in just seconds!

The slime is a good weapon, but it can also clog the hagfish's gills. So a hagfish has to work the slime off its body. It does this by tying itself into a knot! The hagfish can do this because it has no stiff fins or bones. Its muscles push the knot down its body and squeeze off the slime.

A hagfish's eating habits are odd, too. It eats living and dead animals. Its body digests food very slowly. So a hagfish can go seven months between meals.

SKILL PRACTICE Read the item. Write your response.

1. When does a hagfish ooze slime?

   _____

   _____

2. Are there any opinions stated in the last paragraph? How do you know?

   _____

   _____

3. Why does a hagfish tie its body into a knot?

   _____

STRATEGY PRACTICE With a partner, decide which information about the hagfish is important for understanding why some people think the animal is ugly and strange.

Compare and Contrast

Students practice comparing and contrasting by looking at the similarities and differences between two or more people or things.

Make Inferences

Students practice making inferences by using clues in a passage to understand what is being implied or inferred.

DAY 1

Review the *Compare and Contrast* skill with students. Say: **When we compare and contrast, we look at how two or more things are alike and different.** Tell students they are going to read about two types of prickly animals. Then remind students of the *Make Connections* strategy (Week 2). Say: **As you read this passage, think about other animals that have a special way of defending themselves. Think of how those animals are similar to and different from the animals in this passage.** When students have finished reading, have them complete the skill and strategy practice activities. Review the answers together.

DAY 2

Remind students of the *Compare and Contrast* skill. Then tell students they are going to read about the differences between baseball in Japan and the United States. Read the title aloud and, if necessary, explain that it is based on the song "Take Me Out to the Ballgame." The author replaced the American snack *Cracker Jack* with *grilled eel*, a popular Japanese food. Say: **The two countries play the same game, but attending baseball games in Japan is different from attending games in the U.S. Pay attention to those differences as you read.** Then remind students of the *Monitor Comprehension* strategy (Week 1). Say: **One way to monitor your comprehension is to think about the details as you read. Which ones seem most important in helping you understand how the two games are alike or different?** After students finish reading, have them complete the skill practice activity. Then pair students to complete the strategy practice activity. Invite pairs to share their answers.

DAY 3

Review the *Make Inferences* skill with students. Say: **When we make an inference, we use clues from the passage and our background knowledge to figure out information that is not directly stated in the passage.** Tell students they are going to read about meteors and meteorites. If necessary, point out to students the definitions of *meteor, meteoroid,* and *meteorite* in the passage to make sure they understand the differences. Then remind students of the *Make Connections* strategy. Say: **In order to make good inferences, you have to connect what you are reading to what you already know. As you read, use your background knowledge about rocks, space, and Earth to help you infer what is not directly stated.** After students finish reading, have them complete the skill and strategy practice activities. Review the answers together.

DAY 4

Remind students of the *Make Inferences* skill. Then tell students they are going to read a mystery story about a family camping trip. Say: **Solving a mystery often requires making inferences. As you read, pay attention to the clues to solve the mystery of the missing food.** Then remind students of the *Monitor Comprehension* strategy. Say: **A good reader will often reread a passage to make sure he or she understands everything that happened. After you read the passage once, read it again and circle or underline the clues that help you solve the mystery.** After students finish reading, have them complete the skill and strategy practice activities.

DAY 5

Tell students they will practice both the *Compare and Contrast* and *Make Inferences* skills as they read about how chocolate is made. Ask: **Did you know that there are different kinds of chocolate? This passage compares milk chocolate, which is what most candy bars are made of, to dark chocolate. As you read, think about what you already know about chocolate to help you make inferences.** Have students read the passage and complete the skill and strategy practice activities.

Name: _____

Find out how porcupines and hedgehogs are alike and different.

Prickly Critters

Some small animals are just not made for cuddling. For instance, the pointy quills on a porcupine say, "Stay away!" And so do the sharp quills on a hedgehog.

Both animals have short legs and chubby bodies. This means they can't make fast getaways. So when there's danger, they rely on their prickly quills. About 30,000 quills line a porcupine's hide, while a hedgehog has about 5,000 to 7,000 quills on its small body. The quills usually stay flat on both animals. And neither animal can shoot its quills to attack. But they do use their quills in different ways.

An angry porcupine slaps its predator with its tail. This action releases quills that stick painfully in the victim. A hedgehog's tail is too short for slapping, however. So the animal pulls itself into a tight ball, which makes only the spiky quills show. The hedgehog then looks like a real ball of trouble!

Although both animals have quills, some of their other physical features are different. A porcupine weighs between 12 and 35 pounds (5.4 and 16 kg), while a hedgehog usually weighs about 2 pounds (.9 kg). Also, a porcupine has large front teeth, like a rat. The teeth are used to gnaw wood and tree bark. A hedgehog, on the other hand, has a pointy snout that helps it find tasty bugs and slugs.

SKILL PRACTICE   Read the item. Write your response.

1. How does a porcupine differ from a hedgehog?

_____

_____

2. How are the defenses of a hedgehog and a porcupine similar?

_____

_____

3. Name two adjectives that apply to both porcupines and hedgehogs.

_____

STRATEGY PRACTICE   Write about another animal you know of that is *not* made for cuddling.

_____

_____

Notice what is the same and different about American and Japanese baseball.

Buy Me Some Peanuts and Grilled Eel

The United States and Japan are separated by thousands of miles. But the two countries are united by a love of baseball. The game is played by the same rules in both countries. And each team has nine players. The ballgames even begin the same way. Fans stand up to hear their country's anthem and to listen for the players' names. Another similarity is that Japanese and American baseball seasons both last from April to the beginning of October. And in both countries, food is an important part of watching the game. You might munch on a hot dog in either Japan or the United States. But in Japan, you can also choose grilled eel, a Japanese ballpark favorite.

There are a few other differences as well. Only 144 games are played during the season in Japan, compared to 162 games for the season in the United States. And there are 30 American major league teams, but only 12 in Japan. The customs of fans are different, too. In Japan, the outfield seats are divided into two official cheering sections. Fans of the home team sit on one side. Fans of the visiting team sit on the other. The noise never stops! Drums beat, trumpets blow, and the fans sing or shout the same cheers. There is a special cheer for each player, and each team has its own song. But, unlike American fans, Japanese fans sit quietly when their team is not up to bat. Americans like to cheer and jeer through the whole game, no matter who is up to bat.

SKILL PRACTICE   Read the item. Write your response.

1. Tell four ways in which Japanese and American baseball games are alike.

_____

_____

2. Tell three ways in which a Japanese baseball game differs from an American one.

_____

_____

3. Would you like to try grilled eel? Explain.

_____

_____

STRATEGY PRACTICE   Discuss with a partner the biggest difference between American and Japanese baseball.

READ THE PASSAGE   Look for clues that help you make inferences about rocks from outer space.

Meteorites—Rocks from Space

Have you ever seen a streak of light flash across the night sky? You might call it a shooting star. Scientists call it a meteor. A meteor is something that falls through Earth's atmosphere and has a glowing tail. Usually, meteors are rocks that heat up as they fall. As they burn, the rocks glow brightly. Most meteors burn up quickly in the atmosphere and never hit the ground. But if a meteor does crash into Earth's surface, it is called a meteorite.

The rocks that we see as meteors come from different sections of our solar system. However, most come from the part of our solar system between Mars and Jupiter. Scientists call these rocks meteoroids. Like planets, meteoroids orbit the sun, but they are much, much smaller than planets. Sometimes meteoroids have orbits that cross Earth's orbit. Gravity then pulls them through Earth's atmosphere, turning them into the meteors you see streaking through the night sky.

The largest meteorite ever found in the United States is the Willamette Meteorite. This rock crashed thousands of years ago in what is now Oregon, at a speed estimated to be 40,000 miles per hour (64,000 km per hour). You can see the 15-ton (13.6-metric ton) meteorite at the American Museum of Natural History in New York City. It has been on display there since 1906. Just look for a hole-filled rock the size and shape of a small car!

SKILL PRACTICE   Read the item. Write your response.

1. Why has the Willamette Meteorite been on display for more than 100 years?

_____

_____

2. Why can studying meteors be difficult?

_____

_____

3. What did the author do to prepare to write this text?

_____

_____

STRATEGY PRACTICE   Describe what you would do if you saw a meteorite crash into the ground.

_____

Look for clues that explain what happened to the campers' food.

Who Did It?

As Dad showed Mae and Cassie how to set up the tents, many pairs of eyes were watching them. Like spies on a mission, the inky black ravens followed the campers' every move. Dad unpacked containers of food, reminding the girls to keep the containers shut tight. "We don't want raccoons stealing our food," he warned.

"Yeah," said Cassie. "Especially the gooey brownies Mom baked for us."

Dad and Mae went to get the sleeping bags from the car. Cassie offered to stay behind and gather twigs for a fire. She watched her dad and sister disappear around the corner. A few minutes later, Cassie saw Mae and Dad returning. She quickly brushed the crumbs off her shirt.

The girls sat on fallen tree trunks while Dad cooked dinner. They laughed at the ravens somersaulting in the sky. Other ravens carried twigs and acorns up to their nests. Woodpeckers drummed their beaks into tree bark. They were hungry for the bugs inside. Mae was hungry for a brownie. She pulled the top off a plastic container. "That's funny. I thought Mom packed eight brownies. But there are only seven."

After breakfast the next day, all three went for a hike. They were ready for a snack when they got back. "That's strange," said Dad as he brushed a black feather off the picnic table and searched through the food. "The bag of peanuts is gone." He glanced around. "And there aren't any raccoon prints."

SKILL PRACTICE Read the item. Write your response.

1. Why did Cassie offer to gather twigs?

_____

2. Who or what took the bag of peanuts? Why do you think so?

_____

_____

3. What is Dad concerned about? Use text evidence in your response.

_____

_____

STRATEGY PRACTICE In the story, underline the clue that hints at what probably happened to the brownie. Circle the clue that hints at what probably happened to the nuts.

Notice what is the same and different about the two kinds of chocolate.

From Seeds to Sweets

Dark chocolate or milk chocolate? People argue about which tastes better. But did you know that both flavors start as seeds inside large, wrinkly pods? The pods grow on cacao (kuh-COW) trees. Farmers slice open each pod. They scoop out the big cacao beans and spread them under banana leaves for a week. Then the beans are laid out on tables and rooftops to dry. The dried beans are sold to companies that make chocolate.

In chocolate factories, machines clean, mash, and roast the cacao beans. Then ingredients are added to make either dark chocolate or milk chocolate. Dark chocolate has more cocoa butter in it, which gives it a dark-brown color. Milk chocolate is a lighter shade because it has milk in it. These ingredients give the chocolates different flavors, too. Dark chocolate sometimes tastes bitter. Milk chocolate is sweeter.

People have enjoyed chocolate for a long time. About 2,000 years ago, chocolate was a drink mixed with chili peppers. The first candy bar was created in 1847. It was dark chocolate. Then, in 1876, a candy maker added milk to create the first milk chocolate. Today, over 3 million tons (2.7 metric tons) of cacao beans are used every year all over the world!

SKILL PRACTICE Read the item. Write your response.

1. How are dark chocolate and milk chocolate alike?

_____

_____

2. What makes dark chocolate different from milk chocolate?

_____

_____

3. Is chocolate popular worldwide? Use text evidence in your response.

_____

_____

STRATEGY PRACTICE Write something you know about chocolate that helped you understand the passage.

_____

_____

Character and Setting

Students practice analyzing character and setting by looking at the traits and motivations of a character and where and when a passage's events take place.

Theme

Students practice identifying the theme by looking for the central message or lesson in a passage.

DAY 1

Remind students of the definition of *setting*. Say: **The setting is where and when a story or passage takes place.** Confirm students' understanding by choosing a story they are familiar with and asking them to identify the setting. Tell students they are going to read a passage about the world's oldest amusement park, which is in Denmark. Point out Denmark on a map. Then remind students of the *Organization* strategy, which was introduced in Week 4. Ask: **Since this passage tells the history of a place, how do you expect it to be organized?** (in chronological order) Have students read the passage and complete the skill practice activity. Then pair students to complete the strategy practice activity. Invite volunteers to share their responses.

DAY 2

Remind students of the definition of *character*. Explain that there is often more than one character in a passage. Say: **Good readers notice how characters are similar and different. Knowing these traits helps them better understand a passage.** Remind students of the *Visualization* strategy, which was taught in Week 3. Say: **Visualizing the characters is another way to help you better understand and remember the passage.** Direct students to read the passage and complete the skill and strategy practice activities. Review the answers together.

DAY 3

Review the definition of *theme* with students. Say: **The theme is a lesson or viewpoint that the author wants you to think or learn about as you read.** Give examples of themes in familiar stories (e.g., Cleverness is rewarded in "Jack and the Beanstalk"). Have students read the instructions at the top of the page. Then tell students they will read a new version of a fairy tale. Read the title aloud and ask students if they recognize what story this passage is based on ("The Boy Who Cried Wolf"). Point out that both stories are organized similarly. Then direct students to read the passage and complete the skill and strategy practice activities.

DAY 4

Review the definition of *theme* and remind students of the *Visualization* strategy. Say: **Sometimes, visualizing a passage can help you figure out the theme. As you read this passage, picture the events in your mind, especially during the trial.** Have students read the passage and complete the skill and strategy practice activities. Review the answers as a group. Invite students to read the sentence they wrote and to explain how visualization helped them understand the theme.

DAY 5

Tell students they will practice studying character, setting, and theme as they read about a man who must make a decision. Say: **This story is open-ended. This means that we don't know what the final outcome will be. However, you can use clues about Charlie and the setting to help you figure out the choice that Charlie will probably make.** Then remind students of the *Organization* strategy. Say: **This story is organized so that the reader learns about Charlie's problem and has to interpret what Charlie will likely do. Make sure you read carefully to catch important details.** Then direct students to read the passage and complete the skill and strategy practice activities. Review the answers together.

READ THE PASSAGE   Think about the history of Bakken and the people who affected it.

The World's Oldest Amusement Park

If you ever make it to Denmark, you should visit Bakken (BOK-en), the world's oldest amusement park. Like other amusement parks, Bakken has roller coasters, food, and games, but its history is very different from amusement parks and fairs you might know.

Bakken was popular in the late 1500s as a place to get clean water. People in the nearby city could not drink the dirty water near the town, so they went to the springs at Bakken. Soon, merchants and performers showed up. The merchants sold food and crafts, while the performers did tricks for the visitors.

During the mid-1600s, Bakken was closed to the public. It was part of the land that belonged to the king. In 1669, King Frederick III turned Bakken into a private animal park that was like a personal zoo. The next king, King Christian V, made the park larger in 1670. But the park remained private until 1756, when King Frederick V wanted to share the park with everyone.

Once the park reopened to the public, merchants and performers showed up again. Soon, Bakken became one of the most well-known places in Europe. During the 20th century, roller coasters and other typical amusement park rides were added to Bakken. Today, Bakken is the second most popular place for tourists to visit in Denmark.

SKILL PRACTICE   Read the item. Write your response.

1. What did the performers and merchants do at Bakken in the late 1500s?

_____

_____

2. Why was Bakken closed to the public for nearly 100 years?

_____

_____

3. Describe what Bakken looks like today.

_____

_____

STRATEGY PRACTICE   Think about the subject of the passage and then tell a partner why you think the author organized it in chronological order.

READ THE PASSAGE   Pay attention to how Ben and Oscar behave and the different things they do.

A Perfect Job?

Ben and Oscar decided that pet-sitting would be the perfect summer job. So Ben designed a flier, and the boys posted it at the pet store, Petrie's Pet Palace.

A few days later, the boys got their first job. A man named Chuck asked them to feed his lizard. Oscar hoped the lizard would be a giant Gila monster with claws as sharp as razors. Ben imagined the lizard as a Komodo dragon with long shark-like teeth. The boys offered to come by that afternoon so Chuck could give them instructions. They were surprised to see a puny green reptile in a tank full of leaves. Chuck said the lizard's name was Gizzard.

The next day, Ben overslept, so the boys had to rush to Chuck's house. Ben checked on Gizzard while Oscar went to get the crickets to feed him. As Oscar reached for the bag in the fridge, he heard Ben yell. "Oscar, get over here! You won't believe what happened to Gizzard! He shriveled to death! All that's left of him is his skin!"

The boys headed to the pet shop and bought a replacement. When they returned to Chuck's house, Ben started to set the new lizard in the tank. Then he exclaimed with surprise, "Hey, there's Gizzard! And there's the skin! He didn't die—he just molted."

"You should have looked in the tank more closely," Oscar said, frowning. "Now our first pet-sitting job cost *us* $20."

SKILL PRACTICE   Read the item. Write your response.

1. Who are the main characters, and what is their goal?

_____

_____

2. What length of time does the story cover? How do you know?

_____

_____

3. Name two adjectives that describe Ben. Explain why you chose them.

_____

_____

STRATEGY PRACTICE   Underline the part of the story that created the most vivid picture in your mind.

READ THE PASSAGE   Think about what the author is trying to tell you about how people should behave.

The Boy Who Cried "Pirates!"

Long ago, a boy named Johnny lived on a ship that sailed the seas. His father was the captain. Johnny continually begged his father to let him keep watch. "Life on the sea is dangerous," his father said. "Only the most responsible sailors can keep watch for sudden storms or fearsome pirates."

One night after much complaining and begging, the captain allowed Johnny to keep watch. Johnny expected the work to be exciting, but time crept more slowly than a slug. So Johnny decided to have some fun.

"Pirates! Pirates!" Johnny yelled out. Sailors scrambled on deck, only to see Johnny laughing. "Just kidding!" he said as his eyes filled with tears of laughter.

The captain was furious. "Pirates are no joke," he scolded. He made Johnny promise to behave, but Johnny did not listen. Once again, when everyone was asleep, he sounded the alarm. Sleepy sailors hurried to their posts, ready for action. And again, Johnny laughed at the fun of tricking them.

The third time Johnny was on watch, he yawned and stretched, scanning the horizon. To his shock, he saw a pirate ship in the distance. "P-p-pirates!" he stammered. "Pirates!" The sailors merely rolled over in their hammocks. They were sure Johnny was lying again. As the pirate ship edged closer, Johnny's heart beat quickly with fear. He realized this was not a joke.

SKILL PRACTICE   Read the item. Write your response.

1. Why does Johnny claim to see a pirate ship when he doesn't actually see one?

_____

_____

2. Why does Johnny tell the same lie a second time?

_____

_____

3. What is the theme of this story?

_____

STRATEGY PRACTICE   Underline the word or words in paragraphs 2 through 5 that help you understand how the writer organized the passage.

Think about the lesson that the judge teaches Ned and Chef Mario.

Ned's Nose Gets Sued

Ned sat near the window with his pot of boiled noodles. He deeply inhaled the smells of tomato, onion, and garlic that were wafting up through the air from Pasta Perfecto, the restaurant below his apartment. The smell of the sauces transformed his plain noodles into the most delicious of dishes.

Just then, a fist pounded on Ned's door. He opened it to see Chef Mario wagging his finger. "You thief! I know what you're doing! You're enjoying the smell of my food and yet you're paying for nothing! I demand that you pay me for the smells you are stealing!" Ned thought the request was silly. He refused to pay, and so Chef Mario took him to court.

The judge listened as the chef accused Ned's nose of stealing. Ned explained that he was a college student and could not afford to eat at Pasta Perfecto. Finally the judge held up a metal cup and told Ned to put all of his money into it. Ned dropped in a few dollars and a lot of change. The judge shook the cup and spoke. "I rule that the sound of Ned's money pays Chef Mario for the smell of his sauces." Then the judge returned the money to Ned.

Chef Mario stared at the floor. Suddenly he looked up and smiled. "From now on," the chef said, "Pasta Perfecto will give discounts to students!"

SKILL PRACTICE Read the item. Write your response.

1. What is the theme of this story?

_____

2. Why does Ned eat near the window?

_____

_____

3. What lesson does Chef Mario learn?

_____

_____

STRATEGY PRACTICE Write a sentence from the story that was easy for you to visualize.

_____

_____

READ THE PASSAGE   Think about what Charlie says and does in the story.

All Aboard!

Charlie checked the stagecoach before anyone boarded. He squatted on his heels next to the wooden wheels. Each one was bolted tight, and there wasn't a crack to be seen. He climbed to the top of the coach and tugged the leather straps. The mailbags were tightly secured. Then he gave the horses a careful look. Their harnesses and reins showed no signs of fraying.

Once the coach was ready, Charlie yelled, "All aboard!" The passengers climbed into the coach. They sat across from each other, so close that their knees bumped together. Bags jammed the floor. Before Charlie could put the coach in motion, Rory from the town newspaper hurried up to him. He thought Charlie should know that a heavy rainstorm was heading toward the main road.

Charlie carefully considered his options. If he took the usual route, the road might be washed out. The stagecoach's wheels could get stuck in mud. The windows in the coach could not be closed, so the rain would surely soak his passengers.

If he tried to go around the storm, the ride to the next town would take longer. And it was a rutted back road full of holes. The passengers would be bounced around, but they would be dry. Charlie wanted to get to the destination as fast as possible. But he always did what was best for his passengers.

SKILL PRACTICE   Read the item. Write your response.

1. Name two adjectives that describe Charlie. Explain why you chose them.

_____

_____

2. When does this story take place?

_____

3. What is the theme of the story?

_____

STRATEGY PRACTICE   In your own words, explain the problem that Charlie faces. Then write about what clues you found in the passage to help you decide what Charlie will do.

_____

_____

Author's Purpose
Students identify the author's reason for writing about a subject.

Prediction
Students practice using clues from a passage to predict what will happen next.

DAY 1

Review the definition of *author's purpose* with students. Say: **It's important to know why an author wrote something. Understanding an author's purpose helps us pay attention to the details that the author thinks are important. Remind students that the author's purpose might be to entertain, to inform, to teach, or to persuade. Sometimes an author may have more than one purpose. For example, an author may write a funny passage to both inform and entertain you.** Tell students they are going to read a passage about an unusual gift from Egypt's ruler to the king of France. Then remind students of the *Ask Questions* strategy (Week 6). Say: **Asking questions is a good way to set your purpose for reading.** Then have students read the first paragraph and think of a question they have about the rest of the passage. When they have finished, have them write their question in the space provided for the strategy practice activity. Then direct students to finish reading the passage and complete the skill and strategy practice activities. Review the answers together.

DAY 2

Review the common purposes for writing (to inform, to teach, to persuade, and to entertain). Tell students they are going to read a *tall tale*, or a kind of story that uses exaggeration to describe people and things. Then remind students of the *Make Connections* strategy (Week 2). Say: **To understand the exaggerations in a tall tale, you must make connections to what you already know.** Read the first two sentences of the passage aloud. Ask: **What is a rattle?** (a toy that a baby can hold and shake) **Can babies hold tree branches?** (no) **You used your knowledge of rattles, babies, and tree branches to understand that exaggeration.** Direct students to finish reading the passage. If necessary, explain that the Panama Canal is a real waterway that was completed in 1914 so ships would no longer have to sail all the way around South America. Then have students complete the skill and strategy practice activities. For the strategy practice activity, pair students or complete it as a group.

DAY 3

Review the *Prediction* skill with students. Say: **When we make a prediction, we use clues from the text and our own background knowledge to figure out what will happen next.** Tell students they will read a passage about tide pools. Build background, if necessary, by telling students where tide pools are found and about the creatures that live in them. Then remind students of the *Ask Questions* strategy. Say: **Asking yourself questions while you read is a good way to make sure you are following along well enough to make predictions. After each paragraph, ask yourself a question that will help you predict what you will read about next.** Have students read the passage and complete the skill and strategy practice activities.

DAY 4

Tell students they are going to make predictions as they read a passage about a secret agent. Then have students recall the *Make Connections* strategy. Ask: **What do you know about secret agents from books, TV, and movies?** (e.g., They are smart. They use gadgets. They travel the world.) Say: **Use what you know about secret agents to look for clues in the passage that will help you make predictions.** Have students read the passage and complete the skill and strategy practice activities.

DAY 5

Tell students they will practice finding the author's purpose and making predictions as they read about a special part of the brain. Read the title aloud and define *thermostat* (a device that senses and adjusts temperature). Then have students read the passage and complete the skill practice activity. Review the answers together. For the strategy practice activity, pair students or complete it as a group.

READ THE PASSAGE   Think about why the author would want to write about this subject.

Paris, Here She Comes!

In 1824, Egypt's ruler, Muhammad Ali, gave a special gift to the king of France. Muhammad Ali hoped to create a friendship between the two countries. But did the Egyptian ruler give the French king a treasure chest or an ancient Egyptian mummy? No, Muhammad Ali sent the king what no one in France had ever seen—a giraffe!

The giraffe was named Zarafa. Her long trip from the African grasslands to Paris, France, was an odd one. It began with a camel ride! At two months old, Zarafa was six feet (1.8 m) tall, but she willingly sat on a camel's back. The camel carried her 200 miles (320 km) to a small village, where she was cared for until she was old enough to travel down the Nile River. A big boat then carried her across the Mediterranean Sea to the shores of France. A large hole was cut into the boat's deck so Zarafa could stand up straight.

When they reached the shores of France, Paris was still 550 miles (885 km) away! Zarafa had to walk for 42 days over dusty roads and rolling hills. Everywhere Zarafa went, she was a celebrity. By the time Zarafa reached Paris, it had been two years since she left Egypt.

The people of Paris adored Zarafa. Streets were named for her. Women piled their hair high on their heads to imitate her, and men wore giraffe-spotted hats and ties!

SKILL PRACTICE   Read the item. Write your response.

1. Why did the author write this text?

_____

_____

2. Why did the author include the description of Zarafa's trip?

_____

_____

3. What is the purpose of the last paragraph?

_____

_____

STRATEGY PRACTICE   Write the question you asked yourself after you read the first paragraph of the passage. If you found the answer, write it, too.

_____

_____

READ THE PASSAGE   As you read, ask yourself what the author's purpose is for writing the story.

Mighty Stormalong

Have you heard of Stormalong, the tallest, biggest sailor there ever was? When Stormalong was born, he was so big that he was given a tree branch for a rattle. When Stormalong was one year old, his mom and dad took the roof off the house so he wouldn't hit his head on it. Stormalong was taller than most buildings by the time he was two.

Stormalong's mom spent four years knitting a hammock for him to sleep in. It stretched from New Jersey to New York. Stormalong watched the ships sail in and out of the New York Harbor as he swayed in his bed.

When Stormalong turned 10 years old, he joined the crew of the *Humongous.* It was the biggest ship he could find. All went well as long as he stayed in the middle of the ship. But if he leaned to the side just a bit, the ship would lean, too, and the crew would tumble.

Stormalong outgrew the *Humongous* when he was 13. So he built his own ship, the *Gigantic.* It was as fast as it was large. Stormalong decided to sail around the world. He left New York on a sunny day after a large breakfast of sausages as big as canoes. By the time he reached Florida, Stormalong was fast asleep. The *Gigantic* drifted south to Panama, the country that connects North America to South America. That ship was so big and heavy that it pushed right through the land and made the Panama Canal! Stormalong had created a shortcut through North and South America!

SKILL PRACTICE   Read the item. Write your response.

1. Why did the author write this story?

_____

_____

2. What kind of story is this (realistic fiction, fable, tall tale, etc.)? How do you know?

_____

_____

3. What is the purpose of the last paragraph?

_____

_____

STRATEGY PRACTICE   Tell a partner how you used your background knowledge to understand the exaggerations in the story.

Think about what happens next when the tide changes.

A Harsh Home

The ocean waters rise and fall along the rocky coast. This movement is called the *tide*. When the tide comes in, the ocean rises. The rocks along the shore are covered in water. When the tide goes out, some of the salt water stays behind in large holes in the rocks. This creates tide pools. The animals that live in tide pools, such as crabs, sea stars, and mussels, have to adapt to changes in the water. They must face huge waves, the hot sun, and hungry predators.

When the tide is high, animals in tide pools are covered with water, which protects them from the strong sun. The tide also brings in food for the animals to eat. But huge waves can also wash the animals away.

When the tide is low, the animals in tide pools have to adapt to another world. Many of them are no longer covered by water. They are not safe from the sun's heat or hungry animals. The water in the tide pools has less food for animals such as mussels and urchins. Animals in tide pools must keep themselves safe from predators while trying to grab a bite to eat. Mussels are protected by hard shells. When food floats by, a mussel opens its shell to eat. It closes its shell tight when danger approaches. Hungry sea stars will poke and prod a mussel, hoping to find a way into its shell. Crabs hunt for dead plants and animals while hiding from sea gulls. Life in a tide pool is always an adventure.

SKILL PRACTICE   Read the item. Write your response.

1. It is low tide, and sea gulls approach a tide pool where a crab lives. What will the crab do?

   _____

   _____

2. A wave carries a sea star into a tide pool of mussels. What happens next?

   _____

   _____

3. What are mussels doing in tide pools during high tide?

   _____

STRATEGY PRACTICE   Write a question you had while reading the passage. If you found the answer, write it, too.

_____

READ THE PASSAGE   Think about what the characters say and do, and predict what will happen next.

The Double Agent

The stone wall was two feet thick, but that didn't worry Klue. She knew how to enter the office of the secret spy organization. Klue waved her right hand in front of a large rock in the center of the wall. The ring she wore, which looked like a lion's head, lit up. Klue could hear hidden gears whirring into action, and she smiled as the rock walls slid away to show the inside of the office. Two women stood near a desk in the center of the room. Klue knew Jessie Kwan, the brilliant scientist. And Klue knew Admiral Eva Garcia from the photos in her file. Admiral Garcia was new to the secret spy organization. As Klue stepped into the office, the wall closed behind her.

Kwan spoke. "We have a dangerous situation, Klue. Our plans for the sea lab are missing. We think a double agent stole them. We're sending you to chase the thief and recover the plans."

"You can count on me," answered Klue.

"Good! Keep this with you at all times," said Dr. Kwan. She held up a golden spider on a chain. "Press the spider's head to trigger a laser that will cut through anything."

"I'll take that," hissed Admiral Garcia. "Now I don't need your lion ring to get inside the secret base!" She seized the chain, stuffed it deep inside her pocket, and slipped on a gas mask. The room was suddenly filled with a loud hissing sound. Kwan and Klue began to cough.

SKILL PRACTICE   Read the item. Write your response.

1. What will happen now?

_____

2. What will Klue do next?

_____

3. What will Admiral Garcia do with the spider? Why do you think so?

_____

_____

STRATEGY PRACTICE   Describe a story, movie character, or TV show that the passage reminds you of.

_____

_____

READ THE PASSAGE   As you read, stop and think about what the author wants you to learn.

Your Body's Thermostat

If you get really hot, your body sweats to cool down. If you're too cold, your body shivers to warm up. If germs enter your body, you get a fever. Sweating, shivering, and having a fever may seem like bad things, but they are all healthy reactions. They show that your body is working well. And all of those reactions begin in a small part of your brain.

The *hypothalamus* (HY-po-THAL-uh-mus) is only about the size of an almond, but it does very important work. One of its jobs is to control your body temperature. Your body usually stays at a regular temperature, but that temperature can sometimes change. For example, during a fast game of soccer, your body temperature rises. The hypothalamus quickly sends signals to your sweat glands. It says, "Get to work!" When the sweat glands create sweat, your body begins to cool down. It soon returns to a normal temperature.

The hypothalamus also works when you are ill. When nasty germs attack your body, it makes white blood cells. These signal the hypothalamus to raise your body's temperature. You now have a fever. Your skin may look flushed and feel hot to the touch. Your body loses water. The rise in your body's temperature helps to kill the germs. A fever is also your body's way of telling you that you're sick so you can take care of yourself. Your hypothalamus is very hardworking!

SKILL PRACTICE   Read the item. Write your response.

1. Why did the author write this text?

   _____

   _____

2. Reread paragraph 2. What is the purpose of sweat?

   _____

3. On a hot day, you step into a heavily air conditioned store. Use facts from the text to explain what happens to you.

   _____

   _____

   _____

STRATEGY PRACTICE   Ask a partner a question about something from the passage.

Nonfiction Text Features

Students practice identifying and comprehending common features of nonfiction text.

Visual Information

Students examine and evaluate information that is depicted visually.

DAY 1

To review the *Nonfiction Text Features* skill, say: **Nonfiction text often includes certain features that writers use to organize their ideas or information. These features help make the text easier to understand at a glance.** Direct students' attention to the application on the student page. Say: **An application is something you fill out to apply for a job. This application is for a hall monitor position. What are some of its features?** (heading, bulleted list, name and signature lines, etc.) Then review the *Determine Important Information* strategy with students (Week 5). Say: **As you read, think about why the information in the list is important. Why is it set apart with bullets?** Have students read the passage and complete the skill and strategy practice activities.

DAY 2

Review the *Organization* strategy (Week 4) and remind students that good readers pay attention to nonfiction text features to see how information is organized. Say: **A table of contents is a type of nonfiction text that shows the organization of a book, magazine, or other work. The table of contents lists chapters or sections of the book and their page numbers. Call students' attention to the title of the table of contents on the student page. If necessary, explain that a hoax is a trick or a story that has been made up to fool people.** Then have students read the table of contents and complete the skill and strategy practice activities. Review the answers together.

DAY 3

Review the *Visual Information* skill with students. Say: **Visual information can be presented in the form of illustrations, diagrams, graphs, maps, or photos.** Tell students that in this passage, they are going to study a timeline about the history of surfing. Then remind students of the *Determine Important Information* strategy. Say: **When looking at timelines, it is important to pay attention to certain features and visual clues. For example, in this timeline, I see specific dates with blocks of text above them. I think this text must be important for understanding the history of surfing.** Have students study the timeline and complete the skill and strategy practice activities.

DAY 4

Tell students they will practice interpreting visual information as they read an ad. Point out the diagram of the treehouse on the student page. Say: **Diagrams like this are important to people who plan and build buildings. What features does this diagram have that would be helpful to someone building something?** (labels, measurements) **As you study the diagram, pay attention to how the information is presented. Think about other ways you could list or show the features of this treehouse.** Then have students read the ad and study the diagram. When students have finished, have them complete the skill practice activity. For the strategy practice activity, have students work in pairs.

DAY 5

Tell students they will practice both the *Nonfiction Text Features* and *Visual Information* skills as they study the life cycle of the Pacific salmon. Point out the diagram on the student page and say: **Diagrams of cycles show how something goes through the same stages over and over. What do you see on this page that tells you that this is a cycle?** (the word "life cycle" and the arrows between pictures) Then remind students of the *Determine Important Information* strategy. Say: **Good readers often read something that has a lot of information more than once. When you study this life cycle, first read only the bolded names of each stage of the salmon and study the pictures. Then study the diagram again and read the captions.** When students have finished, have them complete the skill practice activity. For the strategy practice activity, pair students or complete it as a group.

READ THE APPLICATION Study the features of the application and think about the information they give you.

Westlake Hall Monitor Application

I, _____, am applying to be a Westlake Elementary School Hall Monitor.

If I am chosen for this position, I agree to:
- report for hall monitor duty on time at 8:00 AM;
- always strive to set a good example for my peers and the younger students;
- show respect for my teachers and all the other people who work at Westlake; and
- keep my grades up and never have lower than a B average.

_____   _____
(Signature)   (Date)

SKILL PRACTICE Read the item. Write your response.

1. What is the purpose of the document?

   _____

   _____

2. Why is there a list?

   _____

3. Who is supposed to sign the document? How do you know?

   _____

   _____

   _____

STRATEGY PRACTICE Explain why somebody who is applying to be a hall monitor would want to read the bulleted list carefully.

   _____

   _____

READ THE TABLE OF CONTENTS   Pay attention to how the sections of the book are organized.

Famous Hoaxes

SKILL PRACTICE   Read the item. Write your response.

1. How can you find out if a creature known as the yeti is discussed in this book?

   _____

   _____

2. In which chapter would you find information about fake web sites? Explain.

   _____

   _____

3. What is the first page number of the chapter about mysterious flying objects? How do you know?

   _____

   _____

STRATEGY PRACTICE   How would a page with a list of all the photographs in the book be useful? Explain your answer.

   _____

   _____

READ THE TIMELINE Study the timeline to learn information about the history of surfing.

The History of Catching a Wave

How much do you know about the history of surfing? The timeline below shows how the sport grew from a Hawaiian tradition to a worldwide fad.

| European explorers observe surfing in Hawaii. | Missionaries in Hawaii forbid the local people to surf. | Surfing comes to different parts of the United States and Australia. | The teen movie *Gidget*, about a group of California surfers, is released. It makes surfing a national fad. | Kelly Slater sets a world record for winning the most surfing competitions. |

1779 **1821** **1901–1915** **1959** **2007**

SKILL PRACTICE Read the item. Write your response.

1. What happened in 1821? How do you know?

_____

_____

2. When and why did surfing become popular in the United States?

_____

_____

3. What is the purpose of the timeline?

_____

_____

STRATEGY PRACTICE How would the timeline be helpful to someone writing a report on the history of sports? Explain your answer.

_____

_____

READ THE ADVERTISEMENT   Study the diagram and think about the information that it presents.

Treehouse?
Why Not a Tree Mansion?

The **Murray Company Tree Mansion** is the best treehouse available today. All the materials you need are included in the kit to help you create a play area that's as big as your imagination.

This diagram shows the different parts of the Tree Mansion and the space you'll need to build it.

CALL NOW for your very own *Tree Mansion!*
800-555-4321

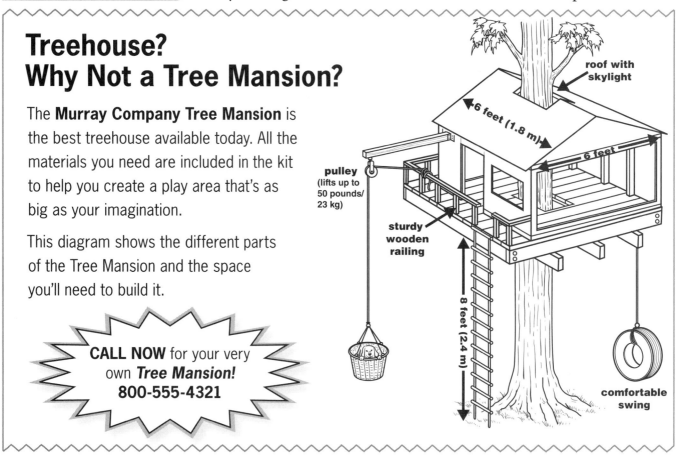

SKILL PRACTICE   Read the item. Write your response.

1. What information is only available in the diagram?

_____

_____

2. Why did the author include measurements in the diagram of the Tree Mansion?

_____

_____

3. What important information is missing from this ad?

_____

_____

STRATEGY PRACTICE   If you had to describe the features of the Tree Mansion without using a diagram, how might you organize the details in writing? Tell a partner.

STUDY THE DIAGRAM   Study the pictures, labels, and captions to learn about the Pacific salmon.

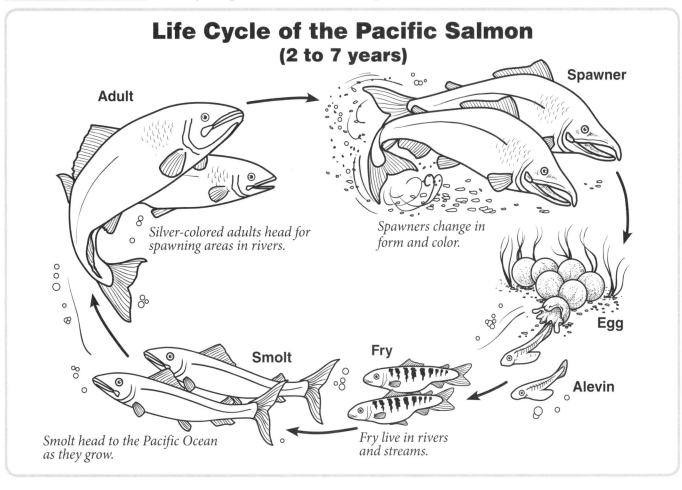

Life Cycle of the Pacific Salmon
(2 to 7 years)

Adult

Spawner

Silver-colored adults head for spawning areas in rivers.

Spawners change in form and color.

Egg

Smolt

Fry

Alevin

Smolt head to the Pacific Ocean as they grow.

Fry live in rivers and streams.

SKILL PRACTICE   Read the item. Write your response.

1. What are the words in italics called? What do they tell the reader?

_____

_____

2. What is a Pacific salmon called in the last stage of its life cycle? How do you know?

_____

_____

3. What is surprising about the Pacific salmon's change from fry to smolt?

_____

_____

STRATEGY PRACTICE   Discuss with a partner the types of people who might find the diagram useful. Explain your thinking.

Main Idea and Details

Students look for the central idea or message of a passage or story. They also find details that best support the main idea.

Sequence

Students look for the order of events or steps in a process.

DAY 1

Review the *Main Idea and Details* skill by saying: **Every passage has a main idea, as does each paragraph in the passage. A paragraph's main idea further explains the passage's main idea. Each paragraph also contains details that support the main idea of the paragraph or passage.** Then remind students of the *Monitor Comprehension* strategy (Week 1). Say: **As you read, stop after each paragraph and think about its main idea. Ask yourself how that main idea supports the main idea of the passage. If the main ideas don't make sense together, read the paragraph again or rethink the main idea of the passage.** Have students read the passage and complete the skill and strategy practice activities. Review the answers together.

DAY 2

Tell students they are going to read a story but that they may not know the main idea until they finish reading. Say: **Fiction, unlike nonfiction, usually does not have main ideas that are directly stated. You will often have to read the entire story before you can decide what the main idea is. To help you decide, check if the details in the story support what you think the story is mostly about.** Then remind students of the *Visualization* strategy (Week 3). Say: **A good way to remember and concentrate on details is to picture them in your mind.** Have students read the passage and complete the skill and strategy practice activities. Review the answers together.

DAY 3

Tell students they are going to learn about the history of chewing gum. Then remind them of the *Sequence* skill. Say: **When you read about the history of something, what you read is often organized by chronological, or time, order. Dates in the text help you better understand the sequence of events that you are reading about.** Then remind students of the *Monitor Comprehension* strategy. Say: **As you read, circle the dates of important events and the order in which they occur.** Have students read the passage and complete the skill practice activity. For the strategy practice activity, say: **Making a timeline is a good way to make sure you understood the sequence of events you read about.** Model by drawing a timeline on the board and filling in the first two dates. Then have students create their own timelines.

DAY 4

Tell students they are going to read about how popcorn is prepared and manufactured before it is ready to be sold. Then remind students of the *Sequence* skill. Say: **The writer explains the steps in making popcorn in the order that they happen. Pay attention to the sequence of events as you read.** Then remind students of the *Visualization* strategy. Say: **Try to visualize details of each step in your mind. This will help you understand the process of manufacturing popcorn.** Have students read the passage and complete the skill and strategy practice activities.

DAY 5

Tell students they will practice both the *Main Idea and Details* and *Sequence* skills as they read about how a shoe company recycles running shoes. Say: **This passage tells about how old shoes become new things, so make sure you understand the sequence of what happens to the shoes and the details about what the old shoes become.** Then remind students of the *Monitor Comprehension* strategy. Say: **Pause after each paragraph to check your comprehension by thinking of the paragraph's main idea.** Have students read the passage and complete the skill and strategy practice activities. Review the answers together.

Name: _____

READ THE PASSAGE   Find the main idea and supporting details in each paragraph.

Sea Homes Made of Wood

Some marine animals live among rocks on seashores. Others choose wood pilings for their home. Pilings are the large posts that support piers, or raised walkways over water. Many sea creatures attach themselves to the pilings and live on or in the wood.

Gribbles and shipworms are two animals that live in pilings. These animals are lucky—they don't have to leave their home to find food. They simply eat their home! Gribbles are tiny shrimp-like animals that tunnel into wood pilings, munching as they go. Shipworms are worm-like clams with a long body and a small shell. Shipworms attach themselves to wood and then move their heads back and forth to rub away the wood. A shipworm feasts on the wood as it burrows deeper and deeper.

Other marine life, such as barnacles, can stay fastened to a piling but need to look elsewhere to find food. Before they are fully grown, barnacles "glue" their heads to the pilings. Then they grow and form a hard shell shaped like a volcano. Barnacles open their shells to look for food. They wave feathery legs that filter bits of floating food out of the water. Anemones (uh-NEM-uh-nees), like barnacles, hang on to pilings. They wave their tentacles to eat. The tentacles are full of stinging cells for snagging food. So, whether a sea creature eats it or lives on it, a wood piling can be a safe and comfortable home.

SKILL PRACTICE   Read the item. Write your response.

1. How are anemones and barnacles alike?

_____

_____

2. Describe how a barnacle changes as it becomes an adult.

_____

_____

3. Write two details about shipworms.

_____

STRATEGY PRACTICE   Write the main idea of each paragraph in your own words.

_____

_____

_____

READ THE PASSAGE   Ask yourself what the story is about and which details help tell the story.

Baseball Bash

Alex and Jack like to play catch while their mom is running errands. Today it's raining outside, but Jack wants to try out his new baseball glove.

The boys toss the baseball back and forth a few times in the living room. Then Alex kicks up his leg and hurls the baseball with a spin. The ball sails through the room. Jack stretches out his arm, but he is too late. The ball flies past him and crashes into a potted plant that breaks into pieces.

"Now look what you did!" yells Jack. He drops his glove and runs to the plant.

Alex hurries to clean up the mess. Jack carefully holds the plant while Alex sweeps up the dirt and broken pieces. Neither boy hears the front door open or notices Mom enter the room.

"What are you doing with that plant?" Mom asks.

"Um, the plant seems too big for its pot," mumbles Jack. "We thought we'd replant it."

"Really? When did you boys start liking plants?" Mom raises an eyebrow and glances at the baseball that is lying where the plant once stood.

"When we started playing catch in the house," admits Alex. "Sorry, Mom. We'll take care of the plant. It needs a new pot."

"Great," Mom says. "And you two can help me in the garden all next week."

SKILL PRACTICE   Read the item. Write your response.

1. What is the story mostly about?

_____

_____

2. Why were the boys playing catch in the house?

_____

_____

3. How does Mom figure out that the boys played ball inside?

_____

_____

STRATEGY PRACTICE   Underline at least three details in the story that were easy for you to visualize.

Daily Reading Comprehension • EMC 3614 • © Evan-Moor Corp.

READ THE PASSAGE   Notice the sequence of events that led to the development of chewing gum.

A Short History of Chewing Gum

Hundreds of years ago, when Native Americans wanted something to chew on, they simply walked to the nearest spruce tree. They scooped off sticky brown resin that oozed from the bark and popped it into their mouths. That changed in 1848, when John B. Curtis took spruce tree resin and added wax and flavoring to it. He turned the resin into chewing gum that he then sold in hunks across New England.

Resin gum with wax was popular, but it didn't last long. In 1869, a man named Thomas Adams created something better. Adams worked with a rubbery sap called *chicle* (CHIK-ul). He discovered that boiled chicle made a good texture for gum. He added flavors to the chicle and named the results. The flavors—"Licorice Blackjack," "Sour Orange," and "Tutti-Frutti"—caught on. His gum, however, had a big problem. It didn't keep its flavor for very long. In 1880, William White added sugar, corn syrup, and peppermint to chicle. The flavors in the gum lasted longer.

Blibber-Blubber, the first bubble gum, was created in 1906, but it was never sold. The gum was so sticky that you could hardly scrape it off your face after it burst! In 1928, Walter Diemer created a better bubble gum. He took five pounds (2.3 kg) of pink gum that he called "Double Bubble" to a grocery store. All of the gum sold in one day.

At the end of the 1940s, Topps Chewing Gum company began to sell bubble gum in a clever way. They printed comic strips on the gum wrappers. And in 1951, they added a trading card to each flat pack of Topps bubble gum. From tree resin to gum with trading cards, people have always loved something to chew.

SKILL PRACTICE   Read the item. Write your response.

1. When was chewing gum invented, and who invented it?

_____

2. What kind of gum was sold 80 years after the first gum? Who created it?

_____

3. What did Topps Chewing Gum do to get people more interested in gum? Explain.

_____

_____

_____

STRATEGY PRACTICE   On a separate piece of paper, make a timeline of events in chewing gum history.

READ THE PASSAGE   Notice the order of steps in the process for manufacturing popcorn.

From Seeds to Snacks

If you were to place sweet corn into a popcorn popper, you wouldn't hear the sound of popping. This is because of all the different varieties of corn, dried popcorn is the only kind that pops. But going from seeds to snacks takes several steps.

The process begins when ripe ears of popcorn are picked and the husks are removed. Then, workers place the ears on conveyor belts that move the corn into steel containers called *cribs*. Some cribs are as long as a city block and three stories high! Millions of pounds of popcorn ears sit inside cribs for several months. Slots on top of the cribs allow air to enter so that the ears can dry. The ears, however, are carefully watched. They can't dry out too much or they won't pop.

When the ears of popcorn are dry enough, they are transferred to a machine called a *scalper*. It quickly strips the kernels off each ear of popcorn. At the same time, a machine called a cleaner gets rid of any dirt on the kernels. Then, the kernels are sorted. The bad kernels are thrown away. Giant fans then blow dust off the remaining kernels. The dusted kernels take one last ride on a conveyor belt. Workers check them and vacuum up any bad kernels that may have been missed. The rest of the kernels are stored in bins until they are ready to be packaged in bags and boxes. Finally, the packages are sold to stores or sent to companies that turn the kernels into delicious popcorn.

SKILL PRACTICE   Read the item. Write your response.

1. What does the scalper do?

_____

2. What is the purpose of both the cleaner machine and the giant fans?

_____

_____

3. After the corn is harvested, which step in the process of making popcorn takes the longest?

_____

_____

STRATEGY PRACTICE   Summarize one step in the process that was easy for you to visualize.

_____

_____

READ THE PASSAGE   Pause as you read to make sure you understand the main ideas and sequence.

Grind Those Shoes!

What can you do with a pair of smelly old running shoes? Give them to Nike®! This well-known company runs a program that recycles used sneakers. Over 25,000,000 running shoes have been reused since 1990.

The program is fairly simple. First, people donate worn-out running shoes. Drop-off sites are located in Nike stores all over the world. Next, the shoes are shipped to a large factory. The shoes are then separated into their three main parts: the rubber soles, the foam cushions, and the fabric uppers. Each shoe part is sorted into a pile of similar shoe parts. Then, each pile is placed on its own conveyor belt. The belt moves the piles to an enormous grinding machine that grinds and disinfects the shoe parts.

These ground-up pieces of soles, cushions, and uppers are then made into materials that can be used to create new sports equipment. Rubber soles become running tracks and new gym floors. Foam cushions are turned into outdoor tennis courts. And the fabric upper parts of the shoes become pads for indoor wooden basketball courts.

Maybe your school or community has a court, track, or floor made of recycled materials. If so, you and your running shoes could be running on top of running shoes!

SKILL PRACTICE   Read the item. Write your response.

1. Write the main idea of the passage in your own words.

   _____

   _____

2. What happens after the old running shoes arrive at the factory?

   _____

   _____

3. Why is it a good idea to recycle old running shoes?

   _____

   _____

STRATEGY PRACTICE   Write a question you have about how running shoes are recycled.

_____

_____

Cause and Effect

Students practice identifying cause-and-effect relationships by looking for what happens (the effect) and why it happens (the cause).

Fact and Opinion

Students determine whether details in a text can be proved (facts) or represent what someone thinks or feels (opinions).

DAY 1

Review the concept of *cause and effect* with students by having them identify a common experience with a clear cause and effect, such as eating lunch because you are hungry or doing well on a test because you studied. Then remind students of the *Determine Important Information* strategy (Week 5). Read the passage title aloud. Say: **This title tells me that the passage will be about koalas. As I read, I'll look for important information that helps me understand why koalas behave the way they do.** Then direct students to read the passage and complete the skill and strategy practice activities. Review the answers together.

DAY 2

Tell students they are going to read a folk tale about a hungry wolf and a smart fox. Review the *Cause and Effect* skill with students by saying: **Sometimes the cause or effect of something might not be directly stated. You must use clues to understand the cause or effect.** Model by reading the first sentence of the third paragraph aloud. Say: **When Fox saw Wolf drooling, it had an *effect* on her. It *caused* her to realize Wolf was hungry, which *caused* her to be scared. And *because* Fox was scared, she knew she had to think fast so she wouldn't be eaten.** Then remind students of the *Ask Questions* strategy (Week 6). Say: **As you read, ask yourself what is happening and why it is happening. These questions will help you understand the causes and effects in the folk tale.** Have students read the passage and complete the skill and strategy practice activities.

DAY 3

Remind students of the *Fact and Opinion* skill. Say: **A fact is something that is true. An opinion is a personal thought, viewpoint, or judgment.** Tell students they are going to read about a special kind of doll from Japan. If possible, show students pictures of a Daruma doll to build background. Then remind students of the *Determine Important Information* strategy. Say: **As you read, look for information about the Daruma doll that helps you determine what is fact and what is opinion.** Have students read the passage and complete the skill and strategy practice activities. Review the answers together.

DAY 4

Tell students they are going to read about some strange inventions. Say: **As you read, pay attention to whether the details given about the inventions are facts or opinions.** Then remind students of the *Ask Questions* strategy. Say: **Asking the right questions can help us figure out if something is a fact or an opinion. Read the instructions for the strategy practice activity aloud and brainstorm with students some questions they can ask themselves to check facts and opinions** (e.g., "Can I look this up in an encyclopedia?" "Does this information tell me how someone feels?"). Have students write their question in the space provided for the strategy practice activity and tell them to refer to their question as they read. Then have students read the passage and complete the skill practice activity. Review the answers together and invite volunteers to share the question they wrote.

DAY 5

Tell students they will practice finding cause-and-effect relationships and will evaluate facts and opinions by reading about the invention of numerals. Remind students of the *Determine Important Information* strategy. Say: **As you read, pay attention to information that tells you how people counted in the past.** Then have students read the passage. When students have finished, have them complete the skill and strategy practice activities. Review the answers together.

READ THE PASSAGE Look for causes and effects that explain how and why a koala lives the way it does.

Calm Koalas

Tucked into the branches of a eucalyptus (yoo-kuh-LIP-tuss) tree in Australia, a koala is forced to live a lazy life. Its diet consists almost entirely of eucalyptus leaves. Eucalyptus leaves contain a lot of moisture. Therefore, a koala doesn't need to leave its tree to find water. But the leaves don't provide much nutrition. As a result, a koala has little energy and must nap between 16 and 20 hours a day.

When a koala is not sleeping, it is eating. An adult koala will chew about 1,000 leaves a day! The koala has special front teeth that help it nip a thin branch off a eucalyptus tree. Then it uses its back teeth to strip the leaves from the branch. The animal chews the leaves into a paste that makes the leaves easier for the koala's stomach to handle.

Eucalyptus leaves are poisonous to other mammals, so they don't dare eat them. But a koala's stomach can break down the poisons in most kinds of eucalyptus leaves. Because of this, the leaves are not harmful. However, there is one kind of eucalyptus leaf that koalas *cannot* eat. That means a koala must smell each leaf before eating it. The animal's strong sense of smell can detect the odor of the poison in dangerous leaves.

SKILL PRACTICE Read the item. Write your response.

1. Why does a koala smell a eucalyptus leaf before eating it?

_____

_____

2. Why do koalas chew the leaves into paste?

_____

_____

3. Why don't other mammals compete with koalas for the eucalyptus leaves?

_____

_____

STRATEGY PRACTICE In your own words, tell how a koala spends its time.

_____

_____

READ THE FOLK TALE Notice the things that happen between Wolf and Fox and why they happen.

The Hungry Wolf and the Clever Fox

One moonlit night, Wolf was lurking in the forest, hoping to find dinner. He hadn't eaten all day, so he was grumpy from hunger. His mood changed when he spied Fox trotting toward her den. Wolf boldly blocked Fox's path, but he spoke to her in a sweet voice.

"Fox, you certainly look beautiful tonight," Wolf said. "Your fur is so glossy."

When Fox saw Wolf's tongue droop and his mouth drool, she knew she had to think fast. Fox pointed to her fur and said, "Why, this old coat is full of ticks and fleas. I'm embarrassed to be seen in it." Fox tried to step away, but Wolf growled deeply.

"Don't move!" he snarled. "I'm hungry, and you look good enough to eat!"

"Mr. Wolf, I'm a skinny old thing," Fox said, jutting out her chin. "You'd be hungry again before you finished swallowing me. But I can show you where to get some delicious cheese. I know where there's a rich, creamy wheel of it as big as your head."

Even though his stomach growled terribly, Wolf was tempted by Fox's description of this magnificent cheese. He walked by her side until they came to a well. Wolf looked down and saw a large, round, yellow cheese floating in the water. As he leaned farther down into the well to gobble up the cheese, he lost his balance and tumbled into the well.

Fox chuckled. With the help of a full moon, she had outfoxed the wolf.

SKILL PRACTICE Read the item. Write your response.

1. Why did Wolf stop Fox?

_____

_____

2. How did Fox trick Wolf?

_____

_____

3. What was the result of Fox's trick?

_____

_____

STRATEGY PRACTICE Write a question you had about the story as you were reading.

_____

READ THE PASSAGE   Notice which details about the Daruma doll are facts and which are opinions.

A Different Kind of Doll

On the first day of my piano lessons, Mom did a strange thing. She gave me a Daruma doll from Japan. Daruma dolls are usually given as gifts to encourage people or wish them luck. The doll doesn't have a body like other dolls. Its body is round with a flat bottom, and it has the face of a strange-looking man.

The doll doesn't have any moving parts, but its bottom is heavy. This means that if you push the Daruma doll over, it will pop back up again. It was fun to play with the doll for a little while.

The doll's body is very pretty. It is painted red and has the Japanese symbol for "good luck" written in gold. But the face is weird! Its eyebrows are bushy and shaped like two black birds. The straight lines under its grim mouth look like a beard, and the eyes are very large. They look like round moons and are completely white. Mom says that the eyes are the reason she bought me a Daruma doll. I have to set a goal for myself and paint a black iris in one of the eyes. When I reach my goal, I can fill in the other eye.

I bet I know what goal Mom wants me to have—to become a good piano player!

SKILL PRACTICE   Read the item. Write your response.

1. Write two facts from the second paragraph.

_____

_____

2. Does the third paragraph contain any opinions? Explain.

_____

_____

3. Cite an opinion from the text. Use quotation marks.

_____

_____

STRATEGY PRACTICE   Write two important facts about a Daruma doll that would help someone understand what it is and how it is used.

_____

_____

READ THE PASSAGE Notice the words that tell you how someone feels or thinks.

Wacky or Wise?

My dad and I found a great web site that describes wacky inventions. Some of them impressed us, but others made us ask, "What was that inventor thinking?"

One of Dad's favorite inventions was the alarm fork. It's supposed to help people eat more slowly. The alarm fork looks like a regular fork except it has two lights on the handle that work like a traffic signal. When the fork's green light is lit, you can take a bite of your food. When the red light flashes, you stop eating and wait. That would drive me crazy!

Another invention was a pair of eyeglasses without earpieces. They looked ridiculous! To wear them, you first glue a magnet onto each side of your head near your eyes. The frame for the glasses has two ends with metal pieces that the magnets attract. But I wonder what happens when you take off your glasses. Will your head stick to the fridge?

There's also a traveling washing machine that washes clothes while you drive. Dad and I think the machine is a good idea, but it seems like too much trouble to use. First, you have to lift your car so you can fasten the machine onto one of the car's wheels. Then you add water, soap, and clothes and hit the road. But you can't drive over 25 miles an hour (40 km per hour), or the machine will break. And you have to stop twice. First, you need to replace the dirty water with clean water for rinsing. And then you have to empty the rinse water so the clothes can spin dry. Washing clothes with rocks in a creek seems easier to me!

SKILL PRACTICE Read the item. Write your response.

1. Is the first sentence of the text a fact or an opinion? Why?

   _____

2. Are there any facts in the third paragraph? Explain.

   _____

   _____

3. What is the writer's opinion of the traveling washing machine? Use text evidence in your response.

   _____

   _____

STRATEGY PRACTICE Write a question that you can ask yourself to check whether what you are reading is a fact or an opinion.

_____

READ THE PASSAGE Notice the facts and opinions about the history of counting, and pay attention to causes and effects that the author describes.

Not as Easy as 1, 2, 3

I learned something amazing today. Numerals have not been around forever—they had to be invented! Thousands of years ago, people who hunted and gathered their food did not use numerals. They counted by carving notches into bones. Each notch stood for "one more." It sounds like hard work to me.

When people began farming, they needed to count crops and animals. They used different tokens for counting. Each token stood for "one" of something. For example, sheep were counted with small disks. One disk stood for one sheep. This worked well enough, until a farmer ran out of tokens!

About 5,000 years ago, people began to live in communities. They ran businesses, owned animals, and paid taxes. People could no longer keep track of things with tokens. Finally, people figured it out. They invented numerals, or written symbols that could stand for different amounts. The first numerals were formed as wedges and circles. The numeral 10 was shown with a small circle, so three small circles stood for 30.

I think doing math can be challenging. Now I see that inventing the numerals for doing math was pretty challenging, too! I also realize just how important numerals are.

SKILL PRACTICE Read the item. Write your response.

1. How did farming affect counting?

_____

_____

2. Why did people invent numerals?

_____

_____

3. Are there any opinions in the second paragraph? Explain.

_____

_____

STRATEGY PRACTICE According to the passage, what are three ways in which people counted?

_____

_____

Compare and Contrast

Students practice comparing and contrasting by looking at the similarities and differences between two or more people or things.

Make Inferences

Students practice making inferences by using clues in a passage to understand what is being implied or inferred.

DAY 1

Tell students they will practice comparing and contrasting by reading about how two sisters behave when they come home from school. Say: **As you read, notice what the sisters have in common and what is different about them. Knowing the similarities and differences will help you understand the passage better.** Tell students they will also practice the *Make Connections* strategy (Week 2). Say: **You can connect what you do after school to what the sisters do.** Have students read the passage and complete the skill and strategy practice activities. Review the answers together.

DAY 2

Tell students they will practice comparing and contrasting by reading about two famous men—the poet Langston Hughes and the movie director Steven Spielberg. Have students read the passage and complete the skill practice activity. Then remind them of the *Monitor Comprehension* strategy (Week 1). Say: **Rereading is a good way to make sure you found all of the important information. Reread the passage and underline the sentences that tell about what Langston Hughes and Steven Spielberg have in common.** Then have students complete the strategy practice activity.

DAY 3

Tell students they will practice making inferences by reading about a type of bird called a *swift*. Say: **When we infer, we use clues from the text and our own background knowledge to figure out information that is not clearly stated. For example, what does the word *swift* mean?** (fast, quick) **Based on their name, what can you infer about how fast swifts fly?** (They are probably very fast.) Then say: **When we use our background knowledge, we are making connections with the text. As you read, think about what you already know about birds to help you better understand swifts.** Have students read the passage and complete the skill practice activity. For the strategy practice activity, help students brainstorm familiar types of birds—what they eat, where they live, etc.—before having students complete the activity independently.

DAY 4

Review the *Make Inferences* skill with students. Say: **When we make inferences, we use clues from the text and our background knowledge to understand information that is not directly stated.** Tell students they are going to read about the Tasmanian devil, a mammal that lives in Australia. Then remind students of the *Monitor Comprehension* strategy. Say: **One good way to monitor your comprehension is to think about the main idea of each paragraph. As you read, pause after each paragraph and tell yourself what the paragraph was mostly about.** Have students read the passage and complete the skill and strategy practice activities. Review the answers together.

DAY 5

Tell students they will practice both comparing and contrasting and making inferences by reading about an unusual animal friendship. Say: **You are going to read about a lion, a tiger, and a bear that live together in a special animal shelter. As you read, connect what you are reading to what you already know about those animals and about animal shelters in general. This will help you understand the information so you can find good comparisons and make good inferences.** Have students read the passage and complete the skill and strategy practice activities. Review the answers together.

READ THE PASSAGE Think about what is the same and what is different about Ellie and Tess.

Sisters After School

As soon as Mom pulls into the garage, Tess and Ellie burst from the car like air escaping from balloons. Tess flings open the door to the house. Ellie closes it gently behind her. Tess tosses her backpack on the kitchen counter, grabs an apple, and kicks off her shoes. One shoe whizzes past the cat, Lulu, causing Lulu to scurry under the table.

Ellie walks into her bedroom, which she shares with Tess. She lays her backpack on her desk and unties her shoes. She carefully hangs her school clothes on the hangers that her mom has decorated. Ellie's hangers have pictures of horses. Tess's hangers are covered with photos of skateboarders. Mom thought the special hangers would help the girls stop throwing their clothes onto the floor. The idea works for Ellie but not for Tess.

Dressed in her favorite sweats, Ellie heads into the kitchen. She always snacks on milk and cookies while doing her homework. She likes finishing her homework before dinner. Tess, however, needs a break after school. Ellie can hear Tess playing their favorite video game, "Return to Wizard Mountain." Between bites of her apple, Tess yells, "Yeah! Got it!" Tess will work on her homework after dinner. But both girls like doing their homework at the kitchen table with the cat purring softly beside them.

SKILL PRACTICE Read the item. Write your response.

1. Name two ways in which Tess and Ellie are alike.

   _____

   _____

2. How do Tess and Ellie differ?

   _____

   _____

3. Which girl do you think is more active and noisy? Explain.

   _____

   _____

STRATEGY PRACTICE Compare what you do after school with what either Tess or Ellie does.

   _____

   _____

READ THE PASSAGE Ask yourself what is the same and what is different about Langston Hughes and Steven Spielberg.

Two Men Who Dared to Dream

What could a poet and a movie director have in common? More than you think! Langston Hughes began writing poetry in high school and soon became one of America's greatest poets. Most of his writing reflects his experiences as an African American. He wrote poems about people who struggled through life but still found things to be happy about. He wrote plays and books about justice for all people, and he wrote kids' books, too. *The Sweet and Sour Animal Book* is an alphabet book of his animal poems. The book was illustrated by kids. "Hold fast to dreams" is a line in a famous Hughes poem. That's exactly what he did throughout his life.

When Steven Spielberg was in middle school, he wanted to make a film. He had an idea for a movie but no money. He started a tree-planting business and made his film with the money he earned. Spielberg never stopped making films, even after many film schools rejected him. Today he is one of the most popular and important filmmakers in the world. His movies are about people who are curious, adventurous, brave, kind, and sometimes bullied. His characters often fight for what is good. Some of his work reflects his Jewish background, such as *Schindler's List*. Spielberg once said, "I don't dream that much at night because I dream for a living." In different ways, both Hughes and Spielberg have inspired people of all ages to reach for their dreams.

SKILL PRACTICE Read the item. Write your response.

1. How do Steven Spielberg and Langston Hughes differ?

_____

_____

2. Name two adjectives that apply to both men.

_____

3. Did both men know at an early age what they wanted to do? How do you know?

_____

STRATEGY PRACTICE Write two of the similarities that you underlined when you reread the passage.

_____

_____

READ THE PASSAGE   As you read, think about what inferences you can make about swifts.

Life in the Sky

Swifts are among the fastest animals on Earth. These small birds live mostly in the air. In fact, swifts can go two or three years without touching the ground! To adapt to life in the sky, swifts depend on their speed and, believe it or not, the saliva in their mouths.

Swifts can fly faster than 100 miles per hour (160 km per hour). That's because their wings are curved like a boomerang. This shape gives them extra speed. They can also flap one wing faster than the other, which allows them to make sharp turns without slowing down. Making fast, sharp turns helps swifts snag flying bugs to eat. Swifts will often fly into clouds of bugs such as gnats or mosquitoes. The birds swoop in and open their wide beaks to catch as many insects as they can.

Swifts also catch bugs to feed their young. The saliva of a swift is sticky, like glue. The bird collects insects in its mouth and holds the insects in a sticky ball of saliva. One food ball can contain nearly 1,000 bugs.

Swifts also use their saliva as glue to build their nests. The birds catch feathers that float in the air and stick the feathers together to form a sturdy nest on the side of a cliff or building. Swifts' short feet are not good for walking or perching on flat surfaces. But their sharp claws allow them to cling to rocks and walls so they can take a brief rest before returning to their lives in the sky.

SKILL PRACTICE   Read the item. Write your response.

1. Where do swifts build their nests?

_____

2. What is special about a swift's saliva?

_____

_____

3. Where do swifts sleep? Use text evidence in your response.

_____

_____

STRATEGY PRACTICE   Tell one way that swifts are different from another bird you know about.

_____

_____

READ THE PASSAGE   Use clues from the passage to make inferences about Tasmanian devils.

Angry Animals

When the sun sets in Tasmania, a large island near Australia, spine-chilling screams pierce the air. The Tasmanian devils are awake and eager to eat. Tasmanian devils are mammals with ferocious appetites and tempers. If there is some meat to eat, dead or alive, these animals will go after it.

Devils hunt alone, eating up to eight pounds (3.6 kg) of food a night. They gulp it down as fast as they can, and they don't share. They are scavengers that usually feed on dead animals such as birds or mammals. Their powerful jaws and sharp teeth can crush the toughest dinner. Every part of their meal gets eaten, including fur, feathers, and bones. Poisons and bacteria in the rotten meat do not harm the devils. They are like nature's garbage disposals. So, even though they may seem disgusting, Tasmanian devils help keep their habitat clean.

Tasmanian devils are famous for their temper tantrums. When devils are bothered or threatened, their ears turn red, and they stomp their feet and bare their sharp teeth. They scream and snap their jaws, too. If their tantrums don't scare away an enemy, they create smelly fluids that make most animals run off. It's easy to see why this creature got its unfriendly name.

SKILL PRACTICE   Read the item. Write your response.

1. Two Tasmanian devils meet. What happens next? Explain.

_____

_____

2. How did Tasmanian devils probably get their name?

_____

_____

3. Why do Tasmanian devils have strong jaws and sharp teeth? Use text evidence in your response.

_____

_____

STRATEGY PRACTICE   Tell the main idea of each paragraph in your own words.

_____

_____

READ THE PASSAGE Think about how the three animals are alike and different. Use clues from the passage to make inferences.

Where the Wild Things Are

Baloo lies on his back, huge and furry. Shere Khan nuzzles his face and rubs his whiskers into Baloo's neck. Leo stretches in the grass near a rock and yawns with a slight roar. The three animals live together in a fenced-in space, and they share a small wooden house. But they are not pets. They are fully grown wild animals. Baloo the bear, Leo the lion, and Shere Khan the tiger were each rescued in 2001 when they were 2-month-old cubs. They were taken to Noah's Ark animal center in Georgia, where they have never been separated. Their young age helped them form an unusual friendship.

Baloo and Shere Khan were named for characters in *The Jungle Book.* They play together during the day while Leo sleeps. When Leo wakes up, the three friends wrestle and play like brothers before Baloo and Shere Khan go to sleep. Sometimes they pile on top of each other for warmth and to show affection.

In the wild, these three would live in different habitats. Black bears usually live in forested areas. African grasslands are home to lions, while tigers survive in the forests and jungles of Asia. But Baloo, Shere Khan, and Leo don't know what it's like to live in the wild. None of these animals hunts for their own food. Instead, they are fed by the humans who care for them. None of the animals knows how unusual—or special—their friendship is.

SKILL PRACTICE Read the item. Write your response.

1. How are the three animals alike?

   _____

   _____

2. How is the relationship of these animals different than if they lived in the wild?

   _____

   _____

3. Leo spends two days with the zoo vet. How do Baloo and Shere Khan feel during this time?

   _____

STRATEGY PRACTICE Write something you already knew about animals that helped you understand what you read in the passage.

_____

_____

Character and Setting

Students practice analyzing character and setting by looking at the traits and motivations of a character and where and when a passage's events take place.

Theme

Students practice identifying the theme by looking for the central message or lesson in the passage.

DAY 1

Tell students they will practice studying character and setting by reading a story about a dentist who is fixing a bear's teeth. Remind students: **The character is whom or what a story is mostly about. The setting is where and when a story takes place. As you read, pay attention to details that tell you what the characters are like and that help you understand the setting.** Then remind students of the *Organization* strategy (Week 4). Say: **One way to organize writing is to describe the problem the characters face and then explain how the problem is solved. As you read this story, try to identify the problem and its solution.** Then direct students to read the passage and complete the skill and strategy practice activities. Review the answers together.

DAY 2

Explain how the characters and setting of a story can affect each other. Say: **The setting can often impact the tone or mood of the story. It can also affect how the characters feel.** Tell students they are going to read a story about two cousins hiking through a redwood forest. You may want to show students photos of giant redwood trees. Then remind students of the *Visualization* strategy (Week 3). Say: **As you read, pay attention not only to visual details, but also the ones that tell you how the place sounds, smells, and feels. Those details will help you better visualize the setting and relate to the characters.** Have students read the passage and complete the skill and strategy practice activities. Review the answers together.

DAY 3

Review the definition of *Theme* with students. Say: **A theme is a lesson or view about life that the author wants to share. You must figure out the theme based on what happens in the passage or on which details the author includes about a topic.** Tell students they are going to read a true story about an explorer who discovered a large cave system. Then remind students of the *Organization* strategy. Say: **True events are often told in chronological order, or the order in which they happen. As you read, look for words and phrases that help you understand the order.** Model by reading the first sentence of the second paragraph aloud and having students identify the signal phrase (*a few days later*). Have students read the passage and complete the skill and strategy practice activities.

DAY 4

Tell students they will practice finding the theme of a passage by reading about a firefighter who must parachute into danger in order to fight wildfires. Say: **As you read, pay attention to how the author describes the main character. What is she like? What does she think about? How does she react to the events of the story? Think about what the author is trying to tell you through the main character and the choices she makes.** Then remind students of the *Visualization* strategy. Say: **Pay attention to the vivid language used to describe the setting and events.** When students finish reading, have them complete the skill and strategy practice activities.

DAY 5

Tell students they will practice thinking about characters and setting and finding the theme of a passage by reading about a woman who is autistic. Say: **Dr. Temple Grandin is a famous woman with autism, a brain disorder that causes people to think in unusual ways and experience the world differently from the way most people do. But this does not mean that autistic people are not smart.** Then remind students of the *Organization* strategy. Say: **Some passages are organized by causes and effects. In this passage, you will learn about how autism affects Dr. Grandin.** Then have students read the passage. When students have finished, direct them to complete the skill and strategy practice activities. Review the answers together.

READ THE PASSAGE Pay attention to the details that describe the characters and the setting.

Dewey and the Dentist

Dr. Brown, the dentist, didn't have to ask his patient, Dewey, to open wide. The sleeping bear's mouth was already open. Dewey was a Kodiak, the largest of all brown bears. He weighed in at 1,600 powerful pounds (725 kg). His teeth were ten times the size of human teeth.

"We'll have to work fast," Dr. Brown told his team of assistants. "We have three hours until the bear wakes up. And I see that he's got four bad teeth."

Dr. Brown worked with tools to remove one of Dewey's bad teeth. All went smoothly for the first hour. Then the power went out. The machine that kept Dewey asleep stopped working. If the bear woke up, he could hurt himself or others in the room.

The zookeeper ran down the long hallway of the bear house. She found the fuse box and flipped switch after switch to restore the power, but nothing happened. Everyone in Dewey's room stared at the huge wild animal, their hearts pounding.

Suddenly, the zookeeper tried a switch she had overlooked. The machine keeping Dewey asleep began whirring. Now Dr. Brown had less than an hour to fix three more teeth. He and his assistants worked quickly. They finished with only minutes to spare before they got out of the room, locked it, and allowed the groggy bear to wake up.

SKILL PRACTICE Read the item. Write your response.

1. What is the setting? How do you know?

_____

_____

2. Write two things you know about the zookeeper.

_____

3. During the power outage, who was probably in danger and why?

_____

_____

STRATEGY PRACTICE What is Dr. Brown's main problem at the beginning of the story? What makes the problem bigger, and how is it solved by the end of the story?

_____

_____

Notice how Jesse's reaction to the setting is different from Max's reaction.

Checking Out Giants

"Come on, Jesse! Let's find ourselves some giants!" yelled Max.

"Everything is giant here," said Jesse softly. "This place is huge." Oak and cypress trees greeted the boys as they started on a trail through the state park. The shady path was just wide enough for the two cousins to walk side by side.

Jesse enjoyed the peace and quiet after two hours in the car with Max. The only sound he heard was the occasional twitter of birds—until Max started complaining.

"We should have watched the Giants game instead of looking for stupid giant trees," Max said. Jesse ignored him and focused on the cool breeze and the smell of damp soil.

"Got any water, Jesse?" Max asked loudly, making Jesse jump. Jesse handed Max an extra bottle from his pack. Max took a swig and then squirted some water on Jesse, laughing. Jesse calmly wiped his face with his shirt and kept walking.

"Check out the size of this thing!" Max yelled. He was the first to spot the huge redwood tree blackened by lightning. Both boys stood at the base of the trunk, staring up.

"I don't think I can even see the top!" whispered Jesse.

Then the boys noticed that fire had carved out a large hollow space at the base of the trunk. They stooped to step through the opening. Inside the hole, they could barely see each other in the darkness.

Max grinned as he ran his hand down the rough interior bark. "We're *inside* a tree!" he exclaimed. "This is way better than some old ballgame!"

SKILL PRACTICE   Read the item. Write your response.

1. How does Jesse feel about the setting? Use text evidence in your response.

_____

_____

2. How does Max show that he is bored?

_____

3. How and why has Max's attitude changed by the end of the story?

_____

_____

STRATEGY PRACTICE   Underline the details that helped you visualize the setting, including sounds, smells, and other sensations.

READ THE PASSAGE   Ask yourself what the author wants you to learn from Jim White's experience.

Deep into the Earth

The year was 1898. Jim White's horse clopped through the desert grasses of New Mexico. As the summer sun set, the teenage cowboy noticed a whirlwind of bats climbing into the sky. Jim watched for a long time as the bats flooded the air. "There's got to be a million of them!" Jim thought. "Their cave must be huge!" He searched until he found the biggest and blackest hole he had ever seen. Jim knew he had to explore it.

Jim returned a few days later with some supplies. Carrying a lantern, he climbed down a wooden ladder into the gloom. Jim crawled over ledges, through tunnels, and into giant chambers. The cave was too large to explore in just a few hours.

Five days later, Jim and a friend dared to spend three days underground. They brought food, water, homemade torches, and a large ball of string to help them find their way out of the dark maze. As the boys explored, they discovered more caves leading to still others. The boys saw amazing rock formations of many different colors and shapes.

Jim had told people about the enormous caverns under their feet. But no one believed that such huge caves could exist. Jim returned to the caves over and over again. Finally, 17 years after Jim had made his discovery, a photographer joined him in the caves. Years later, photos of the caves were published, and people at last began believing Jim.

In 1930, the black hole that Jim White had first climbed into became the entrance to Carlsbad Caverns National Park.

SKILL PRACTICE   Read the item. Write your response.

1. Write the main idea of the text in your own words.

   _____

   _____

2. What conclusion can you draw about Jim White?

   _____

   _____

3. What is the theme of this text?

   _____

STRATEGY PRACTICE   Look back at the story. Underline the words and phrases that indicate that the events are told in chronological order.

READ THE PASSAGE   Think about the problem Erin faces and the choice she makes.

A Blaze to Battle

One hot summer night, lightning struck Columbia Park with a harsh sizzle. It triggered a fire that began spreading across the dry land. An alarm blared at the nearby firefighters' base. It was Erin's first day as a wildfire fighter. In less than two minutes, she was dressed in her fireproof suit and boots. She checked her gear and parachute, and then grabbed her helmet. The plane was waiting.

The wildfire raged in an area full of mountains and trees. There were no highways nearby, so the firefighters had to arrive by air. Erin had fought big house fires before, and she had also parachuted, but this would be her first jump so close to a deadly wildfire.

After a short flight, Dan, the leader, spotted a clearing that was close to the fire. It was a perfect place for the jumpers to land. Dan told Erin to go first.

As Erin stood with her left foot on the step, Dan slapped her shoulder to jump. Erin looked down at the coils of black smoke and froze. Her mind raced with awful questions. What if something happened on the way down? What if she got hurt? Dan noticed Erin's fear. He told her to breathe and focus on the job. She nodded and jumped.

Erin pulled the cord on her parachute, which opened with a loud crack. She watched the ground rise toward her feet. As she prepared to land, she concentrated on what to do first. By the time Erin landed hard on the ground, she was ready to battle the blaze!

SKILL PRACTICE   Read the item. Write your response.

1. What is the theme of this text?

_____

_____

2. What lesson does Erin learn from Dan?

_____

_____

3. Compare how Erin feels before and after she jumps.

_____

STRATEGY PRACTICE   Write two sentences from the story that were easy to visualize.

_____

_____

READ THE PASSAGE   Think about the lesson that the author wants you to learn about autism.

Picture This

Dr. Temple Grandin is autistic, which means she thinks and acts differently from most people. For example, she thinks in pictures. If you say the word *school* to Dr. Grandin, her brain immediately recalls every school she has ever seen. She pictures each school and the books, desks, and rooms inside it! This may sound strange to some people, but Dr. Grandin likes being different.

Thinking in pictures allows Dr. Grandin's brain to work on difficult ideas because she can "see" everything in her mind. That ability helps her design machines and equipment. She first imagines all the pieces of a machine and how they work together. Then she gives them a "test run" in her mind to see if they will work. If the machine does not work in her mind, she changes it until she sees something that does work.

Dr. Grandin uses her ability to make special equipment for handling farm animals. She believes that animals have a right to a comfortable, healthy life. So she has designed many inventions that help animals such as cows and pigs live more comfortably on a farm. For example, she invented a curved corral that calms stressed animals as they walk through it.

Dr. Grandin and others like her teach people that being different can be a positive thing. If we all thought alike, Dr. Grandin believes, nothing new would ever be invented.

SKILL PRACTICE   Read the item. Write your response.

1. How does Dr. Grandin feel about animals? How do you know?

_____

_____

2. What helped Dr. Grandin become successful?

_____

_____

_____

3. What is the theme of this text?

_____

STRATEGY PRACTICE   Reread the passage and underline at least three key sentences that describe effects of Dr. Temple Grandin's autism.

Author's Purpose
Students identify the author's reason for writing about a subject.

Prediction
Students practice using clues from a passage to predict what will happen next.

DAY 1

Review the *Author's Purpose* skill with students. Say: **Authors write for many reasons, including to inform you about a topic, to entertain you with a story, to persuade you to support an idea or activity, and to teach you how to do something. Sometimes a piece of writing can have more than one purpose. For example, an ad informs us about a product, but it also tries to persuade us to buy the product.** Tell students they are going to read about a special event in Providence, Rhode Island. Then remind students of the *Ask Questions* strategy (Week 6). Say: **Asking questions about a passage after you read it is a good way to think about what you have learned and to note what else you would like to know.** Then have students read the passage and complete the skill and strategy practice activities. Invite volunteers to share the question they wrote in the strategy practice activity.

DAY 2

Tell students they will practice finding the author's purpose by reading an essay about people who do not eat meat. Review the common purposes for writing (to inform, to persuade, to entertain, and to give instructions). Then remind students of the *Make Connections* strategy (Week 2). Say: **As you read, think about the main point of each paragraph. Think about how those points make you feel. This will help you understand the author's purpose.** Have students read the passage and complete the skill and strategy practice activities. Review the answers together. Invite students to discuss their responses to the strategy practice activity and whether the passage made them think differently about being a vegetarian.

DAY 3

Review how to make a prediction with students. Say: **When we predict, we use clues from the text and our own background knowledge to think what will happen in the future.** Tell students they are going to read about a boy who enters a fishing tournament. If necessary, describe what a fishing tournament is. Say: **As you read, look for clues that will help you predict what will happen next. These clues might be what the character says or does or something that happens in the story.** Then remind students of the *Ask Questions* strategy. Say: **Asking questions about the topic of a story can help you better understand the story.** Have students read the story. When students have finished, direct them to complete the skill and strategy practice activities.

DAY 4

Tell students they will practice making predictions by reading a story about a young pioneer boy from long ago who is traveling west with his family. Then say: **When you make a prediction, you use clues from the story to figure out what will happen next. You also use your background knowledge. Therefore, it is important to make connections with the text as you read.** Have students read the passage and complete the skill and strategy practice activities.

DAY 5

Tell students they will practice both finding the author's purpose and making predictions by reading a passage about a sister and brother eating popcorn. Say: **As you read, think about why the author wrote this passage and what questions you have about the topic or about details that you read.** Read the directions for the strategy practice activity aloud. Then read the title of the passage aloud and have students write a question. When students have finished, direct them to read the passage and complete the skill practice activity. Review the answers together.

READ THE PASSAGE   As you read the passage, think about why the author wrote it and what she wants you to know.

Fire on the River

If you ever visit Providence, Rhode Island, be sure not to miss WaterFire. WaterFire is a celebration that takes place on most weekend nights between May and October. The event is best known for the many bonfires that are lit on floats in three rivers that run through downtown. WaterFire begins just before sunset. Volunteers paddle out to stacks of logs that have been placed in floating iron racks. Soon, orange flames dance on the water, and the air fills with the fires' smoky perfume.

A Rhode Island artist named Barnaby Evans came up with the idea of WaterFire and set up the first bonfire in 1994. In 1997, WaterFire became a yearly event. Now it is a treasured part of the culture in Providence.

You can stroll along the river banks and visit the booths that sell food and crafts. You can dance to the beautiful music played by live bands. Or you may want to sit down for a tasty meal at a nearby restaurant. Whatever you do, you're sure to be swept away by the magical sights, sounds, tastes, and smells of WaterFire.

SKILL PRACTICE   Read the item. Write your response.

1. What is the author's purpose for writing this text?

_____

_____

2. Think about where Rhode Island is located. Why isn't WaterFire held year-round?

_____

_____

3. Does the first paragraph have a sentence stating the main idea of the text? If so, write it. If not, write the main idea in your own words.

_____

_____

STRATEGY PRACTICE   Write a question that you have about WaterFire.

_____

_____

READ THE PASSAGE As you read, think about what the author is telling you.

Go Vegetarian!

Being a vegetarian, or someone who does not eat meat, has become a popular choice. It is seen as a healthy and responsible way to live. In fact, 1 in every 200 kids in the U.S. is a vegetarian. Most choose to be a vegetarian for the following reasons.

First, a vegetarian diet is good for your health. It usually contains less fat than a diet that includes meat. Eating a low-fat diet helps people stay lean and healthy. A vegetarian diet also provides many vitamins that you can't get from meat. These vitamins protect people from diseases such as diabetes, heart disease, and some types of cancer.

Second, many people who are vegetarians are concerned about the way animals are raised and killed for food. They think the way animals are treated is cruel, and they do not want to be a part of it.

Finally, being a vegetarian can help the planet. Raising animals for food uses more resources than growing fruits and vegetables does. Also, animals put greenhouse gases into the air. These are the gases that cause global warming.

Even eating just a couple of vegetarian meals a week can make a difference, so dig in and eat your veggies!

SKILL PRACTICE Read the item. Write your response.

1. What is the author's purpose for writing this text?

   _____

   _____

2. Write two reasons the author gives for why people become vegetarians.

   _____

   _____

3. Why does the author include the final sentence?

   _____

   _____

STRATEGY PRACTICE Could you be a vegetarian? Why or why not?

_____

_____

READ THE PASSAGE   As you read the story, think about what will most likely happen next.

The Fishing Tournament

"Good luck, Matt!" Mom called from the beach as I paddled my kayak into the bay. She was excited to watch me compete in my first kayak fishing tournament. I was excited, too, but I was also nervous because the waves were big and the wind was blowing hard.

In order to win the tournament, I would need to catch a big halibut. Whoever caught the heaviest one would win a brand-new kayak. Halibut are big, flat fish, and they often weigh over 20 pounds! They like to bury themselves in the sand on the bottom of the bay. Their favorite type of food is squid, but they also eat sardines. I knew how and where to catch a halibut, but today, it would take luck due to the rough, choppy waters.

I slowly paddled to a sandy area where I've caught halibut before. When I arrived, I noticed that five kayakers were already there. "Any luck yet?" I asked one of the kayakers.

"Nothing yet," he replied sadly. I wished him luck and continued paddling until I reached another spot that looked good. When I got there, I took out my favorite fishing pole. That's when I realized I had left all of my squid bait on the beach with Mom.

"Great, now what can I use?" I grumbled to myself. That's when I remembered the fishing lure I had that looked like a sardine. I cast the lure out, allowing it to sink to the sandy bottom of the bay before I started reeling it back in. After about 10 minutes of casting, my lure stopped abruptly and my fishing pole jerked down toward the water. I pulled back hard on the rod and the fight was on! I could tell right away this was a big fish. I grinned and reached for my fishing net.

SKILL PRACTICE   Read the item. Write your response.

1. What will happen next?

_____

2. Why did Matt leave the first site to which he paddled?

_____

_____

3. What is Matt likely to do the next time he fishes for halibut?

_____

_____

STRATEGY PRACTICE   What else would you like to know about kayak fishing tournaments? Tell your partner a question that you would ask Matt.

Look for clues in the passage that tell you what could happen next.

The Brave Pioneer

I'm a smart and brave pioneer. At least that's what I thought when my family and I set out for our long trip west on the Oregon Trail. But then I learned otherwise.

On the first night on the trail, Ma and my sisters slept in the wagon. I slept next to the fire with Pa. But just as I dropped off to sleep, a cricket crawled across my forehead. I didn't sleep at all for the rest of the night. "We slept fine in the wagon," said my sister in the morning.

I thought I was smart and brave, so on the second night, I slept outside again but wore my hat. Just as I dropped off to sleep, a mouse tickled my big toe. I didn't sleep at all for the rest of the night. "We slept fine in the wagon," said my sister in the morning.

I thought I was smart and brave, so on the third night, I slept outside again but wore my boots. Just as I dropped off to sleep, a snake slithered across my hand. I didn't sleep at all for the rest of the night. "We slept fine in the wagon," said my sister in the morning.

I thought I was smart and brave, so on the fourth night, I slept outside again but wore my gloves. Not a single creature touched my skin. But I was so hot that I didn't sleep at all that night. I decided I'd rather be smart and well-rested than brave and tired.

"Don't worry, son," said Pa. "You'll have plenty of chances to be brave on this trip." Then he pointed to the map. "See? There are no bridges across any of these rivers."

SKILL PRACTICE Read the item. Write your response.

1. Why does the author start paragraphs 3 through 5 in the same way?

   _____

   _____

2. Where will the narrator sleep for the rest of the journey? Why?

   _____

   _____

3. How will the narrator have a chance to prove his bravery later in the journey?

   _____

   _____

STRATEGY PRACTICE Tell a partner whether you would rather sleep under the stars or in your own bed and why.

READ THE PASSAGE   As you read, look for clues that tell you what may happen next.

Popcorn Trick

Whenever Rita baby-sat her little brother Oscar, they liked to eat popcorn, peanut butter sandwiches, and cheese and crackers. But today, there was only one package of popcorn. Mom wouldn't be going to the store again for a few days.

Rita and Oscar popped the corn into the microwave. Rita was extra hungry, so she poured most of the popcorn into a light plastic bowl for herself. Then she poured the rest of the popcorn into a heavy glass bowl for Oscar. She hoped Oscar wouldn't notice.

"You have more popcorn than I do," Oscar said.

Rita had to think quick. She'd be in trouble if their mom knew she was cheating Oscar out of his share of popcorn. "I'll prove that I gave you more popcorn," Rita said.

She got the kitchen scale and put Oscar's glass bowl of popcorn on it. It weighed 9 ounces (255 g). Her plastic bowl of popcorn weighed 6 ounces (170 g). "You have 3 ounces (85 g) more."

"But it looks like way less popcorn," said Oscar.

"Watch this," said Rita. She put a slice of bread on the scale. The scale showed 2 ounces (57 g). Then she put another slice on the scale. Now the scale showed 4 ounces (114 g). "See? Two slices weigh more than one. So, whoever has the heaviest bowl of popcorn must have the most," said Rita.

"You're right," said Oscar as he munched his popcorn. He looked forward to telling Mom everything he had learned from Rita about how to weigh things.

SKILL PRACTICE   Read the item. Write your response.

1. What is the author's purpose for writing this text?

_____

2. How does Rita trick Oscar?

_____

_____

3. What will probably happen when Oscar tells Mom what he learned? Why?

_____

_____

STRATEGY PRACTICE   What question might you ask after reading only the title of the passage?

_____

Nonfiction Text Features

Students practice identifying and comprehending common features of nonfiction text.

Visual Information

Students examine and evaluate information that is depicted visually.

DAY 1

Review the *Nonfiction Text Features* skill with students. Say: **Nonfiction writing often includes features or elements on a page that help us better understand what we are reading.** Tell students they are going to read a recipe that explains how to make a fruit smoothie. Say: **A recipe is a kind of nonfiction text. Notice how the text is set up to make the recipe easy to follow.** Then remind students of the *Determine Important Information* strategy (Week 5). Say: **Good readers set a purpose for reading. Then, as they read, they determine what information is important for fulfilling that purpose.** Read the instructions for the strategy practice activity aloud. Then have students read the recipe. When students have finished, direct them to complete the strategy and skill practice activities. Review the answers together.

DAY 2

Tell students they will study the text features of a chart of holidays. Then remind them of the *Organization* strategy (Week 4). Say: **Good readers pay attention to text features and how they are used to organize information. As you read, study how the chart is organized. Think about why a chart of holidays would be organized this way.** Then have students read the paragraph and study the chart. When students have finished, direct them to complete the skill and strategy practice activities. Review the answers together.

DAY 3

Review the *Visual Information* skill with students. Say: **Not all information is presented in words. Pictures, graphs, maps, illustrations, and diagrams can also give us a lot of information about a topic.** Point out the diagram of a plant cell on the student page. Brainstorm with students why a diagram like this is better than just listing and explaining cell parts (e.g., You can see how the parts go together and what they look like.). Then remind students of the *Determine Important Information* strategy. Say: **Good readers don't try to memorize everything they read. They think about what information they need in order to answer a question or perform a task. As you complete the activities, make sure you refer to the diagram to double-check your answers.** Then have students read the paragraph and study the diagram. When students have finished, direct them to complete the skill and strategy practice activities. Review the answers together.

DAY 4

Tell students they will practice interpreting visual information as they read about a boy's comic book collection. Then remind students of the *Organization* strategy. Say: **As you read, pay attention to how the information is organized. Think about why the boy chose to give information in two circle graphs.** Then have students read the paragraph and study the graphs. When students have finished, direct them to complete the skill and strategy practice activities.

DAY 5

Tell students they will practice studying nonfiction text features and visual information as they read a passage about the history of nutrition labels and a sample nutrition label. Say: **Knowing how to interpret and understand a label is very important.** Discuss with students the information that can be learned from nutrition labels (e.g., the amount of sugar, fat, and protein in a food) and why that information is important (e.g., It helps you make good choices about what you eat.). Consider reading the label as a group to help students understand the more difficult features and vocabulary. Then direct students to complete the skill and strategy practice activities. Review the answers together.

Daily Reading Comprehension • EMC 3614 • © Evan-Moor Corp.

READ THE RECIPE   Think about the way the information is presented and how this would help you follow the recipe.

Megan's Sunshine Smoothie (makes two servings)

Utensils
- Blender
- Measuring cups (for both liquid and dry ingredients)
- 4 medium-sized glasses

Ingredients
- 1 cup (.24 L) nonfat yogurt or lowfat milk
- ¼ teaspoon (1 mL) vanilla (optional)
- 2 or 3 ice cubes
- 2 cups (400 g) cut-up fruit such as bananas, strawberries, or pineapple

Directions
1. Put the yogurt or milk, vanilla, ice, and fruit in a blender.
2. Put the lid of the blender on tight.
3. Blend for about 30 to 40 seconds or until the mixture is smooth and creamy.
4. Pour the mixture into glasses and serve.

SKILL PRACTICE   Read the item. Write your response.

1. Why did the recipe writer include a list of utensils?

   _____

   _____

2. You have raspberries but none of the fruits in the recipe. Can you make a smoothie with this recipe? How do you know?

   _____

3. Which ingredient is not required? How do you know?

   _____

STRATEGY PRACTICE   If someone had an allergy to a certain kind of food, what section of the recipe would that person probably pay the most attention to? Why?

   _____

   _____

READ THE CHART   Read the paragraph and study the information in the chart.

Strange Holidays

Have you ever heard of National Underwear Day? How about Sea Monkey Day? These are just a few of the funny holidays that some people celebrate. Some of the days were created to honor favorite foods or events. Other days started as silly ideas. There is now a holiday on almost every day of the year. Perhaps we need a holiday to celebrate all these holidays!

JANUARY	FEBRUARY	MARCH
Jan. 4: Trivia Day	Feb. 5: Bubble Gum Day	Mar. 5: Name Tag Day
Jan. 13: Rubber Ducky Day	Feb. 9: Read in the Bathtub Day	Mar. 13: Earmuff Day
Jan. 24: Compliment Day	Feb. 28: Tooth Fairy Day	Mar. 20: Corn Dog Day
APRIL	**MAY**	**JUNE**
Apr. 5: Deep Dish Pizza Day	May 1: Free Comic Book Day	June 11: Corn on the Cob Day
Apr. 22: Jellybean Day	May 8: No Socks Day	June 21: Go Skateboarding Day
Apr. 30: Hairball Awareness Day	May 30: Hug Your Cat Day	June 24: Handshake Day
JULY	**AUGUST**	**SEPTEMBER**
July 2: "I Forgot" Day	Aug. 7: Mustard Day	Sept. 5: Be Late for Something Day
July 17: Cow Appreciation Day	Aug. 12: Sewing Machine Day	Sept. 12: Video Games Day
July 24: Tell an Old Joke Day	Aug. 18: Bad Poetry Day	Sept. 22: Elephant Appreciation Day
OCTOBER	**NOVEMBER**	**DECEMBER**
Oct. 1: World Smile Day	Nov. 3: Sandwich Day	Dec. 7: Cotton Candy Day
Oct. 13: Bring Your Teddy Bear Day	Nov. 7: Tongue Twister Day	Dec. 21: Crossword Puzzle Day
Oct. 20: Hagfish Day	Nov. 21: World Hello Day	Dec. 26: National Whiner's Day

SKILL PRACTICE   Read the item. Write your response.

1. There is no holiday for May 8. Is this statement true? Explain.

_____

_____

2. Look at January. Which holiday would most appeal to two-year-olds? Explain.

_____

_____

3. Which summer holiday listed in the chart would you like to celebrate? Give a reason for your choice.

_____

_____

STRATEGY PRACTICE   How is the chart organized like a calendar? How is it different?

_____

_____

READ THE INFORMATION   Read the text and study the diagram of a plant cell.

A Plant Cell

The vacuole (VAK-yoo-ohl) is the part of a cell that stores water and gets rid of waste. Animal and plant cells both have vacuoles, but they are much larger in plant cells. When a plant has enough water, the vacuole is firm, which makes the plant firm. A plant that does not have enough water will wilt because the vacuoles in the cells are no longer firm.

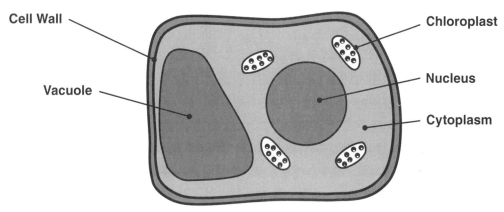

SKILL PRACTICE   Read the item. Write your response.

1. List the parts of the plant cell that are surrounded by cytoplasm.

   _____

   _____

2. According to the diagram, what is the smallest part of a plant cell?

   _____

   _____

3. What is the purpose of the paragraph that accompanies this diagram?

   _____

   _____

STRATEGY PRACTICE   How would the diagram help you study for a test on plant cells? Explain your answer.

   _____

   _____

READ THE INFORMATION   Read the paragraph and study the information in each circle graph.

Junot's Comics

Junot had 100 comic books that he wanted to organize. He created a circle graph to show how many of each subject he had. He created another circle graph to show how many he had from each comic book publisher.

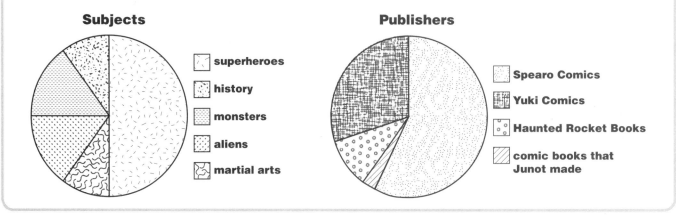

Subjects

- [ ] superheroes
- [ ] history
- [ ] monsters
- [ ] aliens
- [ ] martial arts

Publishers

- [ ] Spearo Comics
- [ ] Yuki Comics
- [ ] Haunted Rocket Books
- [ ] comic books that Junot made

SKILL PRACTICE   Read the item. Write your response.

1. What does the key for the pie chart on the left tell the reader?

   _____

   _____

2. What is Junot's favorite type of comic book? Explain.

   _____

   _____

3. How many different comic book publishers are there in Junot's pie chart? How do you know?

   _____

   _____

STRATEGY PRACTICE   Brainstorm with a partner two other ways Junot might be able to organize his comic books.

READ THE PASSAGE AND LABEL   Study the information given on the nutrition label.

Nutrition Labels

Before 1994, food companies were not required to print nutrition information, or how healthful the food was, in any specific way on the package. This meant that companies could avoid stating clearly how much fat, sugar, salt, or nutrients the food contained. But a new law required all food companies to print the same kind of label on each package to show people exactly what they were eating.

All labels now list food amounts as a percentage of *Daily Value*. The daily value is the amount of something, such as fiber or sugar, people should eat each day as part of a healthful diet.

Nutrition Facts

Serving Size 1 cup (228g)
Servings Per Container 2

Amount Per Serving	
Calories 250	Calories from Fat 110

	% **Daily Value***
Total Fat 12g	18%
Saturated Fat 3g	15%
Trans Fat 3g	
Cholesterol 30mg	10%
Sodium 470mg	20%
Potassium 700mg	20%
Total Carbohydrate 31g	10%
Dietary Fiber 0g	0%
Sugars 5g	
Protein 5g	

Vitamin A **4%**	•	Vitamin C	**2%**
Calcium **20%**	•	Iron	**4%**

*Percent Daily Values are based on a 2,000 calorie diet. Your Daily Values may be higher or lower depending on your calorie needs.

	Calories:	2,000	2,500
Total Fat	Less than	65g	80g
Sat Fat	Less than	20g	25g
Cholesterol	Less than	30mg	300mg
Sodium	Less than	2,400mg	2,400mg
Total Carbohydrate		300g	375g
Fiber		25g	30g

SKILL PRACTICE   Read the item. Write your response.

1. How many calories are in the entire package? Explain.

_____

_____

2. Which mineral or vitamin is most abundant in this product? How do you know?

_____

_____

3. How does the amount of fat compare to the amount of protein in the product? Explain.

_____

_____

STRATEGY PRACTICE   With a partner, discuss why it was a good idea to pass a law that requires all food labels to look the same and give the same type of information.

Main Idea and Details

Students look for the central idea or message of a passage or story. They also find details that best support the main idea.

Sequence

Students look for the order of events or steps in a process.

DAY 1

Review the concept of *main idea and details* with students. Say: **The main idea is what a passage or paragraph is mostly about. Sometimes the main idea is clearly stated, and sometimes it is not.** Details support the main idea. Tell students they are going to read about a period of time called the "Little Ice Age." Then remind students of the *Monitor Comprehension* strategy (Week 1). Say: **Taking notes is a good way to monitor how well you understand what you are reading.** Point out the directions at the top of the page and instruct students to write their notes in the margins or on a separate piece of paper as they read. When students have finished reading, direct them to complete the skill and strategy practice activities. Review the answers together.

DAY 2

Tell students they will practice finding the main idea and details of a passage by reading about an insect called a cicada killer wasp. Then remind students of the *Visualization* strategy (Week 3). Say: **As you read, look for details that are easy to picture in your mind, such as colors and sizes. Make a mental picture of what you are reading about.** Then have students read the passage. When students have finished, direct them to complete the skill and strategy practice activities. Invite volunteers to share their drawings for the strategy practice activity and explain how they knew what to draw.

DAY 3

Review the *Sequence* skill with students. Say: **Good readers pay attention to the order in which events or steps in a process take place.** Tell students they are going to read about how to throw a bocce ball. Explain that bocce is a popular Italian lawn game. Say: **"How to" texts are organized by the steps necessary to make or do something. As you read the passage, number the sentences that give steps for throwing the ball. This will help you better follow the sequence of actions.** Then remind students of the *Monitor Comprehension* strategy. Say: **As you read, look for words that help you understand the order, such as "start by," "at the same time," and "then."** Have students read the passage and then complete the skill and strategy practice activities. Review the answers together.

DAY 4

Tell students they will practice the *Sequence* skill as they read about how a cuckoo hunts and eats hairy caterpillars. Then remind students of the *Visualization* strategy. Say: **As you read, look for strong verbs and concrete nouns to help you picture the order of events and details described in the passage.** Have students read the passage and then complete the skill and strategy practice activities. Review the answers together.

DAY 5

Tell students they will practice both finding the main idea and details and determining sequence by reading about *tektites*, glass pieces formed when meteorites crashed into Earth. Say: **As you read, pause after each paragraph and tell yourself what the paragraph was mostly about. Also, pay attention to the sequence of events mentioned in the passage. Pausing after you read will help you monitor how well you are understanding the information and the sequence of events.** Have students read the passage and then complete the skill and strategy practice activities. Review the answers together.

READ THE PASSAGE   As you read, make notes about the main idea of each paragraph.

The Little Ice Age

Today the world is trying to cope with global warming. But hundreds of years ago, people had a much different problem—a 400-year cold spell! From the 1400s to the 1800s, winters throughout the Northern Hemisphere were colder and longer than they are today. Historians and scientists call this time the "Little Ice Age."

The colder weather created many hardships for people. Crops died and diseases spread. People had to spend a lot more time collecting wood for fires. And occasionally, a huge ice sheet would slide down a mountain and flatten some unlucky village.

Scientists think the Little Ice Age was caused by forces that people could not control. One cause might have been the sun. The sun often has "storms" of energy called sunspots. During the Little Ice Age, there were fewer sunspots than there are today. With fewer sunspots, the sun was releasing less energy to warm the planet. Another natural cause of the cooling might have been volcanoes. During the Little Ice Age, many volcanoes erupted. Their dust and ash could have blocked the sun's light and heat.

Today we are seeing the effects of rising temperatures. The ice sheet in the Arctic Sea is melting. Mountain glaciers are disappearing. Unlike the Little Ice Age, though, scientists think people are contributing to this climate change by burning a lot of coal, oil, and gas.

SKILL PRACTICE   Read the item. Write your response.

1. What is the main idea of this text?

_____

_____

2. Give two details that tell how the Little Ice Age caused hardship.

_____

3. Describe two possible causes for the Little Ice Age.

_____

_____

_____

STRATEGY PRACTICE   Look back at your notes. Write the main idea of the third paragraph.

_____

READ THE PASSAGE   Notice how the details in each paragraph support that paragraph's main idea.

Scary Helpers

Sometimes things that look scary are really quite harmless. Most people would agree that an insect called the cicada (sih-KAY-duh) killer wasp looks scary. This wasp is two inches (5 cm) long with golden wings and black and yellow stripes on its body. Females have a wicked-looking curved stinger. If you see one of these wasps buzzing slowly along the ground, no one would blame you for wanting to run in the opposite direction.

However, the cicada killer is not likely to sting you. The males do not even have stingers. And the females are often too busy to bother with you.

Female cicada killers fly low and slow because they are usually looking for cicadas, the locust-like insects that buzz loudly in late summer. The female cicada killer wants to get a cicada into her underground nest, because that is where she will lay an egg. When the egg hatches into a little worm-like larva, the larva will feed on the cicada.

Cicada killer wasps play an important role in controlling cicadas. Cicadas can damage trees by laying their eggs under the bark. A female cicada killer can get rid of more than 160 cicadas in a season. So these scary-looking wasps are not only harmless, but helpful!

SKILL PRACTICE   Read the item. Write your response.

1. Write the main idea in your own words.

_____

_____

2. What does a cicada killer wasp want to do with a cicada?

_____

_____

3. How are cicada killer wasps helpful to trees?

_____

_____

STRATEGY PRACTICE   On a separate piece of paper, sketch what you think a cicada killer looks like.

Name: _____

READ THE PASSAGE   Number the sentences that give the steps for throwing a bocce ball two different ways.

Throwing a Bocce Ball

Bocce (BOCH-ee) is a game in which two teams score points by throwing or rolling balls toward a target ball called a *jack*. Before every throw, each player must announce which ball he or she is aiming for. Players may either aim for the jack or for one of the other team's bocce balls. A team's goal is to get their balls closest to the jack, and the team whose balls are closest to the jack scores points.

There are two ways to throw a bocce ball, either with a two-step throw or a four-step run. For the two-step throw, start by taking a step forward. At the same time, bring your arm backward. As you begin the second step forward, swing your arm forward and release the ball. You can either roll the ball along the ground or toss it underhanded into the air.

To throw using a four-step run, start the same way. First, take one step, holding your arms at your sides. Then, as you take your second and third steps, swing your throwing arm backward. On the fourth step, swing your throwing arm forward and release the ball. Using the four-step run gives you more power to throw the ball than a two-step throw, but it is harder to control exactly where the ball will land.

SKILL PRACTICE   Read the item. Write your response.

1. How do players score points in the game of bocce?

_____

_____

2. The jack is far away. Which throwing method would you use and why?

_____

_____

3. How could this text be improved by an image?

_____

_____

STRATEGY PRACTICE   Look at the sentences you numbered in the passage. Underline the words that helped you figure out the order of steps in each method of throwing the ball.

READ THE PASSAGE   As you read the passage, pay attention to the order in which things happen.

Cuckoo for Caterpillars!

Have you ever held a hairy caterpillar? If you have, then you know how itchy and uncomfortable the hairs feel on your skin. That's why the hairs are such good protection for the caterpillar. They keep the caterpillar from being eaten—by most animals, anyway. But not by cuckoos. Cuckoos are one of the few birds that can eat hairy caterpillars. They have special ways of dealing with a caterpillar's scratchy hairs.

A cuckoo hunts caterpillars by sitting perfectly still on a tree branch. Then, when the cuckoo spots its "snack," the bird dashes after it with lightning speed and grabs the caterpillar with its beak. Most of the time, the cuckoo will gobble up the caterpillar. But sometimes the bird will rub or beat the caterpillar against a branch before eating it. The bird isn't trying to be mean. It's just trying to remove some of the scratchy hairs.

Cuckoos can eat hundreds of caterpillars in a single day. That's a lot of hair to deal with! And the hairs don't pass through the cuckoo's digestive system. They get stuck in the stomach. After a while, the stomach fills with hair. To get rid of the hair, the cuckoo *regurgitates* it, or coughs it up. That may sound gross, but it's a good way for the cuckoo to make room for more caterpillars!

SKILL PRACTICE   Read the item. Write your response.

1. Your brother puts a hairy caterpillar on your arm. What happens next?

_____

_____

2. What happens to the caterpillar hairs after the cuckoo swallows them?

_____

_____

3. Why does the cuckoo hit the caterpillar against the branch?

_____

_____

STRATEGY PRACTICE   Write at least three words or phrases from the passage that helped you visualize a cuckoo catching a caterpillar.

_____

_____

READ THE PASSAGE   As you read, pay attention to how details are used to support the main idea.

Glass from Space

When you see a piece of glass on the ground, most of the time it is just from an old bottle or other man-made object. But in certain places on Earth's surface, you can find pieces of a special, naturally formed kind of glass. These glass pieces are called *tektites*. They were formed long ago by large meteorites crashing into the ground.

When a meteorite hits Earth's surface, it causes big explosions. Soil, rocks, and other debris are thrown high into the sky. The heat is so great that it melts minerals within the debris into a liquid form. Those liquid minerals create a kind of spray. By the time the spray falls back to Earth, it has cooled into glass.

Many tektites have interesting shapes. They can look like a bottle, a teardrop, a little dumbbell, a ball, or a button. Their different shapes are most likely the result of the liquid minerals being stretched and pulled by the force of flying through the air.

Tektites are found in only four regions on Earth—the United States, eastern Europe, western Africa, and a very wide area that covers much of southeast Asia and western and southern Australia. Scientists think that tektites are not found anywhere else because there were no large meteorite impacts in other places around the world.

SKILL PRACTICE   Read the item. Write your response.

1. Write two things that happen after the minerals melt.

   _____

   _____

2. When does a tektite get its shape?

   _____

   _____

3. What is the first step in the formation of tektites?

   _____

STRATEGY PRACTICE   Draw a star next to the paragraph you would like to understand better. Then write what you need to do to understand it better.

_____

_____

Cause and Effect

Students practice identifying cause-and-effect relationships by looking for what happens and why it happens.

Fact and Opinion

Students determine whether details in a text can be proved (facts) or represent what someone thinks or feels (opinions).

DAY 1

Review the *Cause and Effect* skill with students. Say: **The cause is what makes something happen. The effect is what happens. Imagine that someone throws a rock and it breaks a window. What is the cause?** (throwing the rock) **What is the effect?** (the window breaking) Tell students they are going to read about some special fossils in a place called the Burgess Shale. Then remind students of the *Determine Important Information* strategy (Week 5). Say: **As you read, look for information that helps you best understand the causes and effects described in the passage.** Have students read the passage and then complete the skill and strategy practice activities. Review the answers together.

DAY 2

Tell students they will practice finding causes and effects as they read about colorblindness. Then remind students of the *Ask Questions* strategy (Week 6). Say: **Stop after each paragraph and ask yourself a question about what you have just read. This will help you monitor how well you are understanding the causes and effects of colorblindness.** Have students read the passage and then complete the skill practice activity. Review the answers together. For the strategy practice activity, pair students or complete it as a group.

DAY 3

Tell students they will read about how astronauts have fun in space. Then review the definition of *fact* (something that can be proved) and *opinion* (what someone feels or believes). Say: **Good readers evaluate what they are reading in order to distinguish facts from opinions.** Then remind students of the *Determine Important Information* strategy. Say: **Making notes or marks on a text is a good way to remember important information. As you read, underline information that you think is important for understanding how the author feels.** Have students read the passage and then complete the skill and strategy practice activities. Review the answers together and then invite volunteers to share what they underlined.

DAY 4

Tell students they will practice distinguishing facts from opinions as they read about the dodo, an extinct bird. Say: **Sometimes, opinions may seem like facts. Look for words that tell you how good or bad something is to help you decide whether you are reading a fact or an opinion.** Read the second sentence in the second paragraph of the passage aloud, emphasizing the words "carelessly let them roam free." Say: **The author uses the word *carelessly*, which shows an opinion.** Then remind students of the *Ask Questions* strategy. Say: **Asking questions after you read helps you evaluate whether you understood the facts and opinions in the passage.** Have students read the passage and complete the skill and strategy practice activities. Review the answers together.

DAY 5

Tell students they will practice finding causes and effects and telling the difference between facts and opinions as they read about the Dust Bowl. Build background by pointing out the Great Plains region on a map of the U.S. Have students read the passage and then complete the skill and strategy practice activities. Review the answers together. Invite volunteers to share why they think the information they underlined is the most important.

READ THE PASSAGE   As you read, pay attention to what caused the Burgess Shale fossils to form and be preserved.

The Burgess Shale Fossils

An amazing collection of fossils lies on a ridge in the Canadian Rocky Mountains. These fossils are called the Burgess Shale fossils. They come from animals that existed 505 million years ago, at a time when the only creatures on Earth lived in the sea. The Burgess Shale animals had many weird shapes, with tubes, spines, fans, extra feet, and antennae. They were unlike anything alive today.

The Burgess Shale fossils are amazing for another reason, too. The soft parts of the animals' bodies are preserved in stone. An animal's soft parts almost always rot away or are eaten shortly after the animal dies. This means that most fossils are made up of only hard parts, such as bones, teeth, and shells. What caused the Burgess Shale animals to be so well-preserved?

The fossils are embedded in a very smooth type of rock called *shale*. Shale is made of hardened mud. Scientists believe that the animals were killed in underwater mudslides. The mud buried the animals and covered every part of their bodies. This protected their remains from being eaten by other animals. The mud also protected the soft body parts from air and bacteria, which kept the dead animals from rotting. As a result, the animals' bodies were preserved in a blanket of mud. Over millions of years, pressure turned that mud into shale.

SKILL PRACTICE   Read the item. Write your response.

1. How did the Burgess Shale animals most likely die?

_____

_____

2. How did the Burgess Shale animals differ from today's animals?

_____

_____

3. How do these fossils differ from typical fossils?

_____

STRATEGY PRACTICE   Underline the details in the passage that explain how the Burgess Shale fossils were preserved.

As you read, think about the causes and effects of colorblindness.

Is That Stoplight Red or Green?

Imagine how your life would be if the colors red and green looked the same to you. Some people have a common type of colorblindness called red-green colorblindness. People with this disorder can see most colors, but they cannot tell the difference between red and green.

Most people who have colorblindness are born with it. It is caused by problems with special cells in the eye called *cones*. Cones send signals to the brain that help you see colors. People with red-green colorblindness do not have enough of the kinds of cones that send red and green signals. Some people have enough cones, but the cones do not work properly and do not send any color signals at all.

People with red-green colorblindness can have otherwise normal vision. Some wear tinted contact lenses that help them see reds and greens better. But people with severe red-green colorblindness may not be able to perform certain jobs, such as being an airplane pilot, that require the ability to see all colors clearly.

Currently there is no cure for colorblindness, but new technology may eventually help colorblind people see the world in the same way that most people do.

SKILL PRACTICE   Read the item. Write your response.

1. How can contact lenses help some people who have colorblindness?

   _____

   _____

2. What physical problem causes colorblindness?

   _____

   _____

3. How might red-green colorblindness affect someone who is driving a car?

   _____

   _____

STRATEGY PRACTICE   Write a question you asked yourself about colorblindness while you were reading. Then have a partner find the answer.

   _____

READ THE PASSAGE
As you read, underline the author's opinions about living in space.

Silliness in Space

There's no doubt that traveling into space is the greatest adventure a person can have. But living in space is not always as it appears on TV or in movies. In real life, astronauts must sometimes stay on the International Space Station for many weeks at a time. The station is not very big, and the astronauts don't have a lot of room to move around. And the space shuttle that carries astronauts to the space station is even smaller. Astronauts have to eat, sleep, and do their work in very tight spaces.

However, astronauts still manage to have fun and relax after a hard day's work. They watch movies, play cards, or talk to their friends and family on Earth. Some astronauts even play a musical instrument. That's a valuable talent, no matter where you live!

But the most fun that astronauts have comes from good old-fashioned goofing off. They enjoy doing silly things while weightless, such as somersaults in mid-air. They run in circles, up and down walls, and across the ceiling. They laugh as their hair sticks out in all directions. Astronauts may have a serious job, but they must also have a good sense of humor to handle the pressures of living in space.

SKILL PRACTICE   Read the item. Write your response.

1. How many sentences in the first paragraph are facts? Explain.

_____

_____

2. Is there an opinion stated in paragraph 2? How do you know?

_____

_____

3. What would you most like to do during a visit to the International Space Station? Why?

_____

_____

STRATEGY PRACTICE   Underline the sentences in the passage that explain what astronauts do to relax.

READ THE PASSAGE   As you read, think about which statements can be proved and which cannot. Look for words that signal the author's opinion.

Gone the Way of the Dodo

European sailors traveling along the east coast of Africa first landed on the island of Mauritius (maw-RISH-uss) in the late 1500s. There, the sailors discovered big, gray, slow-moving birds. The birds, which later became known as "dodos," weighed about 50 pounds (23 kg). They had stubby wings and couldn't fly. They built their nests and raised their young on the ground. When the sailors walked up to the dodos, they didn't run away. The sailors thought these birds were the dumbest birds they had ever seen. And this is how one of the worst tragedies in natural history began.

Even though dodos didn't taste very good, the sailors ate many of them because they were so easy to catch. As more Europeans came to live on Mauritius in the 1600s, they brought cats, dogs, and rats to the island and carelessly let them roam free. These animals ate the dodos' eggs and chicks and destroyed their nests. Meanwhile, humans ruined the forests where the dodos lived.

Later, people came to understand why the dodos never ran away. It wasn't because these sweet, gentle birds were dumb. It was because they were trusting. On Mauritius, there were no animals that ate adult dodos. So dodos never had to learn how to escape from danger. That was fine until people came. Then the dodos' trusting nature became a huge problem. By 1663, because of people's carelessness, not a single dodo was left.

SKILL PRACTICE   Read the item. Write your response.

1. Find an opinion statement in paragraph 1. Which words let you know it is an opinion? Explain.

_____

_____

2. Are there any opinions stated in paragraph 2? Explain.

_____

_____

3. Why did the author include so many facts about dodos?

_____

STRATEGY PRACTICE   Write a question that can be answered by using information from the passage.

_____

READ THE PASSAGE As you read about the Dust Bowl, look for causes and effects. Think about which statements are facts and which are opinions.

Dust and Destruction

In the 1920s, wheat farmers on the Great Plains were earning a lot of money. This made many other people want to be farmers, too. But no one thought to stop the farmers from plowing almost all the land and cutting down most of the trees.

Still, everything was fine until 1931. This was the beginning of a terrible *drought, a* long period without rain. The beautiful wheat fields dried up, and the crops died. Then there were no plants to hold down the soil. All that was left was bare, ugly, dry dirt.

Then the wind started to blow. With no trees to block it, the wind gathered up the soil into huge black clouds that traveled for miles. These clouds were called *dust storms*, and they were impossible to escape. Dirt collected in people's houses. It fell into their food. It got into their noses, mouths, and eyes. People wore masks, but the dust still clogged their lungs, causing many people to get sick. The dust even fell waist-high in a few places. Nothing survived being buried in the dust, and farm animals starved from a lack of food. The cruel storms punished everyone and everything. The Great Plains became known as the Dust Bowl.

This was the worst natural disaster ever to strike the United States. But some people believed the farmers deserved what happened to them because they did not care for the soil. They say the disaster could have been prevented if the farmers had been wiser and more careful.

SKILL PRACTICE Read the item. Write your response.

1. Why did the farmers' crops die?

   _____

   _____

2. In paragraph 3, did the author give human characteristics to something that isn't alive? Explain.

   _____

   _____

3. What did people rename the Great Plains duing the 1930s? Why?

   _____

STRATEGY PRACTICE Underline the information in the passage that explains what caused the dust storms.

Compare and Contrast

Students practice comparing and contrasting by looking at the similarities and differences between two or more people or things.

Make Inferences

Students practice making inferences by using clues in the passage to understand what is being implied or inferred.

DAY 1

Review the *Compare and Contrast* skill with students. Say: **When we compare and contrast, we look at the similarities and differences between two or more things.** Tell students they are going to read a passage about different shapes of snowflakes. Remind students to look for words such as *although, alike,* and *common,* which signal that a comparison is being made. Then remind students of the *Make Connections* strategy (Week 2). Say: **When we make connections, we use what we have seen, read, or been told in order to help us better understand the text. As you read this passage, think about what you already know about snowflakes.** Then have students read the passage. When they have finished, direct them to complete the skill and strategy practice activities. Review the answers together.

DAY 2

Tell students they will practice comparing and contrasting as they read about the flag of Nepal. Explain that Nepal is a country in South Asia, and help students find it on a world map or globe. If possible, show students a picture of Nepal's flag. Then remind students of the *Monitor Comprehension* strategy (Week 1). Say: **One way to monitor your comprehension is to identify a part of a passage you do not understand and to think about what you can do to understand it better.** Then have students read the passage. When students have finished, direct them to complete the skill and strategy practice activities. Review the answers together. Invite volunteers to share their responses to the strategy practice activity.

DAY 3

Remind students of what it means to make inferences. Say: **When we make an inference, we use clues from the text and our own knowledge to understand information that is not directly told to us.** Tell students they will read about the 1980 eruption of Mount St. Helens, a volcano in Washington, and the recovery of the affected area. Build background by pointing out the location of Mount St. Helens on a map and, if possible, showing students pictures of the volcano. Then remind students of the *Make Connections* strategy. Say: **As you read, think about what you already know about volcanoes. Connecting the text to your background knowledge will help you make inferences and understand information that is not directly stated in the passage.** Then have students read the passage. When students have finished, direct them to complete the skill practice activity. Review the answers together. For the strategy practice activity, pair students or complete it as a group.

DAY 4

Tell students they will practice making inferences as they read a passage about Ben Underwood, a boy who was blind but learned to use *echolocation,* or the bouncing of sound waves off objects, to find his way around. Then remind students of the *Monitor Comprehension* strategy. Say: **As you read, pause after each paragraph. Think about whether you understood everything, or whether you need to reread in order to make an inference.** Then have students read the passage. When students have finished, direct them to complete the skill and strategy practice activities.

DAY 5

Tell students they will practice both comparing and contrasting and making inferences as they read about types of insects that are eaten in some parts of the world. Say: **As you read, think about how the author compares the taste of insects to other foods and how this helps you make connections to the text.** Then have students read the passage. When students have finished, direct them to complete the skill practice activity. For the strategy practice activity, pair students or complete it as a group.

Name: _____

READ THE PASSAGE   Look for words that tell you that a comparison is being made between different types of snowflakes.

A Closer Look at Snowflakes

After a heavy snowfall, the snow covering the ground looks like a thick white blanket. But when you look closely, you see that the blanket of snow is made of tiny individual snowflakes, each with its own unique shape.

Although no two snowflakes are exactly alike, all snowflakes have some things in common. For example, all snowflakes begin as a water droplet in a cloud. The droplet freezes into an ice crystal that grows as more droplets around it freeze. Also, almost all snowflakes start out with six sides and are shaped like a long, thin column or flat, round plate. Their shapes may quickly change as they grow, but in their earliest stages, all snowflakes look very much alike.

The different shapes that snowflakes can become depends on the air's temperature and the amount of water vapor in the air. Simple column- or plate-shaped flakes form in dry air below 5°F (–15°C). In moister air with temperatures of 5 to 15°F (–15°C to –9°C), snowflakes become lacy, six-pointed stars with many tiny branches. Snowflakes can also take on a needle shape. This kind of snowflake forms when the air is about 20°F (–7°C) and has a lot of water vapor in it.

All snowflakes have one other thing in common. They melt! So if you ever have a chance to study one up close, be sure to look quickly. It won't be around for much longer!

SKILL PRACTICE   Read the item. Write your response.

1. Name three things that all snowflakes have in common.

_____

_____

2. What two factors influence the shape of a snowflake?

_____

_____

3. What does a lacy snowflake have that a column-shaped snowflake does not?

_____

STRATEGY PRACTICE   Describe one thing about snowflakes that you did not know before reading.

_____

READ THE PASSAGE   As you read, think about how the flag of Nepal is different from other flags you know about.

A Flag with a Difference

The use of flags can be traced back thousands of years. Soldiers marching into battle carried *standards*, or tall poles with objects made of cloth, wood, metal, or other materials fastened to the top. Later, cloth pieces or streamers became the most common standard to carry into battle. The flags of today's countries developed from those cloth standards. The colors used on most countries' flags today are some combination of blue, red, white, black, green, yellow, and orange. Most national flags are rectangular. The flag of Nepal is an exception.

Nepal's flag is made up of two triangles, one stacked on top of the other. The top triangle shows a white moon against a red background. The bottom triangle shows a white sun against a red background. The sun and the moon symbolize the hope that the country will last as long as the sun and moon. Red is a traditional Nepalese color, but both sections of the flag also have a blue border that stands for peace.

Nepal's flag developed from the standards of two branches of a family that once ruled Nepal. It is believed that the flag got its present shape in the late 1800s, when the two triangle flags were placed one above the other. The triangles are also meant to represent the shape of the Himalaya mountains—the huge range that covers the country.

SKILL PRACTICE   Read the item. Write your response.

1. How did standards differ from most of the flags used today?

_____

_____

2. What makes Nepal's flag so unusual?

_____

3. What three colors are used in Nepal's flag? Name another nation's flag that uses these same colors.

_____

STRATEGY PRACTICE   Draw a star next to a part of the passage that you did not understand at first. Write what you did to understand it better.

_____

_____

Use clues from the passage and your own knowledge about volcanoes to make inferences about what took place on Mount St. Helens.

Destruction and Recovery

The eruption of Mount St. Helens, a volcano in southwestern Washington, was the most destructive eruption in North America ever recorded. It happened on May 18, 1980. Inside the volcano, hot melted rock, or *magma*, had been rising toward the surface for weeks. This rock was under intense pressure. On the day of the eruption, an earthquake caused the north side of the mountain peak to collapse and slide into the valley. Without the weight of the mountaintop, the pressure inside the volcano was released. As a result, a huge explosion sent steam, dust, rock, and ash soaring into the sky.

In a matter of minutes, the landslide and explosion completely destroyed an area 12 miles (19 km) long by 18 miles (29 km) wide. Thousands of towering old trees were flattened and buried in hot dust, ash, and rock. Fifty-seven people were killed. No large animals close to the eruption survived. The only creatures that lived through the blast were those hidden in underground burrows. And hundreds of homes and miles of highway were destroyed.

Today, life is almost back to normal on Mount St. Helens. Even the areas that were most badly scorched and buried are now blanketed with wildflowers. Deer and elk are thriving. And millions of trees that people planted after the 1980 eruption are already growing tall. Scientists predict that 200 years from now, if the volcano has not erupted again by then, the area should have completely returned to the way it was.

SKILL PRACTICE   Read the item. Write your response.

1. Why did only the animals that lived underground survive the eruption?

_____

_____

2. Why do scientists say that it will take 200 years for the Mount St. Helens region to completely recover?

_____

_____

3. Why are deer and elk now thriving in the area?

_____

STRATEGY PRACTICE   How would you feel if you lived near Mount St. Helens today? Discuss it with a partner.

READ THE PASSAGE   Think about how Ben Underwood changed the lives of other blind people.

"Seeing" with Sound

Ben Underwood was just a baby when he got a rare form of eye cancer. Because of the cancer, doctors had to remove his eyes by the time he was three years old. But Ben never let blindness stop him. He taught himself how to "see" with his ears, just as bats, whales, and other animals do. This type of "seeing" is called *echolocation*.

Ben found his way around by making clicks with his tongue. The clicks traveled to objects and bounced off them. By listening to their echoes, Ben could tell all sorts of things about his surroundings. He could tell how far away something was, what shape it was, and what it was made of. Using his amazing skills, he was able to play kickball and basketball with friends, ride a skateboard, and even play some video games. Ben became a star all around the world. He helped doctors better understand how blind people can learn how to echolocate.

Sadly, Ben's cancer came back. He died in 2009, just a week before his 17th birthday. But because of his talent, more people now understand that a physical condition doesn't need to hold you back. In his short life, Ben became an inspiration to many people—those with and without sight.

SKILL PRACTICE   Read the item. Write your response.

1. How did Ben use echolocation to play basketball?

   _____

   _____

2. Write the sentence from the text that states its theme.

   _____

   _____

3. What was the author's purpose for writing this text?

   _____

STRATEGY PRACTICE   Reread the second paragraph and underline a sentence that helped you make an inference about Ben's personality. Then write the inference you made.

   _____

   _____

READ THE PASSAGE   Think about what it would be like to eat insects, and make inferences about why most Americans do not eat them.

Creepy or Tasty?

How would you like to munch on a fat, pale caterpillar called a witchetty grub? Would you enjoy chowing down on a delicious ant-egg taco? How does a wasp cracker sound to you? Caterpillars, ant eggs, and wasps are just three of the 1,500 different kinds of insects that are eaten by people around the world.

Here in the United States, most people are turned off by the thought of eating insects. But about 80 percent of people in the rest of the world include insects in their diet. Eating insects is not a bad idea. Insects are not only cheap, but they're also good for you. They have a lot of protein, vitamins, and minerals, and they have little fat.

People have different ways of preparing insect dishes. Sometimes the bugs are ground into flour and baked into cookies. Other times they are fried, roasted, boiled, or eaten raw. Depending on how the insects are prepared, their texture may be gooey, chewy, crunchy, or tender. And their flavors can be compared to common foods that even Americans find delicious. For example, witchetty grubs are said to taste like almonds, chicken, or shrimp. Giant red ants, which people eat in Thailand, may taste like bacon. Some Australians enjoy the sweet taste of honeypot ants. And some people compare deep fried bees to sunflower seeds, shrimp, or walnuts. It's all just a matter of taste!

SKILL PRACTICE   Read the item. Write your response.

1. What are three benefits of eating insects?

   _____

   _____

2. Why did the author begin the text by asking three questions?

   _____

   _____

3. Which insects might a person who likes to eat shrimp be willing to try? How do you know?

   _____

   _____

STRATEGY PRACTICE   Would you eat a bug? Why or why not? Discuss it with a partner.

Character and Setting

Students practice analyzing character and setting by looking at the traits and motivations of a character and where and when the passage's events take place.

Theme

Students practice identifying the theme by looking for the central message or lesson in the passage.

DAY 1

Review the definitions of *character* and *setting*. Say: **A character's traits include both what the character looks like and the character's actions and personality. The setting is where and when a story takes place.** Tell students they are going to read a short biography of John Muir, a famous naturalist. Say: **Studying the character and setting of a biography helps us better understand why the author thinks this person is worth writing about.** Explain that John Muir founded the Sierra Club, a national group that organizes outdoor activities and works to protect the environment. Then remind students of the *Monitor Comprehension* strategy (Week 1). Say: **Marking important information in a passage after you read it is a good way to monitor your comprehension. As you read, pay attention to the important events in John Muir's life.** Then have students read the passage. When students have finished, direct them to complete the skill and strategy practice activities.

DAY 2

Tell students they will practice studying character and setting as they read about Annie Oakley, a woman who was famous for her shooting skills. Then remind students of the *Visualization* strategy (Week 3). Say: **Make a mental picture of the events as you read. This will help you better remember the characters and setting.** Then have students read the passage. When students have finished, direct them to complete the skill and strategy practice activities. Review the answers together.

DAY 3

Review the definition of *theme* with students. Say: **The theme of a story is a lesson or moral that the author wants to share. Often the theme is not directly stated in the passage. You must infer the theme based on the events in the passage or by the details that the author includes. For example, if you read a story about a student who cheats on a test and is punished, what might the theme be?** (Cheating is wrong.) Then remind students of the *Monitor Comprehension* strategy. Say: **Good readers notice if their minds start to wander and work to refocus on the text. As you read, pay attention to how well you are able to concentrate on the passage and theme.** Then have students read the passage. When students have finished, direct them to complete the skill practice activity. For the strategy practice activity, pair students or discuss it as a group.

DAY 4

Tell students they will practice finding the theme of a passage as they read about how a doctor invented an important medicine from the venom of a lizard called a Gila monster. Say: **To find the theme, pay attention to what the author tells you about the inventor and how the medicine was created.** Remind students to look for words and phrases in the story that help them visualize what Gila monsters look like and where they come from. Then have students read the passage. When students have finished, direct them to complete the skill and strategy practice activities. Review the answers together.

DAY 5

Tell students they will practice studying characters and setting and identifying the theme as they read a story about a boy and his uncle on a fishing trip. Then remind students of the *Monitor Comprehension* strategy and say: **As you read, think about how the dialogue in the story helps you understand the characters and theme.** Direct students to read the passage and complete the skill and strategy practice activities. Review the answers together.

Daily Reading Comprehension • EMC 3614 • © Evan-Moor Corp.

READ THE PASSAGE   As you read, think about the kind of person John Muir was and the places he loved.

John Muir, a Man with Vision

In 1849, when John Muir was 11 years old, he and his family moved from Scotland to the United States. They settled in Wisconsin, and John immediately fell in love with the prairies, wetlands, oak forests, and lakes. He called it the "glorious Wisconsin wilderness."

John worked hard on his father's farm, plowing fields and digging a well through solid rock. The hard work made him determined and strong. In his spare time, Muir caught turtles and frogs in the streams and lakes. He enjoyed the lovely wildflowers that grew on the prairies. He loved learning, too, and at night he studied and read about many subjects.

As a young man, Muir tried different kinds of work. He built clocks and invented machines that made farming easier. He took classes at the University of Wisconsin. He traveled through Canada and then Florida, studying nature. But at age 29, he suffered a serious eye injury. He was scared that he would never see again. So when his sight returned, Muir knew he needed to follow his dream of exploring and studying nature.

A year later, when John saw the Sierra Nevada mountains in California for the first time, he realized he had found his life's passion. "I came to life in the cool winds and the crystal waters of the mountains," he wrote. Muir dedicated the rest of his life to protecting the wild places he loved so much. He was a gifted writer and used his talent to describe the beauty of the land and convince people that it was worth protecting. In 1892, John Muir founded the Sierra Club, an organization that still works to protect the environment.

SKILL PRACTICE   Read the item. Write your response.

1. How did traveling to the Sierra Nevada mountains change Muir's life?

   _____

   _____

2. Was Muir creative? Use text evidence in your response.

   _____

   _____

3. Approximately how many years ago did Muir start his environmental organization? How do you know?

   _____

STRATEGY PRACTICE   Underline three sentences that tell important events in John Muir's life.

READ THE PASSAGE   Pay attention to the details that describe Annie Oakley and the setting.

Annie Oakley in England

In 1887, on 23 acres (9 hectares) outside London, Buffalo Bill Cody set up his Wild West Show for its first stop on the European tour. He built a huge outdoor arena that could hold 40,000 people. He set up barns for the animals—horses, buffalo, elk, donkeys, steer, bears, and deer. He put up tents to house more than 200 performers, including Native Americans, cowboys, stunt riders from Mexico, and a lady sharpshooter named Annie Oakley.

Annie Oakley was already a star, but she became a superstar in England. During shows, she would skip into the arena blowing kisses. Then she would draw her guns and shoot six glass balls in the air before they hit the ground. She could shoot a playing card in half. She could ride a bike while shooting targets. But once in a while, she would miss on purpose. Then she would pretend to be angry, pouting and stamping her feet. When she hit her target on the next try, the audience cheered. People adored how this dainty, ladylike woman was among the best shooters in the world.

England's royalty loved the show, and Annie got to meet the Prince of Wales and his wife. She knew she was supposed to shake the prince's hand first, but when she was introduced to the couple, she took the princess's hand first. She said, "You'll have to forgive me. I'm an American, and in America, women come first."

SKILL PRACTICE   Read the item. Write your response.

1. Who was the star of the Wild West Show? How do you know?

   _____

   _____

2. What made Annie so unique?

   _____

   _____

   _____

3. Why did Annie shake the princess's hand before the prince's hand?

   _____

STRATEGY PRACTICE   Which part of Annie's act was easiest for you to visualize? Summarize it.

_____

Daily Reading Comprehension • EMC 3614 • © Evan-Moor Corp.

READ THE PASSAGE   As you read the tale, think about the lessons that the villagers learn.

The Terrible Nian

Long ago, there was a dreadful monster, Nian, with the head of a dragon and the body of a lion. Once a year, Nian would storm from his mountain cave to attack the village below. And every year, when Nian was on his way, the villagers scattered to hiding places in the woods and across the river. With no one to stop him, Nian ate the people's farm animals, wrecked their homes, and trampled their crops.

One year, as the people were fleeing their village, an old man appeared. "If you stay here," he told them, "I will show you how to be safe from terrible Nian."

The only person to accept his offer was an old widow. "I have nothing to lose," she said. "We'll face Nian together."

The old man and the old lady worked hard. They hung red paper streamers around the village and lit lanterns in every window. That night, when Nian saw the lights and streamers, he thought a celebration was going on. He sat on the edge of town, waiting for the villagers to leave. Instead, the old man and the old lady rushed out, throwing firecrackers and lighting rockets. Nian fled, howling all the way back to his cave.

When the villagers returned the next day, their homes and fields were unharmed. They thanked the old man for showing them how to frighten Nian. Every year after that, on the night of Nian's return, the villagers worked together to hang streamers, light lanterns, and set off fireworks. The people no longer feared Nian, and Nian never hurt them again.

SKILL PRACTICE   Read the item. Write your response.

1. What is the theme of this tale?

_____

2. Did the villagers get what they wanted? Explain.

_____

_____

3. Is this a modern story? Explain.

_____

_____

STRATEGY PRACTICE   What would be a good tip for helping someone stay focused while reading this tale? How does paying attention to the theme help? Discuss it with a partner.

READ THE PASSAGE   As you read, think about how the medicine called Byetta came to be invented.

Relief from a Lizard's Mouth

Sometimes important discoveries come from the oddest places. Many people suffer from a disease called diabetes (DY-uh-BEE-teez), in which the body doesn't use sugar properly. Diabetes can cause kidney failure, blindness, and even death. In the early 1990s, a doctor named John Eng discovered a substance that could help the body process sugar normally. The substance was in the venom of large orange and black American lizards called Gila (HEE-luh) monsters.

However, Dr. Eng's discovery couldn't help people unless the venom could be converted into a drug. Creating new drugs takes millions of dollars and many years. Dr. Eng couldn't do this on his own. He asked drug companies to help, but none of them were interested. Still, he kept trying. It took two years, but Dr. Eng finally found a small drug company to take on the project. After ten years, the company figured out how to turn Gila monster venom into medicine. The medicine, called Byetta, was released in 2005. It eases the suffering and saves the lives of many people with diabetes.

Dr. Eng learned that the desert areas where Gila monsters live are disappearing. He knew that many other lifesaving medicines are waiting to be discovered in wild plants and animals. So he used some of the money he earned to start a fund that helps college students study plants and animals that could be new sources of medicine.

SKILL PRACTICE   Read the item. Write your response.

1. What is the theme of this text?

_____

_____

2. Name two adjectives that describe Dr. Eng. Explain your choices.

_____

_____

3. Why does Dr. Eng feel passionate about studying plants and animals?

_____

_____

STRATEGY PRACTICE   Underline the words or phrases in the passage that were easiest for you to visualize.

READ THE PASSAGE Notice how the characters react differently to what they see.

Storm or No Storm?

Uncle Carl's little boat bounced on the waves. The sky was overcast, and the temperature was neither too hot nor too cold. In other words, it was the perfect spring day for fishing. And the fish in the lake were biting so well that neither Uncle Carl nor I saw the dark clouds rolling over the line of trees behind us.

When I finally noticed them, I said, "Those clouds look scary. Should we go in?"

Uncle Carl said, "We're fine. I read the *Daily Weather*, the *Weather Examiner*, the *Weather News*, and the *News of the Daily Weather*. They all said there wouldn't be any rain today. So keep fishing. I want to have fish for dinner all week."

"But my eyes tell me those are storm clouds," I said. "And I trust my eyes."

"Don't trust your eyes, Freddie," said my uncle. "Trust the experts who predict the weather."

"Any expert looking at those clouds would say it's going to rain," I said.

"It'll blow over. Keep fishing," my uncle said.

So we did. A few minutes later we saw a flash of lightning. Then a gigantic crash of thunder rattled Uncle Carl's little boat.

Uncle Carl quickly pulled up the anchor. "Reel in. There's a storm coming."

It took us only a minute or two to get back to the dock, but by that time, we were drenched. I think I'm going to keep trusting my eyes.

SKILL PRACTICE   Read the item. Write your response.

1. Where does this story take place?

_____

2. How do the two characters differ?

_____

_____

3. What lesson does Uncle Carl learn?

_____

_____

STRATEGY PRACTICE   Explain how you kept track of who was speaking in the story.

_____

Author's Purpose
Students identify the author's reason for writing about a subject.

Prediction
Students practice using clues from a passage to predict what will happen next.

DAY 1

Review the *Author's Purpose* skill with students. Say: **When we study the author's purpose, we think about the reason why an author wrote a passage. Authors can have more than one reason for writing something.** Remind students of the common purposes for writing (to inform, to entertain, to explain or teach, and to persuade). Then say: **As you read this essay about fortune cookies, stop after each paragraph and think about its purpose.** Then review the *Ask Questions* strategy (Week 6). Say: **Asking questions as you read helps you check if you're understanding the author's main points.** Then have students read the passage. When students have finished, direct them to complete the skill and strategy practice activities. Review the answers together.

DAY 2

Tell students they are going to practice finding the author's purpose as they read about a legendary creature called the Mongolian Death Worm, which supposedly lives in the Gobi Desert. To build background, point out the Gobi Desert on a map. Then remind students of the *Make Connections* strategy (Week 2). Say: **Good readers make connections with a text so they can better understand it. Using information from other things you have seen, read, or done can also help you better understand the subjects you read about.** Then have students read the passage. When students have finished, direct them to complete the skill and strategy practice activities. For the strategy practice activity, you may want to help students brainstorm legendary creatures (e.g., Bigfoot, Loch Ness Monster, Chupacabra) before having them complete the activity in pairs.

DAY 3

Review the *Prediction* skill with students. Say: **When you make a prediction, you use clues from the text and your own experience to predict what will happen next.** Tell students they are going to read about the stages of tooth development. Then say: **Before you read, think of a question you want to find the answer to as you read.** Help students brainstorm questions, such as: *Why do baby teeth fall out? When do you get all your adult teeth?* Then have students write their question in the space provided for the strategy practice activity. Instruct them to look for the answer as they read. When students have finished reading, direct them to complete the skill practice activity. Review the answers together. Invite volunteers to share their question from the strategy practice activity and to discuss the answers, if applicable.

DAY 4

Explain to students that they will practice predicting as they read a story about a pet parrot that gets stuck in a tree. Say: **When making predictions about what might happen next in a story, it is a good idea to pay attention to the things the characters say and do. Their words and actions can give you clues.** Then remind students of the *Make Connections* strategy. Say: **As you read, use what you already know from your own experience to help you check your predictions. If a prediction does not match what you know about the topic, you may need to make a different prediction.** Then have students read the passage. When students have finished, direct them to complete the skill and strategy practice activities.

DAY 5

Tell students they will practice both identifying the author's purpose and making predictions as they read a letter of complaint about a mistake in a book. Then review the *Ask Questions* strategy. Say: **After you read, think of a question you would ask the book's author if you were writing to him about the mistake.** Then have students read the passage. When students have finished, direct them to complete the skill and strategy practice activities. Invite students to share the question they wrote for the strategy practice activity.

READ THE PASSAGE   Think about why the author wanted to write about this topic.

Cookie Wars

No one really knows exactly how, when, or where fortune cookies were invented. One thing is for sure, though. Fortune cookies are not from China. They were created in America. However, they may have been inspired by Chinese or Japanese treats. Some people think that fortune cookies come from mooncakes, small Chinese cakes with messages inside. Others believe that fortune cookies are similar to a traditional Japanese rice cracker that once had a fortune inside it.

Fortune cookies are so popular that two American cities, San Francisco and Los Angeles, fought over the right to be the "home" of the fortune cookie. In 1983, a fake trial was held to determine where the fortune cookie came from. One side argued for David Jung, founder of the Hong Kong Noodle Company in Los Angeles. He claimed to have invented the fortune cookie in 1918.

The other side argued the cookie was invented by Makoto Hagiwara, a man who ran the Japanese Tea Garden in San Francisco in the 1890s. The court sided with Hagiwara. This was no surprise, because the trial was held in San Francisco. People in Los Angeles later held their own trial and decided that *their* city was the home of the fortune cookie.

No matter where fortune cookies are from, it is hard to imagine finishing a meal of Chinese food without cracking open this sweet, crunchy treat and reading its message.

SKILL PRACTICE   Read the item. Write your response.

1. Why did the author write this text?

_____

_____

2. Why did the author explain what mooncakes are?

_____

3. What is the purpose of the first paragraph?

_____

_____

STRATEGY PRACTICE   Write a question that you thought of as you read the passage.

_____

READ THE PASSAGE   Think about the author's purpose for writing this passage.

The Mongolian Death Worm

The sun beat down on the travelers as their camels trudged across the Gobi (GO-bee) Desert's blazing hot sand. The people were tired and almost out of water. They just wanted to get to their campsite. But they would never make it.

So began many of the stories that Richard Freeman and his team had heard about the Mongolian Death Worm. In 2005, Freeman searched for this mysterious creature. It seemed like everyone he spoke to had a story about it. The Mongolian Death Worm was said to be a two- to five-foot-long (.6–1.5 m), red worm-like creature that lived underground. It could spit venom and shoot electricity. Some people claimed that they had seen the worm themselves. More often, however, they knew someone else who had seen it. All of the stories, though, gave the same description of the worm.

Freeman and his group spent a month in the Gobi Desert. The team set traps for the worm. They searched places where it had been seen. They offered a reward to anyone who could show them the worm. They even flew over vast regions of the desert. However, they found no proof of the Mongolian Death Worm.

In the end, Freeman and his team concluded that the tall tales of the Mongolian Death Worm are most likely about a type of legless reptile. But again, there is no proof. For now, the Mongolian Death Worm remains a legend.

SKILL PRACTICE   Read the item. Write your response.

1. Why did the author begin the text with the paragraph in italics?

_____

_____

_____

2. What is the purpose of the third paragraph?

_____

_____

3. What does the author think about the Mongolian Death Worm? How do you know?

_____

STRATEGY PRACTICE   Tell a partner about a legendary creature that you have heard tales about.

Daily Reading Comprehension • EMC 3614 • © Evan-Moor Corp.

READ THE PASSAGE   Look for clues that tell you what is likely to happen to each child's teeth.

Time for Teeth

Bonnie helps take care of her baby brother, Brady. He is only seven months old, but already, two little teeth poke through his bottom gums. He screams sometimes because his gums hurt. Bonnie gives Brady a cold washcloth to chew on, which soothes Brady's gums—and Bonnie's ears. Soon the two teeth will be all the way in, and they won't hurt Brady's gums anymore. But in a few months, more teeth will start coming in.

Bonnie has another brother, Berty, who is four. Like most kids his age, Berty has all 20 of his baby teeth. They will start to fall out when he is five or six, and his adult teeth will start coming in. Berty is already begging Bonnie to tell him how much money the tooth fairy will bring for each baby tooth.

Bonnie is nine and knows all about the tooth fairy, because she has lost eight of her own baby teeth and has already grown eight adult teeth in their place. By the time Bonnie is 12 or 13, she will have a total of 28 adult teeth. All her baby teeth will be gone. But there will still be four more molars waiting to come in, called *wisdom teeth*. Wisdom teeth start growing under the gums at age 10 but don't actually appear until around the age of 17 to 21. Most people have to get their wisdom teeth removed because there is no room left in their mouths. Bonnie is glad she has a big mouth.

SKILL PRACTICE   Read the item. Write your response.

1. What will happen to Brady's mouth in a few months?

_____

_____

2. What will happen to Berty's mouth in the next 18 months?

_____

_____

3. What will happen to the mouths of all three children when they are between the ages of 17 and 21?

_____

STRATEGY PRACTICE   Write a question about teeth that you want to find the answer to. If you found the answer in the passage, write it, too.

_____

_____

READ THE PASSAGE As you read, look for clues that tell you what will happen to Archie.

Come Down, Archie!

I couldn't see our parrot, Archie, but I could hear him. "Yankee Doodle went to town," he sang. It was his favorite song.

Archie was stuck in our maple tree in the backyard—again. This time, it was my brother Peter's fault. He was carrying a tent into the yard, and he had left the door open. Archie flew out. His wings were clipped, so he couldn't get far. But the wind carried him like a kite into the big maple tree. He hopped to a very high branch, and there he sat, singing away.

"That bird is annoying," Peter said as he ducked inside his tent.

Usually, whenever Archie escapes, Dad pulls his ladder from the garage. He climbs the ladder and coaxes Archie down with grapes, Archie's favorite food. But this time, Dad was gone. We were home alone, and we knew Dad wouldn't want us to climb the ladder ourselves. But we weren't sure what time he'd be back. Plus, we had to get Archie down before my sister Katya got home from her soccer tournament. She loved Archie and would cry and be miserable if he wasn't in his cage.

As the afternoon went on, Archie got hungry. "Time for dinner?" he asked in a sad voice, over and over. It was getting dark. I was just about to call the fire department when Dad pulled into the driveway.

SKILL PRACTICE   Read the item. Write your response.

1. What will happen next?

   _____

2. Once Archie gets down from the tree, what will he probably do first? Why?

   _____

3. Why was the narrator about to call the fire department? Would that have worked?

   _____

   _____

   _____

STRATEGY PRACTICE   Describe how you think you would feel if your pet got away.

_____

Daily Reading Comprehension • EMC 3614 • © Evan-Moor Corp.

READ THE LETTER   As you read, think about why the writer wrote the letter and look for clues about what will happen next.

Dear Mr. Steiner,

    I recently bought your book *212 Fun Activities for a Rainy Day*. I see on your web site where you respond to readers, and I want to share my story with you. We tried to follow your directions to make "Ice Cream in a Bag," but it was a disaster.

    You said to mix ½ cup (240 mL) of milk, 1 tablespoon (18 g) of rock salt, and ¼ teaspoon (1 mL) of vanilla in a plastic zip-up food storage bag. Then you said to put that bag inside a bigger zip-up bag with 6 tablespoons (72 g) of sugar and a bunch of ice cubes, and then to shake it. We did that. Can you guess what happened?

    After we tasted the mess, we figured out what was wrong. You mixed up the sugar and salt. The directions should have said to put 1 tablespoon (12 g) of sugar in with the milk and 6 tablespoons (108 g) of salt in with the ice cubes. My dad looked through the rest of the book and found other mistakes in your recipes.

    I see that you are coming out with a new book called *179 Tasty Recipes for Kids to Make and Share*. I hope you tested the recipes first. My dad and I certainly won't be testing them.

                        Respectfully,

                        Tommy Whitehouse

SKILL PRACTICE   Read the item. Write your response.

1. Why did Tommy write this letter?

_____

_____

2. Will Tommy buy Mr. Steiner's new book? Use text evidence in your response.

_____

_____

3. What will Mr. Steiner probably do when he receives Tommy's letter?

_____

STRATEGY PRACTICE   What question would you ask Mr. Steiner if you were writing to him?

_____

Nonfiction Text Features

Students practice identifying and comprehending common features of nonfiction text.

Visual Information

Students examine and evaluate information that is depicted visually.

DAY 1

Review the *Nonfiction Text Features* skill with students. Say: **Certain text features make reading nonfiction easier by helping you identify how the text is organized or where information can be found.** Tell students they are going to read about how to make a simple electric motor. Point out the subheads and then remind students of the *Determine Important Information* strategy (Week 5). Say: **Good readers set a purpose for reading. Setting a purpose helps you determine what information to look for as you read. Subheads can help you find the information.** Then have students read the passage. When students have finished, direct them to complete the skill and strategy practice activities. Review the answers together.

DAY 2

Tell students they will practice reading the text features of a chart as they learn about *portmanteau words,* or words made from the parts of two other words. Remind students of the *Organization* strategy (Week 4). Say: **Writers often organize their ideas in ways that help readers understand the topic. As you read, pay attention to how the author has organized the chart, using features such as columns and boldface words to help you understand the information.** Then have students read the paragraph and study the chart. When students have finished, direct them to complete the skill and strategy practice activities. Review the answers together.

DAY 3

Review the definition of *visual information* with students. Then say: **Sometimes presenting information in words is less effective than using visual aids, such as graphs, charts, diagrams, or maps. For example, a diagram is helpful for showing what something looks like and how its parts fit together. A diagram is often clearer than words alone.** Tell students they will study a diagram that shows one section of the International Space Station. Then remind students of the *Determine Important Information* strategy. Say: **Sometimes when you look at a diagram, you can be overwhelmed because there may not be a clear place to start reading. To give yourself a starting point, think about your purpose for reading and look for the information that is most important based on that purpose. For example, as you study this diagram, look for parts that help you understand what astronauts do inside the space station.** Then have students read the paragraph and study the diagram. When students have finished, direct them to complete the skill and strategy practice activities. Review the answers together.

DAY 4

Tell students they will practice using visual information as they read a flier about traveling through the Grand Canyon. Remind students of the *Organization* strategy. Say: **Writers often put words and visual aids together to help you understand more about a topic. As you read, think about how the text and map together make the information easier to understand.** Then have students read the paragraph and study the map. When students have finished, direct them to complete the skill and strategy practice activities.

DAY 5

Tell students they will practice reading text features and visual information as they study a flowchart about how laws are passed. Explain that a law starts out as a *bill*, or a proposed law written by someone in the House of Representatives or the Senate. Say: **This flowchart shows the different people and groups that must work on a bill before it becomes a law. Good readers look carefully at flowcharts and think about how each piece of information is connected to another.** Then have students read the paragraph and study the flowchart. When students have finished, direct them to complete the skill and strategy practice activities. Review the answers together.

READ THE INSTRUCTIONS   Read the instructions for making an electric motor.

Start Your Motor

You might think of an electric motor as a complicated machine that only an expert could build. But there's not much more to an electric motor than a spinning metal rod and the electricity that makes it spin. Here's how to create your own electric motor:

What You Need

- a flat-head metal screw
- 6 inches (15 cm) of copper wire
- a disc magnet
- a 1.5-volt C battery

What You Do

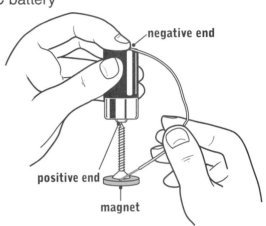

1. Set the flat head of the metal screw on top of the disc magnet.

2. Move the positive end of the battery close to the tip of the screw.

3. Hold one end of the copper wire to the negative end of the battery. Touch the other end of the wire to the disc magnet.

4. Watch what happens to the screw!

SKILL PRACTICE   Read the item. Write your response.

1. What is the purpose of the bulleted list?

_____

_____

2. How does the numbered list help the reader?

_____

_____

3. Would you like to try to make this motor? Explain.

_____

_____

STRATEGY PRACTICE   What information in the instructions would be important for you to take on your trip to the store? Why?

_____

_____

READ THE PASSAGE   Study the text features and information in the chart.

A Word "Smash" (<u>Sm</u>ack + M<u>ash</u>)

You know what the word *squiggle* means, but did you know that it came from two other words, *squirm* and *wiggle*? It's a *portmanteau* (port-MAN-toe), or a word that comes from two other words. Below are some other fun portmanteaus.

Common Portmanteaus	Technology Portmanteaus	Animal Portmanteaus
flounder (<u>floun</u>ce + blun<u>der</u>) People who flounder at a job cannot do that job very well.	**blog (We<u>b</u> + <u>log</u>)** A blog is a journal written on the Internet, or Web.	**beefalo (<u>beef</u> + buf<u>falo</u>)** Beefalo are animals that have a cow and a buffalo as parents.
smog (<u>smo</u>ke + f<u>og</u>) When big factories opened in cities, they produced pollution and gases that mixed with moisture in the air. People started calling this smog.	**infomercial (<u>info</u> + <u>commercial</u>)** Infomercials are very long television commercials that thoroughly explain or demonstrate a product.	**liger (<u>li</u>on + t<u>iger</u>)** A liger is a cat whose father is a lion and whose mother is a tiger.
motel (<u>mot</u>or + ho<u>tel</u>) Motels first became popular in the 1950s, when people began using their cars to travel on vacation or take business trips.	**e-mail (<u>e</u>lectronic + <u>mail</u>)** People use their computers to send over a billion e-mail messages every day.	**cama (<u>cam</u>el + l<u>lama</u>)** A cama is a Middle Eastern animal that has a camel and a llama for parents.

SKILL PRACTICE   Read the item. Write your response.

1. What is the purpose of the underlined letters in the chart?

_____

_____

2. Describe how the chart is organized.

_____

_____

3. Why are the sentences included in the chart?

_____

_____

STRATEGY PRACTICE   In which column would you place the word *spork*, which comes from *spoon* and *fork*? Tell a partner why.

READ THE INFORMATION Study the diagram to learn what one section of the International Space Station looks like.

Living in Space

The International Space Station is an important research station for countries around the world. Many countries worked together to build different sections of the station. One section, called the Service Module, was built by Russia and sent to space in 2000. It was the first part of the space station that was built for people to live in.

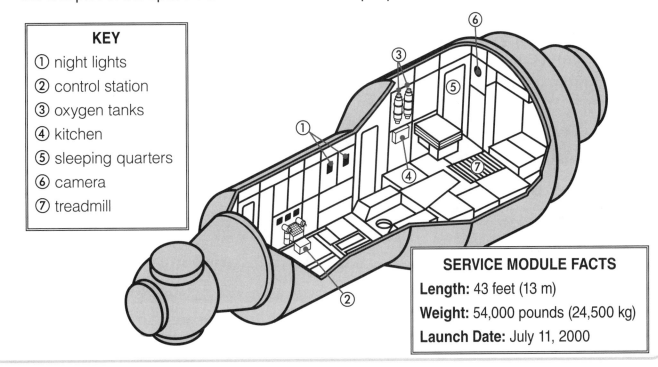

KEY
① night lights
② control station
③ oxygen tanks
④ kitchen
⑤ sleeping quarters
⑥ camera
⑦ treadmill

SERVICE MODULE FACTS
Length: 43 feet (13 m)
Weight: 54,000 pounds (24,500 kg)
Launch Date: July 11, 2000

SKILL PRACTICE Read the item. Write your response.

1. Which number in the diagram shows where the kitchen is located? How do you know?

_____

_____

2. Does the crew sleep closer to the camera or the control station? How can you tell?

_____

_____

3. How does the paragraph support the diagram?

_____

STRATEGY PRACTICE Discuss with a partner why someone other than an astronaut might want to look at this diagram of the Service Module.

READ THE FLIER Read the information and study the map.

Bryan's Rides
We Rent Mules, Horses, and Goats

Did you know that more than 2,000 visitors to the Grand Canyon twisted their ankles last year while hiking? Did you know that another 1,700 stubbed their toes? And over 3,000 people got blisters on their feet! Why risk it? See the Grand Canyon comfortably on the back of a mule, horse, or goat!

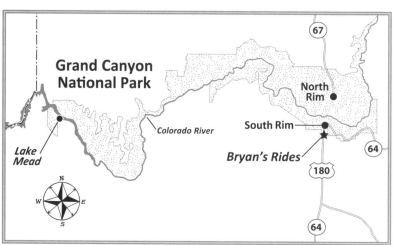

We are located near the park's South Rim, on U.S. Highway 180.

SKILL PRACTICE Read the item. Write your response.

1. What is the name of the park and the name of the river that flows through it?

   _____

   _____

2. What is the map's purpose? How do you know?

   _____

   _____

3. Why is part of the map shaded?

   _____

   _____

STRATEGY PRACTICE Would the text be easier or more difficult to understand if you looked at the map before you read the text? Explain your answer.

   _____

   _____

READ THE INFORMATION   Read the text and study the flowchart to learn how laws are created.

How a Bill Becomes Law

Have you ever wondered what members of Congress do all day? One of their main jobs is to pass laws that help people. The laws come from bills that are written by the senators and representatives we have elected to Congress. Each bill must then go through a long process before it is signed into law by the president.

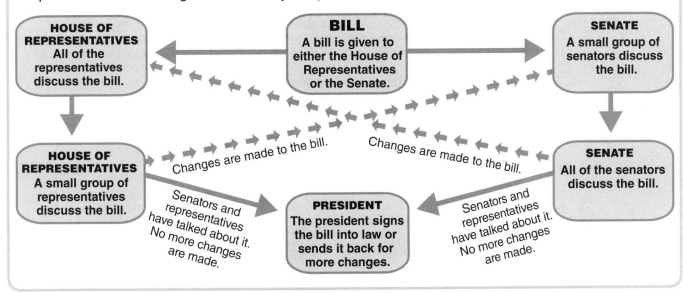

SKILL PRACTICE   Read the item. Write your response.

1. According to the flowchart, what happens to a bill immediately after it is changed by the Senate?

_____

_____

2. When would a bill be rewritten?

_____

_____

3. Based on the flowchart, what is the president's role in determining legislation?

_____

_____

STRATEGY PRACTICE   How would the flowchart help someone who was interested in following the progress of a particular bill?

_____

Answer Key

WEEK 1

DAY 1

Strategy practice sample answer: I didn't understand all the facts in the second section. I reread it slowly, and it made more sense.

1. The article is mostly facts about the Arctic Ocean.

2. They help to guide the reader to the section with the information s/he is seeking.

3. (Accept any two.) The Arctic Ocean does not touch South America, Australia, Africa, or Antarctica.

DAY 2

Strategy practice sample question: How is the seed vault going to survive a worldwide disaster?

1. The Svalbard Global Seed Vault is important because it holds the seeds from many of the world's crops. If a disaster occurs, people will need these seeds to start new crops so they have food.

2. He plans ahead, as shown by his collection of seeds. He is a worrier, because he thinks a disaster will occur.

3. The word *deposit* means to put something in a certain place. I can tell because Dr. Fowler is asking nations to deposit the seeds in the Seed Vault.

DAY 3

Strategy practice sample answer: It helped me focus on the topic of Children's Day.

1. The Japanese believe that this fish is a symbol of strength and good health.

2. As of 1948, Children's Day celebrated both girls and boys. Prior to that year, it only celebrated boys.

3. Allow any response that reflects an activity mentioned in the text and is supported by a reason.

DAY 4

Strategy practice sample answer: The title made me visualize what a dragon looks like and think of stories about dragons.

1. It tells the reader that the way stories describe dragons is not true.

2. "Komodo dragons don't have wings, or smoke coming out of their nostrils, but they have strong tails and a very nasty bite."

3. The main idea of the last paragraph is that Komodo dragons don't usually attack humans.

DAY 5

Strategy practice: Students should describe a comprehension strategy that helps them maintain focus on the main idea of each paragraph.

1. The heading is above a paragraph that tells about Santa Anna's life until age 22.

2. (Accept any two reasons.) Santa Anna was not a good president, because he switched between showing little interest in running a country and being a dictator. He favored the rich, and his bad decisions made the nation poorer.

3. Santa Anna was a Mexican leader who joined the Spanish army at a young age. Later, when Mexico became independent, he served as its president.

WEEK 2

DAY 1

Strategy practice sample answer: One time last winter I wanted to visit my uncle, but it was snowing so hard the roads were closed.

1. The story takes place on a rainy afternoon in Lauren and Henry's home.

2. Lauren pounds her fist into her glove because she is bored and restless.

3. Henry doesn't care about baseball as much as Lauren. I know because he doesn't seem to mind that the game's been rained out and even says, "I hope it rains all day. I'm having a great time."

DAY 2

Strategy practice sample answer: Galileo probably felt mad, like when my brother blamed me for breaking a vase even though it was his fault.

1. The theme is that in the past it was sometimes dangerous to be a scientist who suggested new ideas.

2. The leaders demanded that Galileo support the idea that Earth was the center of the universe.

3. Allow any conclusion that includes text support. Ex. Galileo didn't want to die, so he stopped saying that the Earth wasn't the center of the universe. "He spent the rest of his life in prison."

DAY 3

Strategy practice sample answer: I like to visit the library because there are lots of books to read and games to play.

1. Answers will vary. Ex. A good spot for a community garden would be an empty lot in the city or a park that is no longer used.

2. They meant that the lot wasn't taken care of and was an eyesore.

3. The theme is that something that may seem ugly and appear useless can be made into something useful with some work.

DAY 4

Strategy practice sample answer: I would have told Kate that she doesn't have to exaggerate so much.

1. Accept any three adjectives as long as they are supported by a reason. Ex. conceited, stuck-up, boastful, proud

2. Kate's face turned bright red because she knew that Sarah realized that Kate had made everything up.

3. I think Kate learned that it would be best to tell true stories instead of making stuff up.

DAY 5

Strategy practice sample answer: I would like to study thunderstorms, because I like lightning.

1. The hurricane plane was a way to gather a lot of information from inside a dangerous hurricane without risking anyone's life.

2. Hurricanes form over warm water in the ocean.

3. The more scientists know about hurricanes, the better they can predict them and help save people's lives.

WEEK 3

DAY 1

Strategy practice: Students should underline words or phrases such as *tons of garbage swirl slowly, bottles, bags, nets,* etc.

1. Answers will vary; students must mention lightweight plastic items that would float (plastic bottles, milk jugs, grocery bags, Frisbees, etc.).

2. The sea animals have no reason to expect trash in the water. They think that the moving plastic trash items are other animals to be eaten.

3. Recycling plastic items would reduce the amount of plastic getting into the waterways that eventually empty into the ocean.

DAY 2

Strategy practice: Answers should include words such as *spraying, hot, smelly, popping,* etc.

1. Both skunks and bombardier beetles spray smelly oil at their enemies.

2. When the beetle sprays, it makes a loud pop and a gas that looks like smoke. This reminded people of a bomb, so they named it a bombardier beetle.

3. The beetle's muscles send out a hot, smelly spray aimed right at the predator. At the same time, the bug makes a loud pop and a gas that looks like smoke. The predator probably runs or flies away!

DAY 3

Strategy practice: Answers should include words such as *boomerang, huge, columns, domed tower*, etc.

1. Both are capital cities that have important buildings, government headquarters, and monuments.

2. Both buildings have many columns and windows, but the U.S. Library of Congress has a domed center and is a much older building.

3. People like to visit capital cities and know more about their nation's history. The monuments help them to learn about that.

DAY 4

Strategy practice: Answers should include words such as *copper, difficult to read, lists,* etc.

1. Answers will vary. Ex. The researchers are in a lab at a university. They may be wearing lab coats and are probably wearing gloves. They are laying the pieces out on a long table.

2. The map is in bad shape and the writing is difficult to read.

3. Most treasure maps are made up and are written on paper. This is a genuine treasure map written on metal; it is also thousands of years old.

DAY 5

Strategy practice sample answer: I visualized Tammy as bratty with a pout on her face.

1. (Accept any three.) The school doesn't allow cell phones, she can use the house phone or e-mail to contact her friends, cell phones are expensive, and they want her to wait until she can help pay for one.

2. Both are electronic forms of communication. A text message is sent to a phone number. An email message is sent to an email address.

3. Answers will vary, but students should say that she looks frustrated, discouraged, annoyed, etc.

WEEK 4

DAY 1

Strategy practice: Answers should include words such as *before, next, during,* etc.

1. The first step is to determine where the party will be held.

2. Before the party, you have to get volunteers to spread the word/send invitations, help set up, make the food, get supplies, and plan the activities.

3. Answers will vary; accept reasonable responses.

DAY 2

Strategy practice sample answer: Facts: Root vegetables include beets, carrots, and sweet potatoes. They contain important vitamins and minerals. Opinions: They're delicious! Discovering new foods can be fun.

1. The author really likes root vegetables. I know because the author writes that they taste great, are full of flavor, and will make the reader forget about french fries.

2. (Accept any three.) Eating healthy means you'll be less likely to get sick. You'll also have more energy and will be able to think more clearly and for longer periods of time.

3. Allow either stance as long as it is supported by a reason.

DAY 3

Strategy practice: Students should identify phrases such as *as a result* or *this is because.*

1. After it rains, storm water carries gas, oil, and trash into waterways.

2. The roads and sidewalks cover too much of the ground and keep it from soaking up water. As a result, storm water collects on the pavement and flows through gutters.

3. If no one littered, there wouldn't be trash in the streets to be carried away with the storm water. Then trash wouldn't end up in lakes, rivers, and the ocean.

DAY 4

Strategy practice: 1884: he was born, 1923: he found dinosaur eggs, 1927: he was made an honorary Boy Scout.

1. Andrews went to Asia to search for human fossils.

2. In 1923, he found the first dinosaur egg, which let us know that dinosaurs laid eggs.

3. Andrews sent his discoveries to the American Museum of Natural History in New York. The people there could do more research on the fossils and also display them in the museum.

DAY 5

Strategy practice sample answer: Troy identified the problem and then stated how to fix it. I think his solution will work, because it is easy for people to give 5 dollars.

1. Troy states that the town needs $50,000 for the new library and that each year, more than 10,000 people attend the Pecan Festival.

2. (Accept any one of these.) "This is silly." "People will gladly donate." "This is the only way to raise money for our new library."

3. He thinks that some people will be against his idea because people will refuse to go to the Pecan Festival if it is no longer free.

WEEK 5

DAY 1

Strategy practice sample answer: The *Fast Flyer* is the fastest racer, and it is on sale for a limited time. This is important to know if you are looking for a new racer.

1. The ad's purpose is to get the reader to buy a Fast Flyer.

2. The information inside the starbursts tells about add-ons that can be purchased now or in the future to change the Fast Flyer.

3. The ad shows that the regular price is $799, and the sale price is $499. That means a person can save $300 by buying it during the sale.

DAY 2

Strategy practice sample answer: If I wanted to get one of the prizes for my friend, I would use the chart to know how many candles or boxes of cookies I would need to sell.

1. The Scouts are selling candles and boxes of cookies. I know because those are the items mentioned in the "If You Sell" column in the chart on the left.

2. The chart on the left tells how many candles or boxes of cookies must be sold to qualify for prizes, and the chart on the right tells what prizes are available.

3. A Scout must sell 20 candles to qualify for a prize from Column B.

DAY 3

Strategy practice sample answer: I would use this book in art class because it teaches how to draw comics.

1. Answers will vary; student should acknowledge that this is a book for people who want to draw cartoon/comic books.

2. The text is about coming up with a story, so it would probably appear in Lesson 6: Storyboards and Scripts. That lesson is about creating the storyline.

3. I would turn to page 31 because that's the start of the lesson on drawing people and animals.

DAY 4

Strategy practice sample answer: The picture of the cabin shows what the cabin is made from.

1. The caption lets readers know that they can see the miner's cabin for themselves if they visit the park.

2. In 1892, a fire destroyed a lot of the town. It was the beginning of the end for Bodie.

3. The timeline shows that 20 years passed (1942 to 1962).

DAY 5

Strategy practice sample answer: This recipe is rated 4 stars because people like it. This helps other people decide if it is a good recipe.

1. There are three main parts to make it easy to find information. The top tells you the rating, how long it takes to make, and how many it will feed. The ingredients tell what's needed, and the directions tell how to put the ingredients together.

2. The ingredients list tells you what you need to make the party mix.

3. No, I don't have enough time, because the snack mix has to cook for an hour. The recipe tells me that in two places—at the top and in step 5 of the directions.

WEEK 6

DAY 1

Strategy practice sample questions: Is this story about a dolphin? Is it safe to swim near dolphins?

1. The author wrote this text to inform the reader about how swimming with dolphins helped her sister, who has special needs.

2. Accept any of these sentences: "When my sister Gina was born, she had a problem with her heart. She had five operations before she was three years old. She had trouble walking, playing with other children, and going to school."

3. Yes, Gina enjoyed the trip. I know because the text says that she laughed and clapped when she saw the dolphin, and they swam together all day. Gina was also able to move her body more than she normally did at home.

DAY 2

Strategy practice sample question: How much do solar panels cost?

1. The author wrote this text to inform the reader about solar energy.

2. The summer is the best season because that's when the sun shines the most.

3. The solar panels create power from the sun's rays. In the same

way, the power company creates power from an energy source (coal, natural gas, wind, nuclear).

DAY 3

Strategy practice sample question: Did Mr. Kim get his money back?

1. Answers will vary. Ex. No, this didn't happen, because the neighbors wouldn't make an agreement to switch houses.

2. The author's purpose was to entertain the reader with a funny story.

3. Answers will vary. Ex. Mr. Kim learned that people could surprise him with kindness.

DAY 4

Strategy practice sample answer: It sounds more like football, because the players can pick up the ball with their hands.

1. The author wrote this text to inform the reader about the sport of rugby.

2. Rugby is like soccer because it is played on the same size field, and the ball is kicked between goalposts to earn points.

3. Rugby is like football because its ball is similar in shape, and players kick, carry, or throw the ball down the field. A rugby goal is like a football touchdown, and a rugby drop goal is like a football field goal.

DAY 5

Strategy practice sample question: Can other types of dogs pull sleds, too?

1. Answers will vary. Ex. The family wanted a good family dog; Bo retired from sled racing and needed a new family.

2. Yes, the writer is frustrated because Bo runs so fast that he nearly drags the writer down the sidewalk. The writer states, "it feels like Bo is likely to pull my arms off."

3. Answers will vary. Ex. No, it will take longer than that to train Bo to walk nicely on a leash.

WEEK 7

DAY 1

1. Scientists think that Europa may have water on it. That means it might be able to support life.

2. The text says that 1,300 Earths could fit inside Jupiter.

3. Exploring Europa will be difficult and unlikely to happen soon.

Strategy practice sample answer: The second paragraph, because I have seen ice and played in the ocean.

DAY 2

1. A dog's claws are outside its skin and are made of keratin. The hairy

frog's claws are the toe bones of its feet, which the frog can break so they stick through the skin to use for defense.

2. The ribbed newt can make its ribs poke through its skin. If a predator gets cut by a rib, it will be poisoned.

3. The main idea is that the ribbed newt is another amphibian that uses its bones for defense.

Strategy practice: Students should base their drawings on details from the passage.

DAY 3

1. The father keeps the egg warm for two months. The text says this takes at least 60 days and "During that time, the father doesn't eat, and he must stay very still so he doesn't hurt the egg."

2. The father penguin goes a very long time without any food.

3. As soon as the mother penguin returns, she feeds the chick, and the father goes off to hunt for food.

Strategy practice sample answer: The mother lays an egg. Then the father takes care of it. During that time, he doesn't eat. By the time the chick hatches, the mother has returned, and the father needs to eat because he has fasted for 115 days.

DAY 4

1. A hurricane forms over warm ocean water, usually near the equator. The storm starts spinning north.

2. Hurricane season is six months long. I know because the text says it is June through the end of November.

3. Answers will vary.

Strategy practice sample answer: Step 2 was the easiest to picture because it is similar to steam rising from my school's pool in the winter.

DAY 5

1. The author uses dialogue to discuss how Aunt Hilda has behaved in the past, to announce her arrival, and to show that she says funny things.

2. Hilda gets ready for dinner by putting on her pajamas and going into the guest bedroom.

3. (Accept any two.) June says that Aunt Hilda has washed clothes in the dishwasher and dishes in the washing machine; she says "good morning" when it is afternoon; she gives a woman a tie and a man fancy perfume; she gets ready for dinner by putting on pajamas.

Strategy practice sample answer: She gave everybody the wrong presents.

DAY 1

1. Having cold food or drink touch the roof of your mouth will cause you to get brain freeze.

2. You can push your tongue up against the roof of your mouth to try to warm it quickly.

3. Eating and drinking cold things slowly keeps your mouth from getting too cold too fast and may prevent brain freeze.

Strategy practice sample answer: Eat or drink cold things slowly.

DAY 2

1. Megan was looking forward to riding the Dragon coaster. I know because she said she was sure she was finally tall enough to ride it. It also says she wanted to hurry to the coaster.

2. They stopped at the food court because her dad was thirsty.

3. She smiled and ran up to it because she thought she would be tall enough.

Strategy practice: Students should underline "You must be at least this tall to ride the coaster" and "She stood on the tips of her toes and thought tall thoughts" and "Her father, however, was not smiling."

DAY 3

1. The two opinions in the second paragraph are: "Lake Tahoe is the best spot for camping, skiing, sailing, fishing, and hiking" and "These resorts are much more fun to stay at than the ones in other parts of the country."

2. Accept any three facts. Ex. Lake Tahoe is in the Sierra Nevada, it is along the border of California and Nevada, and thousands of people visit each year.

3. The author states that the best Washoe legend is about a giant bird-like monster that lived in the middle of Lake Tahoe and ate people.

Strategy practice: Underlined sentences will vary, but they should be factual statements about Lake Tahoe, not opinions.

DAY 4

1. *Dog Academy* airs on Thursday nights, and its human stars are Jim and Kalen.

2. Answers will vary. Students must include a reason.

3. The reviewer does not like *Dog Academy* and states, "there are much better shows."

Strategy practice sample question: What other dogs are on the show? Answer: Honkers

DAY 5

1. (Accept any three.) People dislike skunks because they get into trash cans. They may spray people or pets, and the spray smells terrible. Skunks can carry diseases.

2. Skunks are good for a neighborhood because they eat spiders, scorpions, and dead animals.

3. No, the author prefers skunks to spiders and states, "Having a skunk around is much better than being bothered by those creepy creatures."

Strategy practice sample answer: Skunks eat other pests, such as spiders.

DAY 1

1. Chocolate, vanilla, Christmas, and rice puddings are sweet.

2. These three puddings can be served as side dishes: blood pudding, Yorkshire pudding, and noodle kugel.

3. Answers will vary; students must include a reason.

Strategy practice: Responses will vary.

DAY 2

1. With just a quick glimpse, the size of the animal is the best way to tell the difference; the rat will be much larger.

2. The Norway rat's ears are small and its feet are big compared to its body, while the house mouse's ears are big and its feet are small compared to its body.

3. These animals share so many traits because they had a common relative millions of years ago.

Strategy practice sample response: It helped me remember the differences between rats and mice.

DAY 3

1. She will see Carolina getting taken aboard a yellow helicopter.

2. Marcia cares about her sister. She acts quickly to save her sister when she ends up in danger due to a picture Marcia drew.

3. Answers will vary. Ex. Marcia would have seen Carolina riding a horse or a bull.

Strategy practice sample answer: I would have been really surprised to see my drawings come to life. But then I would be proud that I saved my sister's life.

DAY 4

1. He wrinkled his nose because the corn dogs were burned black and probably smelled bad.

2. No, because there's too much salad dressing on the salad.

3. The chicken is going to burn. It should have been defrosted before he put it into the oven.

Strategy practice: Underlined information will vary.

DAY 5

1. Snow skiing and water-skiing are alike because people use long, flat boards to glide across a surface.

2. (Accept any two.) Snow skiing has been around for thousands of years and requires snow. Water-skiing has been around about 100 years and requires water. Snow skiers use two skis; water-skiers use one or two skis that are wider than snow skis. Water-skiers must be pulled by a boat.

3. Water-skiing requires a motorboat to pull the water-skier. There were no motorboats before 1920.

Strategy practice sample answer: Both types of skiers compete in slalom races.

DAY 1

1. (Accept any two.) He could not attend schools with white children; the school he went to did not teach science; most colleges refused to admit him.

2. (Accept any two.) Dr. Julian was determined, hard-working, and intelligent. He didn't give up even when most colleges rejected him. Because he wanted to help others, he created medicines and started a school for chemists.

3. Dr. Julian spent most of his time working in a chemistry lab.

Strategy practice sample response: It helps to understand what Dr. Julian went through to achieve his goals.

DAY 2

1. The story takes place on a hot day in a state park forest.

2. Answers will vary. Ex. Bill cares about Wendy. "'Sorry,' he said, returning and sitting beside his sister. 'I forgot your legs are shorter than mine.'"

3. She becomes more cheerful by the end because she gets a rest, and Bill shares dried strawberries and peanuts with her.

Strategy practice: Underlined details will vary.

DAY 3

1. The cat warned the puppy not to pester the skunk.

2. Answers will vary. Ex. Sometimes it is wise to take the advice of others.

3. Cinder was curious without being cautious. She was convinced that she

knew best.

Strategy practice sample answer: Underline: "I would leave that skunk alone if I were you. You're just asking for trouble." Because the author wanted to show that Rupert sincerely wanted to help Cinder, even though Cinder ignores him.

DAY 4

1. This is a fable because it is fiction that has a moral.

2. By helping others, you may help yourself as well.

3. Hard work will create better results than complaints.

Strategy practice: Responses will vary but should include details from the passage.

DAY 5

1. Greg feels bad because he feels like his family members are amazing, and he is ordinary.

2. The story takes place in the living room of the Rowlands' home.

3. His family wants Greg to know that he is just as special as they are. He helps them to do their amazing tricks. Sometimes greatness is not obvious.

Strategy practice sample answer: The story is in chronological order. It shows how each member of Greg's family appreciates him.

WEEK 11

DAY 1

1. The author wants to inform the reader about how to build a bottle rocket.

2. The numbered list helps the reader to follow the instructions in step-by-step order. The reader knows s/he has to do step 3 before step 4.

3. The reader would find these instructions inside the packaging of the Acme Rocket Launcher.

Strategy practice sample question: How high does the rocket fly?

DAY 2

1. A fourth-grade student wrote this text to persuade the person in charge of the cafeteria to change the lunch menu. I know because the writer uses the word "we."

2. (Accept any three.) We wouldn't need a new menu printed out each week, saving paper. Most of us would rather eat our favorite foods again and again than have many kinds of foods that taste bad. If the meals are fun and delicious, we won't mind. Let's make the food better and the menu predictable.

3. As long as it tastes good, having the same food each day is not boring and would be helpful.

Strategy practice sample answer: No, I disagree, because it would be boring to eat the same type of food each week.

DAY 3

1. He will probably make a tin-can telephone.

2. Answers will vary.

3. She will run away because she didn't like the fact that he wrapped her in aluminum foil.

Strategy practice sample question: What do you think Jason did with the aluminum foil after he finished with it?

DAY 4

1. They would chase the person mowing the lawn. I know because it says that they dislike the sound of motors and are likely to attack.

2. Cold weather would be bad for the bees. That is why they haven't moved north from the hot states. "The bees do not seem to be moving farther north. Some scientists believe this is because the bees only do well in warm climates."

3. You should move indoors as fast as you can.

Strategy practice sample answer: Some bees die after they sting somebody. And some people are allergic to bees.

DAY 5

1. The author wanted to entertain the reader—to tell an interesting story.

2. The other animals' suggestions were based on things they liked to do themselves. They didn't have anything to do with Turtle.

3. Frog told Turtle that she would see a movie with him. I think so because Turtle smiled at Frog's reply.

Strategy practice sample answer: Why does Turtle want to go on vacation? Because he works very hard.

WEEK 12

DAY 1

1. Beans are high in protein, just like meat. I know because the third bullet says "other foods high in protein."

2. The orange is better. I know because the third bullet says to limit fruit juices.

3. The chart says that people who can't have milk should choose to eat and drink things that have added calcium in them.

Strategy practice sample answer: The part that says how much to eat each

day, because that helps you figure out how much you need to buy.

DAY 2

1. Alaska and the Arctic Ocean both have maps. I know because it says "map" indented under those topic headings.

2. I would expect to read about Brazil's natural resources on page 93.

3. The purpose of an index is to list the key words covered by a nonfiction book and tell what pages the terms appear on.

Strategy practice: An index is alphabetical. The table of contents lists things in the order that they appear in the book.

DAY 3

1. The spaghetti and grilled cheese sandwich meals have side dishes.

2. The menu design helps a child to answer questions and follow the arrows in order to pick a meal.

3. Answers will vary; responses must include a reason.

Strategy practice sample question: Do you want a salad? Because the spaghetti comes with a salad.

DAY 4

1. The temperate climate zone has cool winters and warm summers. Accept any one: Parts of the Northeast, the Northwest, and the Midwest have this kind of climate.

2. No, Texas is in three zones. I can tell because of the shading on the map.

3. The Southeast has mild winters, hot summers, and lots of rain.

Strategy practice sample answer: It makes it easier to see where the different climate zones are.

DAY 5

1. Duke wants pet owners to hire him to watch their pets when they go away.

2. You can call the phone number on the flier.

3. The flier states that he doesn't like venomous snakes or geese and that he is not allowed to watch lions, tigers, or bears.

Strategy practice sample questions: What kind of animals do you have? Why do you think geese are mean?

WEEK 13

DAY 1

1. Fungi are interesting living things that will eat almost anything.

2. Fungi get nutrients from whatever they are growing on, often in a damp, warm place. "Fungi take what they need from

whatever they are growing on."

3. There is no one shape or color of fungi. Mushrooms can be small yellow buttons, shiny globs, or red with tiny fibers.

Strategy practice sample answer: Fungi can be many different colors. Fungi can grow in different places. We can eat some types of fungi.

DAY 2

1. Answers will vary; students must include a reason.

2. The second paragraph tells how Milo Mottola got children to draw the images that he made into the carousel animals.

3. Each original drawing hangs in a frame over its animal figure on the carousel, and the kids' signatures are carved into the wooden floor.

Strategy practice: Drawings will vary.

DAY 3

1. A sketch of the balloon is drawn.

2. Each section is formed of strong fabric, and the sections are sealed together to create the character's shape.

3. The balloons are inflated the night before because it takes six hours to fill them.

Strategy practice sample questions: What happens if the balloons float away? Do the balloons ever leak and crash?

DAY 4

1. She twirls the bowling ball twice and slips her fingers into the holes.

2. Carly takes a deep breath just before she approaches the lane to throw the ball.

3. She is pumping her fist and watching the ball.

Strategy practice: Underlined information will vary.

DAY 5

1. No, you need both types of paint. The watercolors are for the background. The tempera paint is thicker and is used to make the flowers.

2. It would be better to use fresh vegetables, because cooked vegetables are soft and might fall apart when you try to press them onto the paper.

3. Answers will vary. Ex. It will look like a vase filled with colorful flowers.

Strategy practice sample answer: The steps are in order, but the supplies are not.

WEEK 14

DAY 1

1. They attend ASSOA because they live too far away from a regular school.

2. The virtual school assemblies help the students to feel like they belong to a class.

3. The tutors are necessary to help the students understand and do their work correctly.

Strategy practice: Underlined information will vary.

DAY 2

1. In Thailand, library books are carried in metal cases by elephants.

2. Books travel by boat in Indonesia because it is a nation made up of 17,000 islands.

3. Camels carry a load of books to a village in Kenya. The librarian sets up a tent and displays the books.

Strategy practice sample question: Do the people still need to have library cards to borrow books?

DAY 3

1. The author is very enthusiastic about the Phillie Phanatic, writing, "No mascot is as 'phun' as the Phanatic!"

2. (Accept any three.) The Phillie Phanatic may dance with the fans, steal their popcorn, sit in their laps, get fans to cheer for the Phillies, and shoot hot dogs into the crowd.

3. The facts are: "Unlike the Phillies, a lot of teams have a mascot that goes with their team name. For example, the Orioles, Blue Jays, and Cardinals all have bird mascots that look like the real birds."

Strategy practice: Underlined information will vary.

DAY 4

1. No, there are only facts given in the second paragraph. All of the statements can be proven true.

2. It is an opinion. Other people may disagree with the statement. No one can prove that Dad's boots are the best.

3. Dad wears chaps to protect his legs from the thorns of cactuses and prickly bushes.

Strategy practice sample question: Do the bad guys always wear black hats?

DAY 5

1. A hagfish oozes slime when it senses danger. It makes it hard for a predator to grasp the fish.

2. "A hagfish's eating habits are odd" is an opinion, because what one person considers "odd" another person might not. "Odd" is not

a quality that can be proven.

3. The hagfish ties its body into a knot to get the slime off its body so that it does not clog its gills.

Strategy practice sample response: "The fish can ooze a bucketful of slime in just seconds!"

WEEK 15

DAY 1

1. A porcupine is larger, has a lot more quills, can release its quills, and eats wood and tree bark. A hedgehog cannot release its quills, can roll itself into a ball, and eats bugs and slugs.

2. Both animals use sharp quills for defense. A predator must get past the quills to eat the animal, so most give up.

3. Answers will vary. Ex. chubby, slow, spiky, prickly

Strategy practice sample answer: My sister has a pet snake called a boa constrictor, and it does not like to cuddle.

DAY 2

1. (Accept any four.) Both countries follow the same rules and have the same number of players. Both games start with the nation's anthem and the players' names. The season is always April to October. Fans enjoy eating in the stadium while watching the game.

2. (Accept any three.) Americans play 18 more games in a season and have 18 more major league teams. Fans are separated into cheering sections in Japan, and there is a special song for each team and a specific cheer for each player. Japanese fans sit quietly when their team is not up to bat.

3. Answers will vary but must be supported by a reason.

Strategy practice sample response: The biggest difference is the way fans act at the game.

DAY 3

1. People want to see it because it is the largest meteorite to ever hit the United States.

2. Studying meteors can be difficult because the majority of them burn up in Earth's atmosphere and never reach the ground.

3. In order to write this text, the author did research. This means that he or she probably read books, web sites, or articles about meteors and meteorites, watched videos, and maybe talked to an expert.

Strategy practice: Answers will vary.

DAY 4

1. Cassie wanted to eat one of the brownies when no one else was looking.

2. A raven probably took the bag of peanuts. I think so because Dad brushed a black feather off the picnic table. Also, the text started out stating that the ravens were watching them.

3. Dad is concerned about animals taking their food. He reminds the girls to keep the food containers shut tight and says, "We don't want raccoons stealing our food."

Strategy practice: Students should underline "She quickly brushed the crumbs off her shirt." Students should circle "as he brushed a black feather off the picnic table."

DAY 5

1. Both kinds of chocolate are made from cacao beans, and the process used to change the beans into chocolate is the same. Both types are popular.

2. Dark chocolate has more cocoa butter in it, is much darker, and is less sweet than milk chocolate.

3. Yes. "Today, over 3 million tons (2.7 metric tons) of cacao beans are used every year all over the world!"

Strategy practice sample answer: I know dark chocolate tastes bitter, because it is my favorite.

WEEK 16

DAY 1

1. The performers did tricks to entertain the visitors. The merchants sold food and crafts.

2. Denmark's king turned Bakken into a private park. He kept animals there like a zoo. Another king reopened it to the public almost 100 years later.

3. Today, Bakken has typical amusement park rides, performers, and merchants. It looks like a modern amusement park.

Strategy practice sample response: It is organized in chronological order because it tells the history of Bakken from the 1500s to the 20th century.

DAY 2

1. The characters are Ben and Oscar. The two boys' goal is to earn money by pet-sitting.

2. The story takes place over the course of about a week. I know because it talks about "a few days later" and "the next day."

3. Answers will vary. Ex. Ben is impulsive, excitable, reckless, etc. I chose these words because he didn't search the tank, he just saw the

skin and jumped to a conclusion.

Strategy practice: Underlined information will vary but should include interesting or vivid details.

DAY 3

1. He is bored and wants to cause some excitement on the ship.

2. He enjoyed the crew's reaction the first time, so he cries out that he sees pirates again.

3. The theme is that if you are a liar, no one will believe you even when you tell the truth.

Strategy practice: Underlined words will vary but should indicate sequence, e.g., "once again," "the third time," etc.

DAY 4

1. A wise judge can find a clever solution to almost any problem.

2. Ned eats near the window so he can smell the delicious foods that Chef Mario is cooking below.

3. Chef Mario learns that being unreasonable made him look silly, and it would be better for his business to encourage students to eat at his restaurant.

Strategy practice: Sentences will vary but should include vivid details from the passage.

DAY 5

1. Answers will vary. Ex. Charlie is careful, thoughtful, responsible, and experienced. I chose these words because he checks the stagecoach and harnesses and also because he thinks about what to do when he hears about the coming storm.

2. This story takes place long ago, before there were cars or asphalt roads.

3. The story's theme is that it is important to take one's responsibilities seriously.

Strategy practice sample answer: Charlie can't decide which way to go. I think he will go around the storm because it will keep his passengers happy, even though it might be a harder route for him.

WEEK 17

DAY 1

1. The author wanted to inform the reader about an actual event.

2. The description of Zarafa's trip makes the text interesting and shows how challenging it was to move a wild animal a long distance in 1824.

3. The last paragraph tells how the people of Paris reacted to Zarafa. It lets the readers know how much the citizens enjoyed her.

Strategy practice sample question: Is a giraffe a good gift for a country?

DAY 2

1. The author wrote the story to entertain readers with a tale about a giant.

2. This is a tall tale. I know because it is filled with exaggerations.

3. The last paragraph tells how Stormalong's ship, the *Gigantic*, created the Panama Canal.

Strategy practice sample response: I knew the author was exaggerating, because it's impossible to build a hammock that stretches from New Jersey to New York.

DAY 3

1. The crabs will hide so that the sea gulls don't eat them.

2. If the mussels sense the sea star, they will close. Then the sea star will poke the mussels to try to get them to open up so it can eat them.

3. The mussels are opening up, hoping that food will float between the two parts of their shells.

Strategy practice sample question: What are the predators in a tide pool?

DAY 4

1. Kwan and Klue realize that Garcia is the doube agent.

2. Klue will try to stop Admiral Garcia and save Dr. Kwan.

3. She will use the spider to make a laser cut through the door of the secret base. I think so because she says she no longer needs the lion ring to get inside the secret base.

Strategy practice sample answer: This story reminds me of the movie *Spy Kids* because it has a double agent.

DAY 5

1. The author wrote this text to inform readers about how the hypothalamus works.

2. Sweat's purpose is to cool your body when its temperature is rising.

3. Your hypothalamus was making you sweat. When you come inside, it stops the sweating because now it's cool. In fact, you may start to shiver if your body cools down too rapidly.

Strategy practice: Questions will vary.

WEEK 18

DAY 1

1. The document is an application to ask to become a hall monitor for Westlake Elementary School.

2. The list states the things that the student must agree to do.

3. The student who wants to be the

hall monitor must sign the document. I know because it starts with "I," and then the person fills in his/her name. The signature shows that the student read the application and is agreeing to its terms.

Strategy practice sample answer: The person should read the list carefully, because it explains the rules that a hall monitor has to follow.

DAY 2

1. I would turn to the index and look for an entry on yeti.

2. Fake web sites would be covered in Chapter 8, because that's the chapter entitled "Hoaxes on the Internet."

3. The first page number is 36. I know because that's where Chapter 4 begins. It covers UFOs, which are unidentified flying objects.

Strategy practice sample answer: It would be a faster and easier way to find photos of the hoaxes that you want to see.

DAY 3

1. In 1821, missionaries told the Hawaiians they couldn't surf anymore. I know because the surfboard for that year points to text that states that information.

2. Surfing became popular in 1959 because it was featured in the popular movie *Gidget*.

3. The timeline helps me to understand the important events in the history of surfing.

Strategy practice sample answer: A timeline shows you important dates in the history of a sport.

DAY 4

1. The diagram gives the dimensions and shows the features of the tree mansion.

2. The author wants the reader to know how much space is needed so the potential buyer can be sure s/he has a space where it can fit.

3. Answers will vary. Ex. The price of the tree mansion is not given; the web site is not listed; where it is made and the seller's address is missing.

Strategy practice sample response: I would make a list of all the features.

DAY 5

1. The captions give the reader information about the Pacific salmon during each life stage.

2. It is called a spawner. I know because that's the boldface label on the fish in the final stage. This is when the salmon lays its eggs.

3. A Pacific salmon fry has stripes and lives in freshwater (rivers and streams).

The smolt loses its stripes and lives in saltwater (the Pacific Ocean).

Strategy practice sample response: This diagram is useful for people who want to study or know more about salmon.

WEEK 19

DAY 1

1. Anemones and barnacles are alike because they attach themselves to wooden pilings and then wave body parts to catch floating bits of food from the seawater.

2. First the barnacle attaches itself to a piling by gluing its head to the wood. Then it forms a hard shell shaped like a volcano, which it opens to get food.

3. Shipworms have a long body. Shipworms eat wood.

Strategy practice sample answers: Paragraph 1—Marine animals can live on or in wood.

Paragraph 2—Gribbles and shipworms live in and eat wood.

Paragraph 3—Barnacles attach to wood and catch food that floats by.

DAY 2

1. The story is about two boys playing catch with a baseball inside the house while their mom is away.

2. It was raining outside, and their mom wasn't there to stop them.

3. She notices that Jack is holding the plant and that there is a baseball where its pot used to be.

Strategy practice: Underlined details will vary.

DAY 3

1. John B. Curtis invented chewing gum in 1848.

2. Walter Diemer created "Double Bubble" gum 80 years after the first gum.

3. Topps Chewing Gum added comic strips and later trading cards to each pack of Topps bubble gum. This encouraged more people to buy gum in order to trade the cards.

Strategy practice: Timelines will vary.

DAY 4

1. It is a machine that strips the corn kernels from each ear of popcorn.

2. The purpose of both the cleaner and the giant fans is to remove dirt from the popcorn kernels.

3. The kernels have to sit in cribs for months while they dry, and that is the longest step in the process of making popcorn.

Strategy practice sample answer: I can picture the huge fans that blow

dust off the kernels.

DAY 5

1. The main idea is that running shoes can be recycled and made into new sports equipment.

2. The shoes are taken apart and their rubber soles, foam cushions, and fabric uppers are separated.

3. It's a good idea to recycle running shoes because new things can be made from them, plus they aren't taking up space in a landfill.

Strategy practice sample questions: How do the shoes get disinfected? Is it a spray or soap that kills germs?

WEEK 20

DAY 1

1. One type of eucalyptus leaf is poisonous to koalas, so they smell each one to be sure it's not the wrong kind.

2. The paste makes it easier for the koala's stomach to digest the leaves.

3. Eucalyptus leaves are poisonous to all mammals except koalas.

Strategy practice sample answer: A koala spends most of the day sleeping. When it is awake, it likes to eat eucalyptus leaves.

DAY 2

1. Wolf was hungry and wanted to eat Fox.

2. Fox told Wolf that there was a huge wheel of cheese at the bottom of a well. It was really the reflection of the full moon.

3. Wolf fell down the well, and Fox escaped being eaten.

Strategy practice sample question: Will Wolf get out of the well?

DAY 3

1. (Accept any two.) The doll doesn't have any moving parts. Its bottom is heavy. If you push the Daruma doll over, it will pop back up again.

2. Yes, the third paragraph has opinions. The writer says the doll's body is pretty, but its face is weird. Both of those are not facts because they cannot be proven true.

3. (Accept any one.) "Mom did a strange thing." "It was fun to play with the doll for a little while." "The doll's body is very pretty." "But the face is weird!" "I bet I know what goal Mom wants me to have."

Strategy practice sample answer: Daruma dolls are given as gifts. They are supposed to bring good luck.

DAY 4

1. It is an opinion. Due to the use of the words "great" and "wacky," the sentence is not a fact that can be proven true.

2. Yes, there are facts in the third paragraph. The only opinion statement is, "They looked ridiculous!" The last sentence is a question.

3. (Accept either sentence as evidence.) The writer does not like the traveling washing machine. The writer states, "it seems like too much trouble to use," and "washing clothes with rocks in a creek seems easier."

Strategy practice sample question: Can this be proved?

DAY 5

1. People created tokens for counting because they needed a way to count crops and animals.

2. People invented numerals because once they started living in communities, they ran businesses and paid taxes. It became too complicated to keep track of big numbers with tokens.

3. No, there are no opinions in the second paragraph. Every statement is a fact that can be proven true.

Strategy practice sample answer: People carved notches into bones, used tokens, and made symbols that stood for different amounts.

WEEK 21

DAY 1

1. (Accept any two.) They both burst out of the car; they both like doing homework at the kitchen table with the cat beside them; both girls' favorite video game is "Return to Wizard Mountain."

2. Answers will vary. Ex. Tess flings open the door to the house, while Ellie closes it gently behind her. Tess tosses her backpack and throws her clothes on the floor, while Ellie lays her backpack on her desk and carefully hangs her school clothes on hangers.

3. Tess is more active and noisy. I can tell based on her behavior, such as flinging open the door, kicking off her shoes, throwing her clothes on the floor, and yelling while playing video games.

Strategy practice sample answer: Just like Tess, I like to relax by playing video games after school.

DAY 2

1. Langston Hughes was an African American poet, and Steven Spielberg is a Jewish filmmaker.

2. Answers will vary. Ex. Creative,

innovative, talented, etc.

3. Yes, the text says that Hughes began writing poetry in high school, and Spielberg wanted to make movies when he was in middle school.

Strategy practice: Chosen similarities will vary.

DAY 3

1. They build their nests on the side of a cliff or a building.

2. A swift's saliva is sticky. It uses the saliva to collect and hold hundreds of bugs in its mouth and to catch feathers that float in the air.

3. They sleep on rocks or walls. "Their sharp claws allow them to cling to rocks and walls so they can take a brief rest."

Strategy practice sample answer: Swifts are faster and smaller than sea gulls.

DAY 4

1. They start screaming and trying to scare each other away from food. They may produce a bad smell. The text says they have a bad temper and won't share.

2. They probably got their name because they are from Tasmania and because they throw temper tantrums, scream, stomp their feet, and snap their jaws.

3. They need strong jaws and sharp teeth to tear apart the dead animals that are their food. "Their powerful jaws and sharp teeth can crush the toughest dinner."

Strategy practice: Answers will vary.

DAY 5

1. They are all wild animals that have never lived in the wild; they are a bonded trio; they were all rescued in 2001 when they were 2 months old.

2. They would not even live in the same habitat in the wild. They would have never met, so they couldn't have developed the relationship they have.

3. Baloo and Shere Khan miss Leo and wonder where he is.

Strategy practice sample answer: I already knew lions are from Africa.

WEEK 22

DAY 1

1. The setting is an operating room at the zoo. I know because the patient is a huge Kodiak bear, and the text mentions a zookeeper.

2. She wants to help make sure Kodiak is okay. She is persistent.

3. If Dewey had woken up, the people in the room would have been in danger. They could have been bitten

or mauled.

Strategy practice sample answer: He doesn't have much time to fix Dewey's teeth. Then the power goes out, but they are able to get power restored so Dr. Brown can finish fixing Dewey's teeth.

DAY 2

1. Jesse appreciates walking among the giant trees in the forest. "Jesse enjoyed the peace and quiet"; "Jesse focused on the cool breeze and the smell of damp soil."

2. Max shows he is bored by complaining, saying he wishes he'd watched the Giants game instead, and squirting water on Jesse.

3. Max is no longer bored and is now enthusiastic about the giant trees. His attitude changes because he and Jesse can fit inside a hole in a massive tree trunk.

Strategy practice: Underlined information will vary.

DAY 3

1. In 1898, Jim White discovered a huge cavern system in New Mexico that is now Carlsbad Caverns National Park.

2. Answers will vary. Ex. He is bold, brave, and determined, because he explored the massive cave system with just a lantern and string.

3. The theme is that when you are telling the truth, if you persist, people will eventually believe you.

Strategy practice: Students should underline words such as *later, finally,* and *years later.*

DAY 4

1. The theme is that you can overcome your fears by focusing on what you need to do.

2. Erin learns from Dan that it is important to focus on the task in order to face a challenging situation.

3. Erin is frightened before she jumps, but after she jumps she is totally focused on getting the job done.

Strategy practice: Sentences will vary.

DAY 5

1. Dr. Grandin likes animals. I know because she has made special equipment for handling farm animals that will improve their quality of life.

2. Dr. Grandin found a way to use her differences as a strength instead of seeing them as a weakness. When she realized that she thinks differently, she figured out that she could approach problems in a way nobody else could.

3. The theme is to view your challenges as opportunities to excel.

Strategy practice: Underlined sentences will vary.

WEEK 23

DAY 1

1. The author wants to inform the reader about an event known as WaterFire.

2. Rhode Island has cold winters. It may be that the rivers freeze.

3. "If you ever visit Providence, Rhode Island, be sure not to miss WaterFire."

Strategy practice sample question: Do they light the bonfires when it rains?

DAY 2

1. The author wants to inform the reader about the benefits of becoming a vegetarian.

2. (Accept any two.) A vegetarian diet is good for your health. Eating a low-fat diet helps people stay lean and healthy. A vegetarian diet provides many vitamins that protect people from diseases. It prevents killing animals. It helps the planet, because raising animals uses up more resources than growing fruits and vegetables does.

3. The author knows that readers may think it's too hard to be a vegetarian and wants to encourage readers to try out a few vegetarian meals a week.

Strategy practice: Answers should show some connection between information in the passage and the students' own lives.

DAY 3

1. Matt will capture and land a large fish.

2. He left the first site because there were already people there, and they said that they weren't having any success catching halibut.

3. He will probably use the fishing lure that looks like a sardine since that seems to be effective.

Strategy practice: Questions will vary.

DAY 4

1. Answers will vary. Ex. This is a literary device called repetition, and the author used it to make a point.

2. He will sleep inside the wagon. He has not been able to get a good night's sleep outside the wagon.

3. He will have to help his family, the animals, and the wagon to cross rivers.

Strategy practice: Responses will vary but should show a connection to the text.

DAY 5

1. The author's purpose is to entertain the reader with an interesting tale.

2. Rita wants to eat more popcorn than Oscar, so she convinces him

that they have equal amounts.

3. Mom will realize that Rita tricked Oscar and may give her a punishment.

Strategy practice sample question: Is this story going to be about magic tricks with popcorn?

WEEK 24

DAY 1

1. The writer wanted to tell the reader what utensils are needed so someone making the recipe could gather everything necessary before starting to make a smoothie.

2. Yes, I can. The recipe calls for fruit "such as," but that doesn't limit it to those three fruits.

3. The vanilla is not required. I know because it has the word "optional" in parentheses after that ingredient.

Strategy practice sample answer: S/he would pay attention to the ingredients to make sure there wasn't anything s/he is allergic to.

DAY 2

1. This statement is false. The holiday for May 8 is No Socks Day.

2. The January holiday that would appeal to two-year-olds would be January 13, which is Rubber Ducky Day. Children that age will not know trivia and may not understand a compliment.

3. Answers will vary. Ex. I'd like Go Skateboarding Day because I am a skater.

Strategy practice sample answer: The chart is like a calendar in that it lists all the months in order. It is not like a calendar in that it does not tell every day of each month.

DAY 3

1. The vacuole, chloroplast, and nucleus are all surrounded by cytoplasm.

2. The chloroplast is the smallest part of the plant cell.

3. The paragraph lets the reader know the purpose of the vacuole.

Strategy practice sample answer: The diagram would help me study because it shows what the plant cell looks like and what each part of the cell is called.

DAY 4

1. The key tells the different kinds of comic book subjects shown in the pie chart.

2. Junot's comic book favorite is superheroes. Half of all his comic books feature superheroes.

3. There are four different publishers, including books that Junot made.

I know because there are four publishers shown in the key/pie chart.

Strategy practice sample response: He could organize them by when they were published or by their titles.

DAY 5

1. There are 500 calories in the entire package. I can tell because there are two servings, and each serving is 250 calories.

2. Calcium is the most abundant. I know because it has the highest percentage of daily value.

3. There are 12 grams of fat, which is more than twice the amount of protein (5 grams).

Strategy practice sample response: This way people can learn how to read a label and always know how healthful or unhealthful their food is.

WEEK 25

DAY 1

1. For 400 years, the Northern Hemisphere's winters were much colder and longer than they are today.

2. (Accept any two.) Crops died, diseases spread, it was hard to collect enough firewood to stay warm, and ice sheets sometimes crushed villages.

3. There may have been fewer sunspots, meaning less warmth from the sun reached the planet. Volcanoes erupted, leaving a lot of dust and ash in the atmosphere that blocked sunlight.

Strategy practice sample answer: The Little Ice Age was probably caused by things that people could not control.

DAY 2

1. Cicada killer wasps look scary, but are harmless to humans and are actually helpful to trees.

2. A cicada killer wasp wants to carry a cicada to her nest so that when her egg hatches, her larva can feed on it.

3. One cicada killer wasp kills 160 cicadas each season. This keeps those cicadas from damaging trees by laying their eggs under their bark.

Strategy practice: Drawings will vary but should include details mentioned in the passage (stripes, a curved stinger, etc.).

DAY 3

1. The points are scored based on which balls are closest to the jack. One team earns all the points.

2. I would use the four-step run so that I could throw the ball farther.

3. Answers will vary. Ex. An image of a game in progress would help the reader to see what the jack and bocce balls look like.

Strategy practice sample answer: *first, at the same time, second, then*

DAY 4

1. Answers will vary. Ex. My skin will itch from the caterpillar's hairiness.

2. The hairs get stuck in the bird's stomach. Then the cuckoo coughs up the hair.

3. It beats the caterpillar on a branch in order to get rid of some of its hairs.

Strategy practice sample answer: *dashes after it; beat the caterpillar against a branch; eat hundreds of caterpillars in a single day*

DAY 5

1. The liquid minerals create a spray that falls to Earth and then cools into glass.

2. Tektites get their shape in midair. The liquid minerals take shape as they fly through the air.

3. The first step is a meteorite crashing into Earth and sending up soil, rocks, and other debris.

Sample answer for the last paragraph: I would like to know why meteors have only hit those four places on Earth.

WEEK 26

DAY 1

1. The Burgess Shale animals probably died in underwater mudslides.

2. They had many weird shapes and body parts such as tubes, spines, fans, antennae, and extra feet.

3. Their soft body parts were preserved, which is almost unheard of for fossils.

Strategy practice: Students should underline sentences from the third paragraph of the passage.

DAY 2

1. Tinted contacts can help these people to see the colors red and green better.

2. The eye does not have enough cones that send red and green signals to the brain. Or if the eye has enough cones, sometimes they don't work right or send color signals.

3. The person may not be able to tell if a stoplight is red or green.

Sample question and answer: What are the two main causes of color-blindness? not having enough cones or having cones that are damaged or don't work properly

DAY 3

1. Five of the sentences are facts because they make statements that can be proven true. Only the first sentence is an opinion.

2. Yes, the author states that being able to play a musical instrument is a valuable talent, which is an opinion.

3. Answers will vary.

Strategy practice: Students should underline sentences from the third paragraph.

DAY 4

1. Answers will vary. Ex. The word "worst" lets me know it's an opinion, because people can disagree about what the worst tragedies in natural history are.

2. Yes. It is a matter of opinion about whether or not the dodos tasted good.

3. The author included a lot of facts so that the reader really understands what the dodos were like and how they became extinct.

Strategy practice sample question: What were two ways that people brought about the dodo's extinction?

DAY 5

1. There was a long drought, or dry spell, and most of the plants died. Then there were no roots to hold the soil in place. The dirt blew around and buried any plants that were still alive.

2. Yes, the author acted as if the dust storms were human with this sentence: "The cruel storms punished everyone and everything." Storms aren't cruel; they are part of nature, and they aren't trying to punish anyone.

3. There were so many dust storms that people renamed the area the Dust Bowl.

Strategy practice: Students should underline "This was the beginning... without rain." "Then there were no plants...the soil." "With no trees...for miles."

WEEK 27

DAY 1

1. (Accept any three.) Every snowflake begins as a water droplet inside a cloud. It freezes into an ice crystal and gets larger as droplets around it freeze. It starts out with six sides and initially looks very much like every other snowflake. It melts when exposed to warmth.

2. The amount of water vapor in the air and the air's temperature affect the shape of a snowflake.

3. Lacy snowflakes look like six-pointed stars with many tiny branches.

Strategy practice: Answers will vary.

DAY 2

1. Standards were made of cloth, wood, metal, or other materials fastened to the top of a long pole.

Over time, fabric streamers became the most common type of standard.

2. Nepal's flag is unusual because it is made of two triangles.

3. The three colors are red, white, and blue. The United States, Great Britain, Australia, and France have flags made of the same three colors.

Strategy practice: Answers will vary.

DAY 3

1. The animals that lived underground were not hit by the hot dust, ash, and rock that fell on the area during the eruption. Although their burrows were buried, after the eruption ended, they dug their way out.

2. Scientists have been studying volcanic eruptions and keeping records about them for centuries. They know how long it takes for a region that's been devastated by an eruption to recover.

3. Plants are growing in the area, and that is what deer and elk need to survive.

Strategy practice sample response: I would wonder when the next eruption might happen.

DAY 4

1. Ben made clicks with his tongue and listened to the sounds that bounced back from the ball or the players in order to tell where they were in relationship to him.

2. "But because of his talent, more people now understand that a physical condition doesn't need to hold you back."

3. The author wanted to inform the reader of a true, inspiring story about a person with a disability.

Strategy practice sample answer: "Ben became a star all around the world." I can infer that Ben was generous with his time.

DAY 5

1. (Accept any three.) Insects are cheap; they are good for you; they contain a lot of protein, vitamins, and minerals; they are low in fat; many people think that they taste good.

2. Answers will vary. Ex. The author thought that asking the reader questions was a good hook to make the person want to keep reading.

3. The person might try witchetty grubs and bees. I know because the text says that people compare the taste of these insects to shrimp.

Strategy practice: Responses will vary.

WEEK 28

DAY 1

1. He found his life's work: writing about the beauty of nature and convincing people to protect it.

2. Yes, Muir was creative. "He built clocks and invented machines that made farming easier." OR "He was a gifted writer."

3. He started it more than 120 years ago. I know because I took the current year and subtracted 1892, the year he started the Sierra Club.

Strategy practice: Answers will vary.

DAY 2

1. Annie Oakley was the star; I know because of the first line in paragraph 2, which says she became a superstar in England.

2. A female sharpshooter was a rarity. Her skills were amazing; not only was she accurate, she was fast. She could shoot six glass balls in the air before they reached the ground.

3. Annie wanted to show that women were not second-class citizens in America.

Strategy practice: Answers will vary but should include vivid language from the passage.

DAY 3

1. The theme is that when people work together to face their fears, they can accomplish their goals.

2. Yes, the villagers got rid of the monster Nian, who had been attacking their village annually.

3. No, I think that this story came from long ago, because people today do not think monsters or dragons are real. Also, it sounds like a fairy tale, and they were written long ago.

Strategy practice sample response: Rereading paragraphs is a good way to stay focused. By paying attention to the theme, you can look for details that support that theme.

DAY 4

1. The theme is that perseverance pays off in the end.

2. Answers will vary. Ex. I think Dr. Eng is determined and generous because he worked for so many years to try to help people.

3. He discovered Byetta by studying the Gila monster and believes that there are more cures to be found in plants and other animals.

Strategy practice: Answers will vary but should include concrete language from the passage.

DAY 5

1. This story takes place on a lake during the day, probably in the summertime.

2. Freddie trusts what he can see; Uncle Carl relies on the experts to tell him what to think.

3. Uncle Carl learns that just because something is published in the newspaper doesn't mean it's 100 percent correct. OR Uncle Carl learns that it's better to trust his own senses than rely on someone else's opinion even if that someone is an "expert."

Strategy practice sample answer: I looked for a new paragraph and quotation marks to know who was speaking when.

WEEK 29

DAY 1

1. The author wrote this text to inform the reader about the ongoing disagreement about the origin of fortune cookies.

2. The author knew that the reader might not know what mooncakes are, so s/he described them.

3. The first paragraph explains that no one knows how, when, or where fortune cookies were invented. This sets up the disagreement that will be explained in the rest of the paragraphs.

Strategy practice sample question: Which company makes the most fortune cookies today?

DAY 2

1. The author had two purposes for the first paragraph. One was to set up a feeling of suspense so the reader would want to continue. The other was to indicate that this paragraph is fiction, while the rest is nonfiction.

2. The third paragraph tells the reader all the different things that Freeman and his team did to try to prove the existence of the Mongolian Death Worm.

3. Answers will vary. Ex. The author thinks that if it existed, there would be some sort of proof.

Strategy practice: Responses will vary.

DAY 3

1. Brady will have more baby teeth come in.

2. Berty's baby teeth will fall out as his adult teeth start to come in.

3. Each child will have four more molars called wisdom teeth come into his or her mouth.

Strategy practice sample question and answer: How many adult teeth do people have? Most people have 32 adult teeth, including their wisdom teeth.

DAY 4

1. Dad will climb the ladder and use grapes to get Archie out of the tree.

2. He will look for food because he is hungry.

3. The narrator thought that the fire department would come and get Archie out of the tree. No, that probably wouldn't have worked, because fire departments do not get animals out of trees, and Archie would be unlikely to go to a stranger anyway.

Strategy practice sample answer: I would be glad, because my parrot is annoying and is never quiet.

DAY 5

1. Tommy wrote the letter to tell the author that there are errors in the book he just published.

2. No. Tommy says he hopes the author tested the recipes because "My dad and I certainly won't be testing them." This implies he won't get the book.

3. Answers will vary. Ex. He will ignore it. OR He will write back and apologize or explain how the errors were introduced, etc.

Strategy practice sample question: Is it difficult to write recipe books for kids?

WEEK 30

DAY 1

1. The bulleted list lets the reader know what items are needed to make the motor. The reader can't get started until these items are available.

2. The numbered list tells the reader the order in which to do the steps to make the motor work.

3. Answers will vary. Ex. No, I am not really interested in motors.

Strategy practice sample answer: If you went to the store, you would need the list of things under the "What You Need" heading.

DAY 2

1. The underlined letters tell the reader which part of each of the two words is used to form the portmanteau.

2. The chart is organized in columns of categories based on the type of portmanteau (common, technology, or animal).

3. The sentences explain what the portmanteau means or how it is used.

Strategy practice sample response:
I would place *spork* in the first column because it is a common portmanteau, not a technology or animal portmanteau.

DAY 3

1. The number 4 shows where the kitchen is. I know because of the key.

2. When I look at the diagram, it is clear that the sleeping quarters are closer to the camera than the control station.

3. The paragraph supports the diagram by telling the reader that it is the Service Module of the International Space Station.

Strategy practice sample response: People who build service modules might want to know what features this module has.

DAY 4

1. It is Grand Canyon National Park, and the Colorado River flows through it.

2. The map shows readers where Bryan's Rides is located so that they can find their way to the business and rent animals.

3. The shaded part of the map is Grand Canyon National Park.

Strategy practice sample answer: It is easier to recognize some of the information on the map after you read the text because the text tells you some of the things to look for on the map.

DAY 5

1. It goes to the House of Representatives.

2. A bill is rewritten when it is rejected by the House of Representatives, the Senate, or the president.

3. The president either signs a bill into law or refuses to sign it. When that happens, it goes back to Congress for changes.

Strategy practice sample answer: The person could find out which stage of the process the bill was in.